The Practice of Writing

By the same author

DAVID LODGE

The Practice
of Writing

ALLEN LANE
THE PENGUIN PRESS

ALLEN LANE

THE PENGUIN PRESS

Published by the Penguin Group

Penguin Books USA Inc., 375 Hudson Street, New York, New York 10014, U.S.A.

Penguin Books Ltd, 27 Wrights Lane, London W8 5TZ, England

Penguin Books Australia Ltd, Ringwood, Victoria, Australia

Penguin Books Canada Ltd, 10 Alcorn Avenue, Toronto, Ontario, Canada M4V 3B2

Penguin Books (N.Z.) Ltd, 182–190 Wairau Road, Auckland 10, New Zealand

Penguin Books Ltd, Registered Offices: Harmondsworth, Middlesex, England

First American edition

Published in 1997 by Allen Lane The Penguin Press, a division of Viking Penguin, a division of Penguin Books USA Inc.

10 9 8 7 6 5 4 3 2 1

Many of the selections in this book have been previously published; acknowledgments appear on pages x–xi.

LIBRARY OF CONGRESS CATALOGING IN PUBLICATION DATA

Lodge, David.

    The practice of writing : essays, lectures, reviews, and a diary / David Lodge.

    p. cm.

    Includes index.

    ISBN 0-7139-9173-9

    1. Lodge, David, 1935– —Aesthetics. 2. Fiction—History and criticism—Theory, etc. 3. Fiction—Film and video adaptations. 4. Authorship. I. Title.

PR6062.036A6   1997

823.009—dc20   96-38927

This book is printed on acid-free paper.

∞

Printed in the United States of America

Set in Plantin

For Jeswyn and Martin

Contents

Preface

This is a collection of occasional prose pieces about literary fiction, drama and television adaptation. Nearly all of them were written after 1987, when I gave up my academic career to become a full-time writer. A few of the essays bear the traces of my involvement in academic literary studies, including structuralist and post-structuralist critical theory; but the dominant emphasis of the book as a whole is on the *practice* of writing, in several different ways. The novelists discussed at the greatest length here interest me because they had an influence on my own creative writing, and/or because their struggles with the craft of fiction, and with the stresses and strains of the writer's life, seem to me exemplary. Most of the other essays draw directly and anecdotally on my personal experience of writing fiction, screenplays and a stage play.

Since I retired from academic life, I have found that this is the kind of criticism I most enjoy writing (and reading): criticism that tries to demystify and shed light on the creative process, to explain how literary and dramatic works are made, and to describe the many different factors, not always under the control of the writer, that come into play in this process. Writing about one's own work carries with it certain risks, including that of seeming egocentric, but I have never felt that there was any conflict or contradiction between being a self-aware creative writer and an analytical, formalist critic at the same time – on the contrary. T.S. Eliot drew the vital connection between the two activities in his essay: "The Function of Criticism": "Probably . . . the larger part of the labour of an author in composing his work is critical labour; the labour of sifting, combining, constructing, expunging, correcting, testing; this frightful toil is as much critical as creative."

The proliferation of Creative Writing courses in tertiary education in recent years, at both graduate and undergraduate levels, suggests that an emphasis on the practice of writing, both for its own sake and as a tool to enhance critical skills, may supersede the fashion for Theory which began in the late nineteen-sixties, and now seems to have exhausted the energy and interest of even its devotees. I hope this book will have some interest and value, therefore, for students and teachers of literature, creative writing and media studies. But it is intended for the general reader as well, and put together with his or her interests in mind.

Most items were written for a variety of specific occasions – contributions to journals, introductions to books, public lectures, conference papers, etc. – and where it seemed appropriate I have described the original contexts in headnotes. I have also added footnotes and postscripts where I felt the need to qualify or add to what I said in the original versions. Some items are published here for the first time. The others were first published (sometimes under different titles) as follows: "The Novelist Today: Still at the Crossroads?" in *New Writing*, edited by Malcolm Bradbury and Judy Cooke, Minerva in association with the British Council, 1992; "Fact and Fiction in the Novel: an Author's Note" in *Tensions and Transitions (1869–1990): the mediating imagination*, edited by Michael Irwin, Mark Kinkead-Weekes and A. Robert Lee, Faber 1990; "The Lives of Graham Greene" in the *New York Review of Books*, 8 and 22 June 1995; "*Lucky Jim* Revisited" as the Introduction to the Penguin Twentieth Century Classics edition of *Lucky Jim* by Kingsley Amis, 1992; "Sex, Creativity and Biography: the Young D.H. Lawrence" in the *New York Review of Books*, 13 February 1992; "Henry Green: a Writer's Writer's Writer" in the *New York Review of Books*, 25 March 1993; "The Making of 'Anthony Burgess' " in the *Times Literary Supplement*, 27 February 1987; "What Kind of Fiction Did Nabokov Write? A Practitioner's

View" in *Cycnos* (University of Nice), Vol. 12, No.2, 1995; "Creative Writing: Can It/Should It Be Taught?" in *Letters* (Royal Society of Literature), No.6, Summer 1995; "The Novel as Communication" in *Ways of Communicating*, edited by D.H. Mellor, Cambridge U.P., 1990; "Adapting *Nice Work* for Television" in *Novel Images: literature in performance*, edited by Peter Reynolds, Routledge, 1993; "Through The No Entry Sign: Deconstruction and Architecture" in the *Guardian*, 8 April 1988; "Harold Pinter's *Last To Go:* a structuralist analysis" in *Harold Pinter: a Casebook*, edited by Lois Gordon, Garland, 1990. I am grateful to the editors concerned for the initial invitations/provocations to write these pieces, and to Mr Harold Pinter for permission to reprint the text of his sketch, *Last To Go*.

PART ONE

Novelists, Novels and "The Novel"

The Novelist Today:
Still at the Crossroads?

This essay started life as a talk given to a seminar at
the University of East Anglia held in November 1990
to mark the twentieth anniversary of the well-known
M.A. in Creative Writing programme at that
institution. It was revised and expanded for
publication in the anthology *New Writing*, edited by
Malcolm Bradbury and Judy Cooke, in the spring of
1992. All such "State of the Novel" addresses are
necessarily provisional, always in danger of being
invalidated by new developments. This one was itself
in part a reassessment of an earlier essay of my own,
but while it was at the proof stage of its first
publication I felt obliged to insert a new paragraph
to take account of the impact of the deepening
economic recession on literary publishing. In
reprinting it here I have added a few further
reflections in a footnote and a postscript.

One can consider the situation of the contemporary novelist either aesthetically or institutionally. Under the aesthetic I include questions of genre, of formal and stylistic choice or fashion – what French critics call *écriture*. In the category of the institutional I include questions about the material conditions of writing, how writing today is produced, circulated, received and rewarded. The two are, of course, connected.

Both the aesthetic and the institutional state of writing today can be viewed from the perspective either of the critic or of the creative writer. As I function in both capacities, this is for me a splitting of the subject in a double sense. For most of my adult life, from 1960 to 1987, I combined an academic career as a university teacher and scholar with writing novels. I tried to keep a balance between these two activities; and throughout this period I published, more or less by design, a novel and a work of literary criticism in alternation. In 1987 I retired from university teaching, and although I expect to go on writing literary criticism, I doubt whether much of it will be oriented towards an academic readership. One component of that decision was a feeling that it was becoming harder and harder to make meaningful connections between an academic criticism increasingly dominated by questions of Theory, and the practice of creative writing.

Both the critic and the creative writer can address themselves to the subject of writing either descriptively or prescriptively. My own preference has always been for the descriptive. Nothing, it seems to me, is more futile or arrogant than for critics to tell novelists what they should write about or how they should write about it or what it is no longer possible to write. Writers themselves may be excused for doing this as a way of defending or publicizing or creating a receptive climate for their work or the work of their friends. There is a long and honourable tradition of discourse about the state of writing known as the manifesto, but for reasons I shall come to I do not think it is appropriate to the present literary moment, and I certainly do not have one to proclaim.

So these are the coordinates of my observations: aesthetic/ institutional, critical/creative, descriptive/prescriptive.

About twenty years ago I published an essay called "The Novelist at the Crossroads" which was aesthetic, critical and descriptive in orientation: that is, it was intended as a descriptive survey of the forms of contemporary fiction, drawing indirectly on my experience as a novelist but written essentially within the conventions of academic criticism. My starting-point or springboard was a short but potent book of prescriptive criticism by the American academic critic Robert Scholes, called *The Fabulators*. (It is, incidentally, difficult to imagine an ambitious young scholar of Scholes's ability choosing today to write a book about contemporary fiction; he or she would almost certainly be working in the field of Theory, or applying Theory to the revisionist reading of classic texts.) The realistic novel was obsolete, Scholes argued; writers should leave realism to other media, such as film, which could imitate reality more faithfully, and instead develop the purely fictive potential of narrative. His prime example was John Barth's *Giles Goat-boy*, a huge allegorical romance that presented the modern world as divided into an East Campus and a West Campus, which the hero, conceived by a virgin impregnated by a computer program and brought up as a goat, has a mission to save. Lawrence Durrell, Iris Murdoch, John Hawkes, Terry Southern and Kurt Vonnegut were the other chief exemplars of a kind of writing that Scholes called "fabulation".

To resist, or at least question, this manifesto, I invoked Scholes's own generic theory of the novel, expounded in an earlier book that he had co-authored with Robert Kellogg, *The Nature of Narrative*: that the novel was generically an unstable mixture of the fictional and the empirical, of romance and allegory on the one hand and history and mimesis (realistic imitation of ordinary life) on the other. Granting that the viability of the traditional realistic novel had been called in question on several grounds (for instance, the bizarre, extreme, absurd nature of modern "reality"), I suggested that the excessive cultivation of the fictional through fabulation was not the only possible response. A writer might equally well decide to develop the *empirical* style of narrative exclusively – as in the so-called non-fictional novels of Capote (*In Cold Blood*) and Mailer (*Armies of the Night*), and in the experimental autobiographical novels of B.S. Johnson.

The contemporary novelist was therefore in the situation of a man (or woman) at a crossroads. Before him stretched the way of traditional realism, now alleged to be a very boring route, and possibly a dead end. To the left and right were the ways of fabulation and non-fictional narrative. Many writers, I suggested, unable to choose between these three routes, built their hesitation into their fiction, made the problems of writing a novel the subject of the novel. I called this the problematic novel; later it was christened (by Robert Scholes again I seem to remember) metafiction, a name that achieved wider currency. An important example of this kind of novel, it seemed to me, was Doris Lessing's *The Golden Notebook*, in which a blocked novelist writes about various aspects of her life, including her own writing, in various differently coloured notebooks and then unites her fractured imagination in a Golden Notebook. I concluded my essay with a "modest affirmation of faith in the future of the traditional realistic novel." It was probably not coincidental that I was about to publish such a novel myself (*Out of the Shelter*). But the essay was essentially a plea for aesthetic pluralism. There was, I argued, no dominant style or *écriture*, such as obtained in the Fifties, or the Thirties: "We seem to be living through a period of unprecedented cultural pluralism which allows, in all the arts, an astonishing variety of styles to flourish simultaneously."

Twenty years later, I think that generalization still holds good; but I am also struck by how sturdily traditional realism has survived the obsequies pronounced over it by Scholes, and by a number of other writers and critics in the Sixties and Seventies, and how clearly it remains a serious option for the literary novelist today. (By realism I mean not only a mimetic representation of experience, but also the organization of narrative according to a logic of causality and temporal sequence.)

Fabulation in Scholes's sense has certainly flourished in the

last twenty years, encouraged by the discovery and dissemina-
tion of South American magic realism in Europe and the USA.
In British writing, Salman Rushdie, Angela Carter, the later Fay
Weldon come to mind in this connection. The blurb's description of Rushdie's *Satanic Verses*, for instance, suggests a family
resemblance to *Giles Goat-boy*:

> Just before dawn one winter's morning a hijacked jumbo jet
> blows apart high above the English Channel. Through the
> debris of limbs, drinks trolleys, memories, blankets and
> oxygen masks, two figures fall towards the sea without
> benefit of parachutes: Gibreel Farishta, India's legendary
> movie star, and Saladin Chamcha, the man of a thousand
> voices, self-made man and Anglophile supreme. Clinging to
> each other, singing rival songs, they plunge downward, and
> are finally washed up, alive, on the snow-covered sands of an
> English beach. A miracle; but an ambiguous one, because it
> soon becomes apparent that curious changes are coming over
> them. Gibreel seems to have acquired a halo, while, to
> Saladin's dismay, his legs grow hairier, his feet turn into
> hoofs, and there are bumps burgeoning at his temples.

The combination of the exploding jumbo jet, as real and
topical as yesterday's newsreel, and the miraculous survival and
mythical metamorphosis of the leading characters, is typical of
fabulation. It aims to entertain us with the humorous extravag-
ance and inventiveness of its story while offering this as a kind
of metaphor, or objective correlative in T.S. Eliot's now rather
outmoded jargon, for the extreme contrasts and conflicts of
modern experience. Humour is a very important component of
this kind of writing, for without humour it is apt to become
portentous, laboured and ultimately boring; and of course a
sense of humour is absolutely essential for an appropriate
reading of it – a faculty Ayatollahs are notoriously lacking in.
The model for this kind of fiction is Rabelais' *Gargantua and
Pantagruel*, and for its poetics Bakhtin's theory of the carnivalesque.

Fabulation has certainly flourished in the last twenty years,
but it has not conquered the fictional scene. It remains a

marginal form of fiction, at least in Britain.*

The non-fiction novel, which applies fictional techniques, such as free indirect style, scenic construction, present-tense narration, prolepsis, iterative symbolism, etc., to factual narratives, was always more of an American than a British genre. The poetics of this form of writing were formulated by Tom Wolfe in his anthology *The New Journalism*, and in that anthology he included only one specimen by a British writer (Nicholas Tomalin). Tom Wolfe's own *Radical Chic* and *The Right Stuff* are classics of the genre, along with Norman Mailer's *The Executioner's Song*. The nearest approximation to this kind of writing in English outside America is perhaps the Australian Thomas Keneally's *Schindler's Ark*, which demonstrated its generic ambiguity by being published as non-fiction in the USA and winning the Booker Prize for best novel in 1982. There has been in Britain in recent years, however, something of a renaissance of literary travel writing, much of which perhaps belongs in this category of the non-fiction novel. Names that come to mind in this connection: James Fenton, Jonathan Raban, Bruce Chatwin, Redmond O'Hanlon, and two Americans who have made their homes in Britain, Paul Theroux and Bill Bryson. Such writing combines factual reporting with cultural and philosophic musing and a slightly teasing autobiographical subtext, both components of modern fiction. Probably the most prestigious and influential outlet for new writing in England today is the paperback book-cum-magazine *Granta*, and it may be significant that its travel number, featuring several of the writers I have named, was its best-selling issue; also that Richard Rayner, author of the very funny *Los Angeles Without a Map*, worked for *Granta* when he wrote it. This book describes the bizarre, mainly sexual adventures of a narrator

---

* This sentence now seems unduly dismissive, and perhaps reflects a personal prejudice in favour of realistic fiction. Angela Carter's reputation and influence have risen steadily since her untimely death in 1992. Salman Rushdie, to his enormous credit, has not allowed the infamous *fatwa* to silence him or stifle his creativity, and his distinctive kind of magic realism remains a potent force in contemporary fiction. Other writers who have made their mark in recent years pursuing various kinds of "fabulatory" fiction include Jim Crace, Jeanette Winterson, Ben Okri, Louis de Bernières, Lawrence Norfolk and Will Self.

indistinguishable from the real author; it reads like autobiography but was shortlisted for the *Sunday Express* Fiction prize in 1988.

There have certainly been many examples of the problematic or metafictional novel produced since I wrote my essay, and still more examples of novels which have a strain of metafiction in them, without being primarily metafictional in motivation. For example, Margaret Drabble's novels from *The Ice Age* onwards, Malcolm Bradbury's *The History Man*, Martin Amis's *Money* and my own *How Far Can You Go?* are all novels primarily focused on developments in contemporary society, but all refer to and in some cases actually introduce the author into the text, as a character on the same ontological level as the fictional characters: a device which exposes the fictionality of texts in a peculiarly drastic way, and invariably reveals some anxiety about the ethical and epistemological nature of fictional discourse and its relationship to the world.

Indeed I would say that my model or metaphor of the crossroads now seems to me inadequate chiefly because it doesn't allow for such mixing of genres and styles within a single text. Such mixing, what one might call "crossover" fiction, seems to me to be a salient feature of writing today. That is to say, relatively few novelists are wholly and exclusively committed to fabulation or the non-fiction novel, or metafiction. Instead they combine one or more of these modes with realism, often in a startling, deliberately disjunctive way. Vonnegut's *Slaughterhouse Five* (1970) was an early and influential American example of crossover fiction. British examples would include some of Doris Lessing's later work (for instance *Briefing for a Descent into Hell*), Julian Barnes's books from *Flaubert's Parrot* onward, and D.M. Thomas's *The White Hotel*. Foregrounded intertextuality, the overt citation or simulation of older texts in a modern text, has frequently been used to achieve the crossover effect in this period, from John Fowles' *The French Lieutenant's Woman* at the beginning of it, through Peter Ackroyd's *Hawksmoor* and *Chatterton*, to Antonia Byatt's recent *Possession*. My own *Small World* might be mentioned in this context. But one has also to say that a great many of the most admired novels of the present time are written wholly in the discourse mode of traditional realism, employing either first-person character-narrators or covert authorial narrators in a way designed to create an illusion of the reality of the story that is not fundamentally challenged or questioned within the text.

In 1989 I was chairman of the judges for the Booker Prize, Britain's premier literary prize. We read, or at least scrutinized, over a hundred new novels. The great majority of them were written within the conventions of fictional realism. The shortlist of six that we selected were all realistic novels. I should say that it was a matter of great regret to me that Martin Amis's *London Fields* was not shortlisted, due to the strong objections of two members of the jury. Had it been, our list would have looked somewhat different, for there are important metafictional and fabulatory elements in this novel. None of the six novels we ended up with could be said to deviate from the conventions of moden realistic narrative.

They were: Kazuo Ishiguro's *The Remains of the Day*, which of course was the eventual winner, John Banville's *The Book of Evidence*, Rose Tremain's *Restoration*, James Kelman's *A Disaffection*, Margaret Atwood's *Cat's Eye*, and Sybille Bedford's *Jigsaw*. Five of them, though we didn't notice this at the time we selected them, are first-person narratives, and the sixth, Kelman's *A Disaffection*, is written from a single point of view, often in interior monologue. First-person narration appeals to contemporary novelists because it permits the writer to remain within the conventions of realism without claiming the kind of authority which belongs to the authorial narrative method of the classic realistic novel. In the case of the Bedford and the Atwood, the voice of the narrator is hardly distanced from that of the implied author; in the Ishiguro, the Banville and the Tremain, the narrators are very different from their authors, created by rhetorical means. These three are virtuoso feats of writing, but they are not formally innovatory. Indeed Banville's novel is perhaps the most conventional he has written, in form. Of the six, Kelman's was regarded as carrying the flag of the avant-garde, but though I greatly admired this novel, and was indeed its chief advocate on the jury, I did not see it as formally adventurous. It is written in a mixture of interior monologue and free indirect style, rather like the early chapters of *Ulysses*, but quite without Joyce's mythic design or the stylistic experiments of the later chapters of *Ulysses*. Its aesthetic motivation is entirely mimetic. It challenges the reader primarily by its content and use of Glaswegian dialect, not by its narrative form.

In short, the aesthetic pluralism I sought to defend in my "Novelist at the Crossroads" essay seems to me to be now a generally accepted fact of literary life. It is sometimes described as a post-modern condition, but if so then we can no longer use post-modernism as a term for a new kind of avant-garde experimentalism. The astonishing variety of styles on offer today, as if in an aesthetic supermarket, includes traditional as well as innovative styles, minimalism as well as excess, nostalgia as well as prophecy.

The triumph of pluralism also no doubt has something to do with the absence of any dominating literary critics or school of criticism actively engaged with the interpretation and evaluation of contemporary literature, a function performed in earlier periods by Eliot, Leavis and the American New Critics. This is partly due to the increasing professionalization of academic criticism and its preoccupation with Theory. It is criticism which defines literary movements, determines or sets up debates about what is important and what is not important, what is in and what is out. What we have now is a literary situation in which everything is in and nothing is out.

This situation has an upside and a downside. The upside is that the literary world is open to anybody with talent. When you have a dominant *écriture* there is a danger that good work that is unfashionable will be neglected, and mediocre work will enjoy an inflated reputation because it is fashionable. The Thirties and Fifties provided plenty of examples. The downside is that, in the absence of any consensus about aesthetic value, some other value system will take over. And given the nature of our society it is not surprising that a somewhat materialistic notion of success, as measured by sales, advances, prizes, media celebrity, etc., has filled the vacuum. To state it summarily: success has supplanted fashionableness as the reference point of the literary world; or, if you like, success has become an index of fashionableness. It was not always so. In the heyday of modernism, you could hardly be considered an important literary writer if you were commercially successful. It is interesting that Martin Amis, widely regarded as the representative novelist of his generation, has written two novels called *Success* and *Money*.

I am now of course viewing my subject under its institutional aspect, and I am well aware that what I am talking about may be partly an effect of a change in my own position within the institution, inasmuch as I have in recent years enjoyed some success of the kind I have just referred to; but I don't think it is entirely a subjective impression. It is a commonplace that the literary novel acquired a new commercial significance in the 1980s, and of course it is no coincidence that it was a decade dedicated to Enterprise culture and the deregulation and internationalization of high finance. In this climate publishing houses became desirable objects for financial mergers and takeovers. Prestigious literary writers became valuable assets, like brand names in the commodity market, worth far more than the income they actually generated – though they could, in certain circumstances, generate a good deal. The literary bestseller was born, a concept that would have seemed a contradiction in terms to F.R. and Queenie Leavis. Umberto Eco's *The Name of the Rose* was a paradigm case. Salman Rushdie's *Midnight's Children* was another. In the 1980s the Booker Prize, which had made little or no impact on sales in the previous decade, suddenly developed the power to make any book that won it a bestseller. Publishers began to search and compete for potential literary bestsellers. In consequence, literary novelists have probably been, in the recent past, better rewarded financially than at any earlier time in this century. It never has been, and it never will be, possible for everybody who would like to earn their living as a full-time writer to do so, but in the 1980s it seemed to be a more attainable ambition than ever before.

The economic recession of the early 1990s has changed this picture considerably. While the market was buoyant, the large advances commanded by bestselling authors led to a general enhancement of novelists' financial rewards. In today's harsh economic climate, however, many of those huge advances have not been earned, while the sales of less commercial fiction have apparently plummeted. Novelists are finding it harder to place their work and to earn a living from it. There has been a painful shakeout of personnel in the publishing industry and a corresponding shakeout in publishers' lists. Whether this is altogether a bad thing depends, of course, on what books are being eliminated by the financial squeeze. There are so many novels published in Britain that a great proportion of them never get properly reviewed, and never thus really enter into the public consciousness at all. It's possible that some novels of real distinction are being published, but not being noticed, because they are swamped by a mass of decently competent, but not really *necessary* novels. In any event, the effects of the structural changes in the publishing of literary fiction that occurred in the 1980s will not quickly disappear.

The novel has from its very beginnings had an equivocal status, somewhere between a work of art and a commodity; but in the twentieth century, under the impact of modernism, it seemed to split into two kinds of fiction – the highbrow novel of aesthetic ambition, which sold in small numbers to a discriminating élite, and the popular or middlebrow novel of entertainment, which sold in much larger numbers to a mass audience. Now the gap seems to be narrowing again, and this has changed the attitude of the literary writer towards his audience and his peers – and his work.

The successful marketing of literary fiction depends upon a collaboration between the writer, the publisher and the mass media. Publisher and writer have a common interest, and the media have been very eager to collaborate with them for their own reasons. Developments in print and communications technology in the last decade have led to a vast expansion and diversification of media outlets – newspapers, magazines, supplements, TV channels and radio stations. They all have an inexhaustible appetite for raw material; discussion and gossip about books and writers is a cheap source of such material.

So, if you are a novelist with any kind of reputation, publishing a new novel no longer consists of sending off the manuscript to your publisher and waiting for the reviews to appear nine months or so later. It means delicate negotiations, probably via your agent, over terms, possibly an auction. Once the contract is signed it means consultation with the publisher over the timing of the book's publication, the design of the jacket and other details of production. You might be asked to talk to the firm's sales force, or to a convention of booksellers. Around the time of publication you will be asked to give interviews to press and broadcasting media, perhaps to do bookshop readings, signings, attend literary festivals. If you are lucky enough to win or even just be shortlisted for a major literary prize, that will lead to more publicity events. And there will be yet more interviews, readings, signings, etc., if and when the book is paperbacked, turned into a film or TV series, and published in foreign countries. You may be invited to tour foreign countries by the British Council, reading from your work or lecturing on the state of the novel. It is an interesting and significant fact that at the very moment when post-structuralist academic criticism has been proclaiming the Death of the Author as a theoretical axiom, an unprecedented degree of public attention has been focused on contemporary authors as living, breathing human beings.

Some authors collaborate in this process more enthusiastically than others; but very few eschew it entirely. Why? For a number of reasons. The present climate encourages writers to think of themselves not only as artists, but as professionals in a business partnership with their publishers. If the publisher has invested a large advance in a book the writer may feel a moral obligation to help sell it, as well as self-interest. The writer may get some ego-gratification from contact with admiring readers, or from the performance element in public readings. He or she may be glad to get out of the house, away from the loneliness of the study, and to travel abroad at someone else's expense.

There are obvious dangers in this new literary lifestyle – I speak as one who has knowingly exposed himself to them. There is the danger that all the media exposure will encourage the vanity, jealousy and paranoia to which writers are constitutionally prone in any case. There is a danger that all the interviews, readings, lecture tours, signing sessions, festival attendances, etc., will consume time and energy that should have been dedicated to the production of new work. There is, perhaps most importantly, a danger that the writer's raised consciousness of the market dimension of his or her work will interfere with the artistic dimension, making the work less innovative, less ambitious, less inclined to explore new territory, than it might otherwise have been. Indeed it is possible to argue that there is a direct connection between the power of the media and the market in today's literary world, and the aesthetic pluralism, in which realism remains a dominating force, of contemporary fiction. J.G. Ballard made a waspish comment to this effect recently in reviewing a biography of William Burroughs in the *Guardian*:

> At a time when the bourgeois novel has triumphed, and career novelists jet around the world on Arts Council tours and pontificate like game-show celebrities at literary festivals, it is heartening to know that Burroughs at least is still working away quietly at Lawrence, Kansas, creating what I feel is the most original and important body of fiction to appear since the Second World War.

"Arts Council" here is presumably a slip for "British Council". The Arts Council doesn't send British writers jetting around the world, it sends them pottering round the country on British Rail, or sets them up as Writers in Residence in regional community centres, though I don't suppose Ballard approves of such enterprises either. The really interesting phrase in this passage is "career novelist". It seems to be formed on the model of "career woman": a somewhat sexist phrase, now becoming rare, used to denote a woman who has sacrificed or subordinated the traditional female occupation of homemaking and childrearing to the pursuit of a career of a traditionally masculine kind, involving the acquisition of power and wealth. Implied in Ballard's locution there is a distinction between writing as a vocation and writing as a profession, writing as the pursuit of importance and writing as the pursuit of success. I must confess that I find William Burroughs a very unconvincing specimen of literary importance, but let us not be distracted by that questionable value judgement from what Ballard is saying.

There are, undoubtedly, dangers in the current literary situation of the contamination of literary values by considerations of fame and money. But they differ only in degree, not in kind, from what has always been the case, at least from the eighteenth century onwards, when writers became professionals, and ceased to rely on patronage, and the printing press turned fiction into a mass-market commodity. It has always been necessary for novelists to struggle to reconcile, in their ways of working, pragmatic institutional considerations with aesthetic integrity. It has always been necessary to be an artist while writing your novel, and a man (or woman) of business when publishing it. All one can say is that the conditions of modern cultural production and circulation make this balancing act particularly difficult, and require from the writer a particularly clear head.

What cannot be denied, I think – and it is perhaps what Ballard means by the triumph of the bourgeois novel – is that contemporary writing, whatever particular style or mode it follows, whether realist or nonrealist, whether fabulation or metafiction or non-fiction novel, or a combination of all of these, is likely to be reader-friendly. The contemporary writer is interested in communicating. This was not always the case. Romantic writers saw their art as primarily self-expression; modernist writers as the making of symbols, or verbal objects. Contemporary critical theory tells us that the very idea of communication is an illusion, or fallacy, though it is not clear what it thinks it is doing when it tells us that. Contemporary writers, however, perhaps partly as a result of the explosion of methods and techniques of communication in modern society – satellite telephone links, video, fax machines, photocopiers, computers, etc. – and certainly because of their greater professional involvement in the publishing and marketing of their fiction, and its adaptation to other media such as TV and film, cannot but see themselves as engaged in a process of communication with an actual or potential audience. This it seems to me is, for good or ill, an irresistible effect of living in the modern world, and it has undoubtedly had an effect on the form of contemporary fiction.

POSTSCRIPT

The "structural changes in the publishing of literary fiction" in the 1980s, referred to above, have continued to have a powerful effect in the 1990s – generally perceived as culturally damaging. I write this in the last days of 1995, which has been a particularly turbulent and anxiety-ridden year for publishers, booksellers and authors. The Reed-Elsevier conglomerate put its entire publishing division (which includes my own publishers, Secker & Warburg) up for sale in the summer. Other publishing groups, notably HarperCollins and Penguin, announced drastic "downsizing" of their operations with corresponding staff redundancies. Autumn saw the collapse of the Net Book Agreement (which stipulated that books must be sold at the cover price set by the publisher), as a number of key publishers and booksellers decided that retail discounting was the only way to galvanize a sluggish market. There were widespread fears that this development would put small bookshops out of business and disadvantage writers and publishers of books of minority interest. The layman might be forgiven for supposing that the publishers who took this drastic step were making a loss under the NBA; but in most cases they had in fact been modestly profitable. What seems to have happened is that the big conglomerates who bought up publishing houses in the 1980s expect them to yield the same kind of profits as any other commercial or industrial operation – twelve or fifteen percent rather than five or six per cent – and put intense pressure on their chief executives when these targets are not reached. But it is doubtful whether general publishing can ever yield such a level of profit in the long term – which is why it was traditionally a "gentlemanly" business, pursued as much for cultural as for financial motives.

Meanwhile the pursuit of the "literary bestseller" continues unabated – indeed it has become even more frantic, as publishers struggle to satisfy both the accountants breathing down their necks and their own sense of cultural mission. In a remarkably prescient article published in *The American Scholar* in 1989 (and reprinted in *The Author*) the American publisher, Gerald Howard, commented on the phenomenon as follows:

> there is a palpable Faustian element to the bargain: the huge distribution mechanism and the celebrity-hungry media machine that function to make these splashy successes possible extract their own costs and compromises and create much confusion of literary values and financial value.

Nothing could illustrate the truth of this observation more

vividly than the story of the publication of Martin Amis's *The Information* in 1995. For the British and Commonwealth rights in this novel he obtained from HarperCollins an advance of nearly half a million pounds, a figure far in excess of anything that had been paid before to a literary novelist (as distinct from a writer of popular genre entertainments), but in the process severed longstanding relationships with his previous publishers, his agent Pat Kavanagh, and one of his closest friends, Julian Barnes (Kavanagh's husband). The most significant aspect of the whole affair was that the negotiations and their personal repercussions were widely reported in the press, with a good deal of unpleasant gloating over the recent break-up of Amis's marriage and determined efforts to whip up envy and disapproval in the literary community. The collusion of the mass media with the cult of literary success in the Eighties has turned sour in the Nineties. The recession has hit the media as hard as book publishing, and *Schadenfreude* sells broadsheet newspapers as surely as scandal sells tabloids.

In consequence the reception of the novel was completely dominated and warped by the controversy that surrounded it before its publication in March 1995. The fact that it is a story of literary envy and rivalry between two novelists, one failed, one prodigiously successful, further blurred the boundary between art and life. The reviews were mixed. Some reviewed the advance rather than the novel. Its commercial success or failure is unknown, and is likely to remain so – publicly quoted sales figures for books being among the most unreliable statistics in the modern world. (Apart from the accuracy of the raw numbers, their interpretation depends on knowing whether they refer to retail sales at the cover price, retail sales at a discount, "hard" sales to bookshops, returnable sales to bookshops, specially discounted sales to bookshops, massively discounted sales to bookclubs, and what are the proportions and combinations of these types of sale.) The general perception of the trade is that *The Information* is unlikely to earn out its advance. It might conceivably have done so if it had won the Booker Prize, but Martin Amis is famous for not winning the Booker Prize, and duly didn't win it again in 1996. He was, of course, fully entitled to try and get as much money as he could for his novel. Whether HarperCollins did him, or themselves, or literary publishing in general, any favours by paying him nearly half a million pounds for it is, however, debatable. As noted above, they were among the publishers who announced substantial redundancies later in the year.

Fact and Fiction in the Novel:
An Author's Note

This essay was originally written for a collection of essays compiled in honour of Ian Gregor, Professor of English at the University of Kent, and presented to him in 1990 to mark his retirement. This explains the occasional flourish of scholarly jargon and allusion in what is an essentially personal and anecdotal essay. Ian was a personal friend of long standing, from whose always entertaining conversation I gleaned, among other things, the title of my novel *How Far Can You Go?* (it is dedicated to him for this reason). Sadly, he died in November 1995.

And here I solemnly protest, I have no intention to vilify or asperse anyone; for although everything is copied from the book of nature, and scarce a character or action produced which I have not taken from my own observations and experience; yet I have used the utmost care to obscure the persons by such different circumstances, degrees and colours, that it will be impossible to guess at them with any degree of certainty; and if it ever happens otherwise, it is only where the failure characterized is so minute, that it is a foible only, which the party himself may laugh at as well as any other.

Henry Fielding, *Preface to* Joseph Andrews *(1742)*

Is it possible for an ordinary person to climb over the area railings of no. 7 Eccles St., either from the path or from the steps, lower himself from the lowest part of the railings till his feet are within 2 feet or 3 of the ground and drop unhurt? I saw it done myself but by a man of rather athletic build. I require this information in detail in order to determine the wording of a paragraph.

James Joyce, *letter to Mrs William Murray, 2 November 1921*

"Hey," I said. "When you, do you sort of make it up, or is it just, you know, like what happens?"
"Neither."

Martin Amis, Money *(1984)*

I

There is a passage in my novel *Small World* (1984) which affords a convenient, if somewhat ribald, introduction to this complex subject. The situation is that Professor Morris Zapp, of Euphoric State University, USA, en route from a conference in Rummidge, England, to the Rockefeller Study Center at Bellagio, on Lake Como, is delayed in Milan by a public services strike, and is offered hospitality for the night by Fulvia Morgana, a rich Marxist professor of cultural studies whom he met on the plane from London. Her interest in him had quickened when she realized that his ex-wife, Désirée, was the famous author of a best-selling feminist novel in the style of Erica Jong or Marilyn French, called *Difficult Days*. Was it autobiographical, Fulvia inquired. In part, he replied. Now, in Fulvia Morgana's palatial house just off the Via Napoleone, after partaking of a delicious dinner for two, Morris Zapp becomes uneasily aware that Fulvia has plans to seduce him.

> "Don't let us talk any more about books," she said, floating across the dimly lit room with a brandy glass like a huge bubble in her hand. "Or about chairs and conferences." She stood very close to him and rubbed the back of her free hand over his crotch. "Is it really twenty-five centimetres?" she murmured.
>
> "What gives you that idea?" he said hoarsely.
>
> "Your wife's book . . ."
>
> "You don't want to believe everything you read in books, Fulvia," said Morris, grabbing the glass of cognac and draining it in a single gulp. He coughed and his eyes filled with tears. "A professional critic like you should know better than that. Novelists exaggerate."
>
> "But 'ow much do they exaggerate, Morris?" she said. "I would like to see for myself."
>
> "Like, practical criticism?" he quipped.

Fulvia did not laugh. "Didn't you make your wife measure it with her tape measure?" she persisted.

"Of course I didn't! That's just feminist propaganda. Like the whole book."

He lurched towards one of the deep armchairs, puffing clouds of cigar smoke like a retreating battleship, but Fulvia steered him firmly towards the sofa, and sat down beside him, pressing her thigh against his. She undid a button of his shirt and slid a cool hand inside. He flinched as the gems on one of her rings snagged in his chest hair.

"Lots of 'air," Fulvia purred. "*That* is in the book."

"I'm not saying the book is entirely fictitious," said Morris. "Some of the minor details are taken from life – "

" 'Airy as a beast ... You were a beast to your wife, I think."

"Ow!" exclaimed Morris, for Fulvia had dug her long lacquered nails into his flesh for emphasis.

" 'Ow? Well, for example, tying 'er up with leather straps and doing all those degrading things to 'er."

"Lies, all lies!" said Morris desperately.

"You can do those things to me, if you like, *caro*," Fulvia whispered into his ear, pinching his nipple painfully at the same time.

"I don't want to do anything to anybody, I never did," Morris groaned. "The only time we ever fooled around with that S/M stuff, it was Désirée's idea, not mine."

"I don't believe you, Morris."

"It's true. Novelists are terrible liars. They make things up. They change things around. Black becomes white, white black. They are totally unethical beings. Ouch!" Fulvia had nibbled his earlobe hard enough to draw blood.[*]

Fulvia Morgana is making an elementary mistake here about the relationship of fiction to reality. Because the fiction corresponds to historical fact in some respects (for example, the male character's chest hair), she assumes that it does in every respect. Most novelists are familiar with this reaction from readers, even quite sophisticated readers, whom they meet face to face. The

---

[*] *Small World: An Academic Romance* (London, Secker & Warburg, 1984) pp. 134–5. All page references are to this edition.

physical presence of the writer, with his or her personal history available for interrogation, seems to push aside the willing suspension of disbelief, the aesthetic appreciation of elegant narrative structure, the ludic delight in the proliferation of meaning, in favour of a beady-eyed curiosity about the "true story" behind the fiction. Spouses of novelists, or other relatives and close acquaintances, are apt to suffer this curiosity in a particularly trying form, as Morris Zapp discovers.

For the record, this episode in *Small World* has no source in my own experience, but was generated entirely by the needs and possibilities of the narrative. Admittedly I was once resident at the Rockefeller Study Center at Bellagio – but *after* writing the novel, not before (a circumstances that has a story of its own attached to it). I certainly met no one like Fulvia Morgana on the way to anywhere. *Small World* is subtitled "an academic romance", a designation that plays on the recognized genre-term "academic novel" and also indicates what kind of romance is invoked – not the Mills and Boon kind, but the kind studied and loved by academics: Heliodorus, the stories of King Arthur, the *Faerie Queene*, *Orlando Furioso*, the late plays of Shakespeare, and so on. As one of the characters says, "Real romance is a pre-novelistic kind of narrative. It's full of adventure and coincidence and surprises and marvels, and has lots of characters who are lost or enchanted or wandering about looking for each other, or for the Grail, or something like that" (p. 258). *Small World* in this way claims the licence to be highly fictive, as the epigraph from Hawthorne says: "When a writer calls his work a Romance, it need hardly be observed that he wishes to claim a certain latitude, which he would not have felt himself entitled to assume had he professed to be writing a novel."

But *Small World*, of course, *is* a novel, a comic novel. The passage between Morris Zapp and Fulvia Morgana is designed to contribute both to the romance theme and the comic effect. Morris Zapp is re-enacting the situation of the errant knight lured into an enchanted castle and trapped in the toils of a seductive sorceress. The name Fulvia Morgana echoes that of Morgan Le Fay in Arthurian legend. In her mirrored bedroom Fulvia snaps handcuffs on to Morris Zapp's wrists and removes his underpants, rendering him powerless to escape. Travesty turns into farce as the terrified Zapp hears Fulvia's husband, Ernesto, letting himself into the house and climbing the stairs. In a reversal of the outraged-husband stereotype, Ernesto greets Morris Zapp genially and prepares to join him and Fulvia between the crimson sheets of the circular bed. Reversal is indeed the keynote of the whole episode. There is a reversal of normal seduction roles in Fulvia's hot pursuit of the reluctant Morris. There is a reversal of "normal" sado-masochistic roles in that Fulvia, while inviting Morris to hurt her, actually hurts him. Thus in the very process of trying to re-enact *Difficult Days*, to force reality to fit the fiction, she is in fact reversing the fiction, just as Morris claims Désirée reversed the facts.

It is important to note, however, that the reader does not know whether Morris Zapp is telling the truth, *and neither do I*. I know nothing more about Désirée's novel, or the sexual side of their marriage, than is fragmentarily revealed in the pages of *Changing Places* and *Small World*, and for my purposes as a novelist it was not necessary to determine how accurate an account of the Zapp marriage is given in *Difficult Days* or by Morris Zapp in his conversation with Fulvia Morgana. In short, there is no source for this episode, either fictional or factual, against which its truth could be checked.

This does not, however, mean that there are no factual sources for other episodes in *Small World*, or that the whole novel is not full of discrete facts culled from my observation of the real world. Of course there are and of course it is.

2

It has long been recognized by historians and theorists of the novel that, in this kind of writing, "fiction" is bound, in a peculiar and complex way, to the world of "facts". In his classic study, *The Rise of the Novel*, Ian Watt stressed the referential or pseudo-referential character of the language of the earliest major English novelists, Defoe and Richardson, who presented their invented stories as real documents – letters, confessions, and so on – of which they posed as the editors. These stories were fictional, but formally indistinguishable from "true stories". The telling of them is full of facts of the kind that constitute reality for an empirically minded culture. The novel, according to Watt, rose in response to: "that vast transformation of Western civilization since the Renaissance which has replaced the unified world picture of the Middle Ages with another very different one – one which presents us, essentially, with a developing but unplanned aggregate of particular individuals having particular experiences at particular times and particular places."[*]

More recent, Foucauldian attempts to locate the origins of the novel in the Renaissance have focused on the same problematic. Robert Weimann, for instance, has argued that, whereas the medieval narrative writer was a quasi-anonymous mediator of stories authorized by tradition ("I fynde no more written in bokis that bene auctorized," Malory says on winding up the *Morte D'Arthur*), the Renaissance writer saw himself as the maker or begetter of an original discourse put together from heterogeneous sources and models, entailing a fusion or confusion of fiction and history. "The 'fained image' of the *fabula* was rendered in terms of that different type of discourse which, as *historia*, was 'bound to tell things as they were'."[†]

In his *Factual Fictions: The Origins of the English Novel* (1983), Lennard J. Davis argues that the novel emerged out of a new kind of narrative writing, the precursor of modern journalism, which he calls "news/novels discourse" – the reporting of recent or current events in broadsides, pamphlets, ballads, criminal confessions, and so on, made possible by the invention of the printing press. The characteristic feature of this discourse is that it foreshortens or collapses the distance between language and reality, and thus between the audience and the matter of narrative. Whereas medieval narrative presented a story for the sake of its moral, which had to be allegorically interpreted, in news/novels discourse the medium is the message, the words efface themselves as signifiers and strive to coincide with the events they signify, the human interest of which is taken for granted, like the contents of a newspaper. Novelists perceived that by imitating the form of this new kind of documentary writing they could exert an exciting new power over their

[*] Ian Watt, *The Rise of the Novel* (Harmondsworth, Penguin Books, 1963) p. 32.
[†] Robert Weimann, "Appropriation and Modern History in Renaissance Prose Narrative", *New Literary History*, XIV, 1983, p. 478.

readers, giving to fictitious characters and events an unprecedented illusion of reality.

This theory of the rise of the novel, like Watt's, seems to
apply more readily to Defoe and Richardson than to their great
contemporary Henry Fielding who mocked the technique of
pseudo-factual writing in *Joseph Andrews* ("He accordingly eat
either a rabbit or a fowl, I never could with any tolerable
certainty discover which"),* and himself employed an ostenta-
tiously literary style full of echoes of and allusions to classical
mythology and scripture. However, as Davis points out, Fielding was a journalist before he was a novelist, and he integrated
the facts of a real event (the Jacobite Rising of 1745), as it
unfolded, into his fictional *History of Tom Jones* and made
adjustments to his original design to accommodate them. He
thus established a precedent that was followed and developed
by later novelists such as Scott, Thackeray and George Eliot.
(Compare the Porteus riots in *Heart of Midlothian*, the Battle of
Waterloo in *Vanity Fair* and the Reform Election in *Middlemarch*.) And although Fielding's characters may seem to us like
stock types, to his contemporaries they were often recognizable
portraits of real people, in spite of the precautions he claims to
have taken in his Preface to *Joseph Andrews* (see the first
epigraph to this essay).

The ambivalent and contradictory relationship between fact
and fiction in the early novel persists into its classical and
modern phases. Novelists are and always have been split
between, on the one hand, a desire to claim an imaginative and
representative truth for their stories and, on the other hand, a
conviction that the best way to secure and guarantee that
truthfulness is by a scrupulous respect for empirical fact. Why
else did James Joyce take such pains to establish whether his
fictional character Leopold Bloom could plausibly drop down
into the basement area of no. 7 Eccles Street?

Novels burn facts as engines burn fuel, and the facts can
come only from the novelist's own experience or acquired
knowledge. Not uncommonly, a novelist begins by drawing
mainly on facts of the former kind and, when these are "used
up", becomes more reliant on the latter. Joyce's progress from

---

* Henry Fielding, *Joseph Andrews* (1742), Ch. XV.

the realistic and autobiographical *Dubliners* and *A Portrait* to the increasingly encyclopaedic *Ulysses* and *Finnegans Wake* is an example. So is the career of George Eliot, who began with *Scenes of Clerical Life*, so closely based on the Nuneaton of her childhood that "keys" to "Janet's Repentance" were soon in circulation in the town, and ended with the massively researched *Daniel Deronda*.

Inasmuch as fact and fiction are opposites, one could say that the novel as a literary form is founded upon contradiction, upon the reconciliation of the irreconcilable, something novelists have endeavoured to conceal by various kinds of diversionary mystification: framing narratives, parody and other kinds of intertextuality, and metafictional devices such as Martin Amis's introduction of himself into his own fiction, to be questioned about his writing by his own character. The question John Self asks "Martin Amis" (see my third epigraph) is the question Fulvia Morgana asks Morris Zapp about his wife's novel. It is the question readers always ask novelists, and his answer is the one they always give. I gave it, anticipating the question, in the Author's Note that prefaces *Small World*.

> Like *Changing Places*, to which it is a sequel, *Small World* resembles what is sometimes called the real world, without corresponding exactly to it, and is peopled by figments of the imagination. Rummidge is not Birmingham, though it owes something to popular prejudices about that city. There really is an underground chapel at Heathrow and a James Joyce pub in Zurich, but no universities in Limerick or Darlington; nor, as far as I know, was there ever a British Council representative in Genoa. The MLA Convention of 1979 did not take place in New York, though I have drawn on the programme for the 1978 one, which did. And so on.

At first glance this looks like a familiar defensive manoeuvre to disclaim any representation of real people and institutions that might take offence. But the Note also informs readers that some components of the book they might suppose to be invented are in fact "real". I wanted my readers to know, for instance, that the panel discussions at the MLA Convention in Part V, on "Lesbian-feminist Teaching and Learning" and "Problems of Cultural Distortion in Translating Expletives in the Work of Cortazar, Sender, Baudelaire and Flaubert", were not parodies but the real thing. I wanted them to know that the Dublin pub painstakingly dismantled and re-erected in Zurich in memory of James Joyce, who wrote most of *Ulysses* in that city, was not some strained conceit of mine but a fact: a fact that says much about the curious intertwining of high culture and popular culture in our epoch, about the reification of literary reputations and the deification of dead writers, a process in which the academic literary profession is deeply implicated.

If *Small World* had a single point of origin, it was the James Joyce Symposium of 1979, held in Zurich, which I attended, and where I first made acquaintance with that pub, thronged with Joyceans from every corner of the globe, knocking back tumblers of draught Guinness and discussing textual cruces in *Finnegans Wake* at the tops of their voices, while outside on Pelikanstrasse the burghers of Zurich went decorously about the serious business of making money, and across the river in the red light district, where my hotel (chosen at random) was situated, squeaky-clean prostitutes stood on the well-swept street corners, one per corner in the methodical Swiss way. What strange conjunctions and piquant contrasts the lives of modern academics encompassed, it struck me, as they toted their conference papers and lightweight luggage around the global campus. There might be a novel in it.

From Zurich I flew direct to another conference in Israel, an experience that provided much of the local colour for the conference organized by Morris Zapp in Part IV of *Small World* (p. 298):

> Now it is mid-August, and Morris Zapp's conference on the Future of Criticism is in full swing. Almost everybody involved agrees that it is the best conference they have ever attended. Morris is smug. The secret of his success is very simple: the formal proceedings of the conference are kept to a bare minimum. There is just one paper a day actually delivered by its author, early in the morning. All the other papers are circulated in Xeroxed form, and the remainder of the day is allocated to "unstructured discussion" of the issues raised in these documents, or, in other words, to swimming and sunbathing at the Hilton pool, sightseeing in

the Old City, shopping in the bazaar, eating out in ethnic restaurants, and making expeditions to Jericho, the Jordan valley, and Galilee.

I always feel a twinge of guilt when I reread this passage, for those who hosted and attended the conference that was its "source" know that it was in fact an extraordinarily hard-working affair, and that the sightseeing and other hedonistic diversions mentioned in the passage from *Small World* were indulged in only after we had been released from long days in smoke-filled seminar rooms, or during an optional four-day tour of Israel after the conference had disbanded. But for the purposes of the novel this conference had to be the one in which the institution of the international conference would demonstrate most spectacularly its "ways of converting work into play, combining professionalism with tourism, and all at someone else's expense" (p. 231). I suppose this is what Morris Zapp means when he says that novelists are totally unethical beings: when the truth of fact and the needs of fiction conflict, the novelist will always favour the latter.

But, broadly speaking, the academic-comedy-of-manners level of *Small World* is derived from the world of "fact", while the interlaced plots (of quest and adventure and love and mysterious origins and identities) are derived from the world of fiction. The challenge, the "game" of writing the novel, was to nudge and fiddle these two planes into a near-perfect fit with each other, and the Chapel of St George at Heathrow was invaluable for this purpose because it is both a real and a romantic place. I discovered it (not without difficulty, for few people at the airport can direct you to it) one Sunday morning in November 1981 while I was waiting for a flight to Warsaw, where I was to attend (what else?) a conference. I had already started work on *Small World*, and the underground chapel, secreted amid the labyrinthine ways of Heathrow, with its chivalric patron saint and its low roof curved like the passenger cabin of a wide-bodied jet, immediately offered itself as a location for my story. Although it was a non-denominational chapel, the Catholics seemed to have taken it over, making it a congenial place for my young Irish hero, Persse McGarrigle. There was a statue of Our Lady against the wall, and a red sanctuary lamp burning on a side altar. As I sat there, a priest clothed in vestments came in. I said, "Is this going to be a Catholic mass?" He said, "Yes, d'you want communion?" I said, "How long will it take?" He said, "As quick as I can make it." Perhaps he too had a plane to catch. His rapid recitation of the liturgy was punctuated with burps from indigestion. I did not use this incident in *Small World*, but I did take note of the petition board at the back of the chapel, especially a poignant, scribbled prayer from what sounded like an Irish girl in trouble. Only slightly modified, it found its way into *Small World* and gave rise to Persse's meeting with his cousin Bernadette. The petition board also became an important property in the story of Persse's pursuit of Angelica. When Howard Schuman adapted *Small World* for Granada TV's six-part serial, he framed the whole narrative with Persse's tape-recorded "confession" in the chapel of St George, and these sequences were actually shot there.

When you are working on a book, everything that happens to you is considered for possible exploitation in the work-in-progress. After my visit to Poland I introduced a Polish character into *Small World*, Wanda Kedrzejkiewicelska, a young lecturer at the University of Lodz, specializing in British absurdist drama, which she finds not at all funny but a sombrely realistic analogue of life in Poland. I wrote a scene or two for her, one in which she is shown queueing for sausage for her husband's dinner and reading *The Birthday Party*, shoving before her with her foot a capacious bag equally handy for carrying books and foraging for food, dreaming longingly of a projected visit to a British Council Summer School at Oxford that would bring her into the plot. Later I decided that the trip to Oxford would never materialize, that Wanda would spend the entire novel travelling about Lodz by tram, getting off to join any likely-looking queue, poignantly excluded from the plot and the fun the other characters were having. But the character of Wanda herself obstinately refused to come alive, and it became obvious to me that the plight of the Polish academics I had met, and of the Polish nation at large, was too grim for incorporation into my light-hearted satire on the global campus; so I cut her out of the novel.

3

"Rummidge is not Birmingham, though it owes something to popular prejudices about that city."

Fictitious place names are, of course, one of the novelist's most transparent devices for incorporating fact into fiction. The elaborately coded topography of Hardy's Wessex, for instance, or Arnold Bennett's Five Towns, is not designed to deceive anybody as to the real locations of their novels, but to avoid the logical contradiction, and perhaps legal risks, of putting fictional characters in places that at a given time were occupied by historical individuals. The implied rules governing this matter cast an interesting though indeterminate light on the relations of fact to fiction in the novel. You can invent an imaginary London street, but you cannot have a capital of England that is not London. You can have an imaginary Oxford or Cambridge college, but it would seem awkward, to say the least, to have an ancient English university that was not Oxford or Cambridge. You can site a university in a city that doesn't actually have one (though there are risks entailed in this practice; I understand that the Institute of Higher Education in Limerick, of whose existence I was unaware when I wrote *Small World*, is at present seeking university status, and that there have been high-level discussions in Ireland about what to call it in view of the rather prejudicial image of my fictitious University College Limerick.)* You can, it seems, have a provincial city or town with a fictional name (Middlemarch, Casterbridge, Rummidge) occupying the same geographical space as an actual city or town, and closely resembling the original in every respect except inhabitants.

In January 1969 I took leave of absence from the University of Birmingham to take up the post of visiting associate professor at the University of California, Berkeley. At that time, both campuses, like most campuses, were in the throes of the student revolution; but whereas Birmingham's "occupation" had been a relatively mild-mannered and good-humoured affair, in Berkeley there was something like civil war in progress, with police chasing demonstrators through the streets with shotguns and

---

* The University of Limerick was established in 1989.

clouds of teargas drifting across the campus. And if Birmingham was timidly responding to the vibrations emanating from Swinging London, Berkeley was at the leading edge of the Permissive Society, the Counter-Culture, Flower Power and all the rest of the 1960s baggage. Out of this experience I constructed a comic novel, *Changing Places: A Tale of Two Campuses*, centring on an exchange between two university teachers of English Literature at that particular moment in history: Philip Swallow, an undistinguished lecturer at the University of Rummidge in the damp and grey English Midlands, and dynamic, abrasive professor Morris Zapp from the State University of Euphoria (familiarly known as Euphoric State) on the sunny west coast of America, who end up swapping wives as well as jobs. The plot was a narrative transformation of the thematic material and the socio-cultural similarities and differences I had perceived between Birmingham and Berkeley. I did not go to Berkeley on an exchange scheme and, unlike my main characters, I took my wife and family with me across the Atlantic. (When I explain this to people like Fulvia Morgana I detect on their faces a look of surprise mingled with disappointment, even resentment, as if they feel they have been conned.) The plot is completely fictional, though the background events of student protest and civil disturbance are closely based on actual events which I observed. Several of the "quotations" which make up Chapter 4 of the novel, entitled "Reading", were transcribed from real journals and documents.

Changing Places also has its carefully worded Author's Note:

Although some of the locations and public events portrayed in this novel bear a certain resemblance to actual locations and events, the characters, considered either as individuals or as members of institutions, are entirely imaginary. Rummidge and Euphoria are places on the map of a comic world which resembles the one we are standing on without corresponding exactly to it, and which is peopled by figments of the imagination.[*]

[*] *Changing Places: A Tale of Two Campuses* (London, Secker & Warburg, 1975).

The fictitious and jokey place names licensed me, I hoped, to exaggerate and deform reality for literary purposes. Rummidge is more dourly provincial, Euphoria more "far out" than their respective models. The University of Rummidge in particular is a much smaller and dimmer place than the University of Birmingham, and its undistinguished English Department, which seems never to have had more than one professorial chair in its entire history, could not conceivably be confused with the large and flourishing School of English (rated in the country's top six by the UGC in 1986, and the only one outside Oxbridge to achieve top marks for research in a recent UFC survey) in which I have had the privilege of working for most of my professional life.

At the time of writing *Changing Places*, I had no plans for a sequel, but when, about ten years later, I conceived the idea of a "global campus" novel, it seemed an obvious move to incorporate some of the characters from the earlier book, and to throw the wilder shores of the international conference circuit into relief by starting the story at a rather depressed and depressing conference at Rummidge. For this opening sequence I drew on memories of several comfortless gatherings in halls of residence belonging to various British universities. (The unseasonable snow that exacerbates the privations of the Rummidge conferees was suggested by the experience of returning from a blossom-laden Washington in late April 1981 to an England totally immobilized by a freak snowstorm – it took us longer to travel from Heathrow to Birmingham than from Washington to London.)

When I began work on a novel about the impact of Thatcherism on universities and industry, intertextually related to the so-called Industrial Novels of the nineteenth century, Rummidge offered itself once more as the setting with a certain inevitability. What point would there be in creating another fictitious Midland industrial city with a university in it? But *Nice Work* is a more sober and realistic novel than its carnivalesque precursors, and the physical setting became less of a caricature and more of a likeness of Birmingham in its composition. The membrane between fact and fiction, between "Birmingham" and "Rummidge", has undoubtedly become thinner and more transparent with the passing of time, and I was concerned that it might be actually ruptured by the recent television serialization of *Nice Work* (which I scripted) because it was filmed entirely on location in Birmingham, including the campus of the University. This was a great bonus for the production team, but I was slightly surprised that the University agreed to it, and so, I think, were some of my former colleagues. The administration evidently decided that the PR advantages of displaying its impressive campus on television would outweigh any negative feedback from the satirical elements in the story and, having seen the finished product, I think they were probably right.*

Watching *Nice Work* being filmed was a fascinating but at times disorienting experience, for I was seeing many scenes that I had invented being returned to the "real" locations which had given rise to them – not only on the academic side of the story, but also on the industrial side. Most of the foundry sequences in Episode One, for instance, were shot in the very first foundry I visited while researching the novel (in which my own awed and appalled reactions are transferred to Robyn Penrose). One Sunday morning in March 1989 I drove from my house in Edgbaston to the main entrance of the University, and there, like a dream or hallucination, was a traffic jam I had invented three years earlier: an articulated lorry was drawn up across the road, blocking the passage of other vehicles, while placard-waving pickets of the Association of University Teachers engaged the driver in earnest discussion of their grievances. A girl student rushed up beside me. "Oh dear!" she cried. "Is the University closed?" She hadn't taken in the signboard, with its fake heraldic shield, that read: *University of Rummidge*. "It's only a TV film," I reassured her. I didn't tell her that I had written the script.

4

I doubt whether I could have countenanced the use of the

---

* Since this was written, the University announced the result of a MORI poll it commissioned into the effect of the series on viewers' perception of Birmingham University. 61 per cent of viewers apparently felt "that the campus featured in the programme is attractive". And even though the story is about a lecturer at "the University of Rummidge", a majority of all viewers mentioned spontaneously that the programme was filmed at Birmingham.

Birmingham campus as a location for the filming of *Nice Work* if I hadn't retired from my post there a couple of years previously. The paradoxes and contradictions of my position had been acute enough while "Rummidge" was just a verbal construct, confined and consumed within the covers of a book, or books. To have collaborated in a re-creation of the fictional place that would be visually indistinguishable from its real-life model while performing a professional role in the latter would, I think, have placed an intolerable strain on the distinction I always tried to preserve, however artificially, between my life as an academic and my life as a novelist. The writer who works in an institutional environment on which he draws for material and inspiration is peculiarly sensitive to the conflicting imperatives and interests of the world of fact and of the world of fiction. Crossing and recrossing the frontier between the two worlds, one is apt to feel like a double agent, always vulnerable to the accusation of treachery, always fearful of being "exposed". I will conclude these ruminations with a personal anecdote, not entirely creditable to myself, but illustrative of the point.

It will be recalled that in the passage from *Small World* with which I began, Morris Zapp is on his way to the Rockefeller Study Center at the Villa Serbelloni in Bellagio, on Lake Como. Since there is no reference to this place in the Author's Note, readers might be forgiven for supposing that it is an invention of mine. It is in fact a real institution, which offers hospitality for periods of about a month's duration, mainly to scholars, but also to writers, artists, musicians and so on, and their spouses, in surroundings of great luxury, elegance and outstanding natural beauty, in order that they can work on some suitable project, with no more distraction then the occasional walk or game of tennis, and civilized social intercourse over meals and after dinner. Several friends and acquaintances of mine who had stayed there had spoken highly of its attractions and urged me to apply. At some time early in the 1980s I did so, in my capacity as a novelist. I had just started *Small World*, and it seemed to me that the Villa Serbelloni would be a very appropriate place to work on this book. In the event, I was too late with my application to be accepted for the coming year, but the Rockefeller Foundation in New York encouraged me to reapply in the future. This I did, but in the meantime two things

had happened. First, I had nearly finished *Small World*. Second,
I had incorporated the Villa Serbelloni into it. For the more I
had discovered and thought about the place in connection with
my original application, the more irresistible it had become as a
setting for part of my story, and I accordingly sent Morris Zapp
to stay there (p. 151):

> Morris was shown into a well-appointed suite on the second
> floor, and stepped out on to his balcony to inhale the air,
> scented with the perfume of various spring blossoms, and to
> enjoy the prospect. Down on the terrace, the other resident
> scholars were gathering for the pre-lunch aperitif – he had
> glimpsed the table laid for lunch in the dining-room on his
> way up: starched white napery, crystal glass, menu cards. He
> surveyed the scene with complacency. He felt sure he was
> going to enjoy his stay here. Not the least of its attractions
> was that it was entirely free. All you had to do, to come and
> stay in this idyllic retreat, pampered by servants and lavishly
> provided with food and drink, given every facility for
> reflection and creation, was to apply.
>
> Of course, you had to be distinguished – by, for instance,
> having applied successfully for other, similar handouts,
> grants, fellowships and so on, in the past. That was the
> beauty of the academic life, as Morris saw it. To those that
> had, more would be given.

As readers of the novel will know, a punishment awaits
Morris's hubristic enjoyment of this ultimate academic freebie:
later in the story he is kidnapped by Italian political extremists
while jogging in the grounds of the Villa, and held to ransom.
Since I knew I would have finished the book before I got to
Bellagio, I could not make it the project of my second
application. Accordingly, I applied this time in my capacity as
academic literary critic, proposing to work on an article on the
form of Jane Austen's novels, commissioned for inclusion in *The
Jane Austen Companion*, edited by J. David Grey, A. Walton Litz
and Brian Southam (published by Macmillan in 1986).

The two sides of my schizophrenic existence were now set on
a collision course, though I did not know it. I vaguely supposed
that my novel would either be published well before my arrival
at the Villa Serbelloni, in which case I would have to grin and

bear the amusement and/or dispproval of my hosts and fellow guests, in a manner to which I was accustomed; or (preferably) it would appear after my departure, in which case nothing need be said about it. A better plot-maker than I, however, contrived that the novel was published on 19 March 1984, just a couple of weeks before I set off to spend my appointed month at Bellagio. I flew straight from a hectic fortnight of interviews, bookshop promotions and anxious scrutiny of the review pages to the peace and beauty of the Italian Lakes.

The Villa Serbelloni, I was glad to discover, corresponded in every particular to my description of it in the novel, based on data obtained from various informants. But professional satisfaction at this achievement was qualified by a certain unease about my own position there. The charming and gracious Italian administrators of the Villa knew nothing of *Small World*; neither did my fellow-guests, most of whom had flown direct from North America and were not aficionados of contemporary fiction. Indeed, nobody knew even that I was a novelist, for I appeared on the current list of residents, supplied by the Foundation in New York, as a Professor of English Literature, working on Jane Austen. (There was a nice additional irony here, since Morris Zapp was also a Jane Austen man – in his own words, "*the* Jane Austen man" – before he converted to deconstruction.) What was I to do? It has never been my style to invite discussion of my fiction. I certainly didn't feel like volunteering the information that I had just published a satirical novel about academic globe-trotters in which one of the chief characters was kidnapped while jogging in the grounds of the Villa Serbelloni. So I said nothing about it; and of course the more time that passed, the more difficult it became to say anything.

The time passed very agreeably. Villa life proved as comfortable and civilized as it was reputed to be. The sun shone; the company was agreeable. A jolly professor of nursing from Winnipeg proposed that we all collaborated on writing a thriller to be called *Murder at the Villa Serbelloni*, and was disappointed by my lack of enthusiasm for the project. My wife, freed from her teaching job by the Easter holidays, arrived to share the last two weeks of my stay. She has her own very good reasons for not advertising the fact that she is married to a novelist (*vide* the conversation between Fulvia Morgana and Morris Zapp, above), and was only too pleased to preserve my "cover", but I suffered from a lingering sense of guilt, or bad faith, and occasional spasms of longing to confess. It seemed to me that it was only a matter of time before I was found out.

One day a fellow guest who had gone to Milan to meet his wife returned without her (her flight had been delayed) but with a Penguin copy of *Ginger, You're Barmy*, which he had picked up from the airport bookstall. He confronted me with it and genially accused me of hiding my light under a bushel. My cover was partly blown, but still nobody seemed to have heard of *Small World*. The Study Center is also used for short, select international conferences, and on two occasions during April about thirty people flew in from various parts of the world, including Britain, for this purpose, and joined us at meals. I was sure one of them would have a copy of *Small World* in their luggage, or at least a newspaper cutting, for the book had been widely reviewed in England; but this never happened. The Villa itself did not subscribe to British newspapers, but it did take the *London Review of Books* and it seemed to me that this was the most likely medium through which news of *Small World* would travel to Bellagio. No review had appeared in the pages of that journal, however, by the time my period of residence came to an end. I shook hands with our hosts and fellow guests with my guilty secret still intact, resolving that as soon as I got home I would write a letter to the chief administrator, confessing all and donating a copy of *Small World* to the Villa's library.

This I did, and in due course both letter and book were received and acknowledged with great good humour. But amongst the heap of mail that awaited me on our return home was the latest issue of the *London Review of Books*, containing a review by Frank Kermode of *Small World*, which must have arrived in the library of the Villa Serbelloni shortly after I left. It was, I am glad to say, a very favourable review, but that wasn't what struck me most forcibly about it. It was entitled – by whom, I do not know, nor upon what whim, or with what telepathic insight, for it was not the most obvious of headings – "Jogging in Bellagio".

The Lives
of Graham Greene

This review-article, originally published in two parts
in the *New York Review of Books* (8 and 22 June
1995), discusses the following: *The Life of Graham
Greene. Volume 2: 1939–1955*, by Norman Sherry.
London, Cape, 1994. New York, Viking, 1994;
(reference is also made to *Volume 1: 1904–1939* of this
biography, London, Cape, 1989); *Graham Greene:
The Man Within*, by Michael Shelden, London,
Heinemann, 1994; published with revisions, as
Graham Greene: The Enemy Within, New York,
Random House, 1995; *Graham Greene: Three Lives*,
by Anthony Mockler, The Guynd by Arbroath,
Hunter Mackay, 1994; *Graham Greene: Friend and
Brother*, by Leopoldo Duran, New York,
HarperCollins, 1994. I have incorporated into the
closing section of this article parts of a memoir
contributed to the *Times Literary Supplement*, 12 April
1991, shortly after Greene's death, entitled "Graham
Greene: a Personal View."

I

If Graham Greene had never published any novels he would surely be remembered as one of our century's finest book reviewers, film critics, and occasional essayists. In 1953 he wrote a characteristically shrewd and witty review[*] in the *New Statesman* of the first volume of Leon Edel's monumental life of Henry James. He observed:

> It is a testing volume, for here the greater part of the material has been supplied with incomparable glamour and cunning by the subject himself, in *A Small Boy and Others* and *Notes of a Son and Brother*. Mr Edel, with great scholarship and freedom from undue reverence, works his way in and out of this luminous smoke-screen: he never allows James to escape completely into the sense of glory.

One is inevitably reminded of the smoke-screen behind which Graham Greene himself hid from inquisitive journalists and would-be biographers for most of his life, while allowing them just enough glimpses of personal trauma and wayward behaviour – like the famous experiments with Russian roulette – to keep public interest in himself simmering. The review ended on a note that seems today even more pregnant with self-referential significance. Looking forward to future volumes of Edel's life, Greene wonders how the biographer will cope with the middle years of Henry James, about which the novelist himself vouchsafed little information:

> It was in these abandoned years behind the façade of the social figure . . . that the greater ambiguities stand like the shapes of furniture in a great house shrouded in dust sheets. Now the lights are about to go on, a hand will twitch at the

---

[*] Reprinted in *Reflections* (London, Reinhardt Books in association with Viking, 1990), a collection of occasional prose by Graham Greene, selected and introduced by Judith Adamson.

sheets, and James himself, who nosed with such sensitive curiosity around the secret in *The Sacred Fount*, would surely be the last to complain of a detective of such gravity and honesty, even if he should have to come to deal with what James might have considered the "all but unspeakable."

Greene did not take so benign a view of such biographical detective work when, much later, it was focused on himself. By the early 1970s, however, he seems to have decided, or to have been persuaded by his family, that the best way to discourage intrusive investigators was to commission an authorized biography. Accordingly, he invited Norman Sherry, the author of two scholarly books about Joseph Conrad which Greene had read and admired, to be his official biographer. Sherry being at this time professor of English Literature at Lancaster, one of Britain's less fashionable new universities, this was the equivalent of a leading actor in some provincial repertory theatre suddenly being offered the coveted starring role in a major Hollywood picture.

At the time it must have seemed like a miraculous blessing, but in the event it turned out to be more like a curse, or cross. Setting himself the herculean task of retracing his subject's every journey (Greene was one of the century's great literary travellers), Sherry suffered many trials and tribulations, experiencing temporary blindness, succumbing to dysentery in the same Mexican village as Greene himself, and nearly dying from some tropical disease that required the removal of part of his intestines. (One is reminded of the ominous remark of the colonial official in *Heart of Darkness* – "men who come out here should have no entrails.") Sherry also surrendered the security of his tenured university chair without any compensating enrichment by way of royalties – according to a recent report in *Publishers Weekly* (27 February 1995), he is £78,000 in debt to his publishers.

Greene, for his part, suffered frequent misgivings about the whole enterprise, and by Sherry's own admission dreaded their occasional interviews. He vainly tried to set limits to Sherry's freedom of investigation, and even on occasion tried to pretend that he had never intended him to write an exhaustive and thoroughly documented life at all. He made a somewhat chilling prophecy, two-thirds of which has already been fulfilled, that he would live to read Sherry's first volume, but not the second, and that Sherry himself would not live to read the third. At about the same time that he commisioned Sherry, Greene befriended a Spanish priest and university lecturer in English literature, Leopoldo Duran, who had written a doctoral dissertation on the religious element in his novels. Greene encouraged Duran to take notes on their occasional trips through Spain, perhaps hoping to make him into a Boswell whose admiring testimony would act as a counterbalance to Sherry's "objective" biography.

Duran noted that Greene always became depressed when the topic of Sherry's book was raised between them, and recorded that the novelist also warned him about "an unauthorized biographer by the name of Mockler." When Anthony Mockler began serializing his biography in 1989 in an attempt to scoop Sherry's first volume, Greene took legal action to silence him. The effort to control and curtail the uncovering of his private life was, however, doomed to be only temporarily successful. Little more than three years after Greene's death in April 1991, Mockler released the first volume of a revised version of his suppressed book, and Michael Shelden, an American academic and author of books on Cyril Connolly and George Orwell, published one of the most destructive literary biographies of recent times, bristling with "all but unspeakable" revelations and speculations.

Sherry tells a story wonderfully evocative of the novelist's perturbation at the prospect of all this posthumous raking through his private life. Greene was seeing Sherry off at a railway station after one of their interviews, and they were alone on the platform when Greene mentioned that he had heard that his wife, Vivien, intended to write a book about their marriage:

> Once Greene had said that, his face took on a look of total dismay, and he opened his mouth and sang high-pitched from an old music-hall song: "Shovel the dust on the old man's coffin and take up your pen and write." He sang with

such melancholy that I stood the entranced spectator of another's mortal sadness.

Even in his own lifetime, when Sherry's monumental first volume appeared in 1989, covering the years 1904–1939 in Greene's life, the novelist must have wondered whether he had not damaged rather than safeguarded his reputation by authorizing a biography and collaborating with the biographer. Two things stand out in one's memory of that book, neither of them flattering to the subject. One is the source of Greene's obsession with betrayal. He had, of course, himself written about his discovery of evil in the bullying to which he was subjected at Berkhamsted School, of which his father was headmaster, and the special stress he suffered as a result of belonging to both "sides" in the inevitable and eternal war between teachers and taught in such an institution. But Sherry, with great pertinacity and investigative skill, uncovered the fact that Greene eventually broke the schoolboy code by naming his tormentor, a boy called Carter, who was consequently expelled. It is a type of betrayal which surfaced in Greene's first novel, *The Man Within* (1928), and continued to haunt his imagination for the rest of his life.

The other memorable feature of Sherry's first volume was its account, extensively documented by reference to Greene's correspondence and diaries, of his extraordinary emotional and sexual life, especially his courtship of and marriage to Vivien Dayrell-Browning. The story is told in more condensed form, but with some new details, by Shelden and Mockler.

When he was an undergraduate at Oxford Greene became editor of the *Oxford Outlook*, and contributed to the issue for February 1925 an article on sex, religion, and the cinema which was to have fateful consequences. "We are most of us considerably oversexed," it began. "We either go to Church to worship the Virgin Mary or to a public house and snigger over stories and limericks; and this exaggeration of the sex-instinct has had a bad effect on art, on the cinematograph as well as on the stage." Greene had of course been brought up in the Church of England, but at this stage of his life was a non-believer. A young woman who had recently been converted to Roman Catholicism, and who worked for the Oxford publisher and bookseller

Blackwells, wrote to reprimand the author of the article for using the word "worship," instead of "venerate," to describe Catholic devotion to the Virgin Mary. Greene invited Vivien Dayrell-Browning to tea, and subsequently took her to a movie starring Greta Garbo (probably, the knowledgeable editor of *The Graham Greene Film Reader* surmises, *Joyless Street*).*

The ironies in this episode are almost too thickly clustered to disentangle. Greene himself suffered chronically from that dissociated sensibility in sexual matters which he rather priggishly diagnosed in his undergraduate article: the mixture of fascination and disgust with the sexual act, and the related tendency to stereotype women as either Madonna or whore. These motifs recur again and again in his fiction. He identified Vivien as a Madonna and fell in love with her in high romantic style. She was only nineteen, emotionally immature, a virgin who by her own admission found the idea of physical sex repugnant. She did not want to marry Greene. She did not want to marry anybody. But he set himself to win her, and he succeeded by the sheer force of his will, exercised through a deluge of letters – he wrote some two thousand to her in a thirty-month period, sometimes three a day.

For her sake he undertook instruction in the Catholic faith, and was received into the Church. He even at one stage tried to allay her sexual timidity by proposing a celibate marriage. According to Mockler, Vivien made a bizarre counterproposal: that her mother should adopt Greene so that they could live together as brother and sister. Greene squashed that idea, but in drawing an enticing picture of their honeymoon he implied that they would have separate bedrooms. Unable to resist such gallantry and ardour, Vivien capitulated and agreed to marry. Greene was happy and triumphant. However, within a year of the marriage, Sherry discovered, he was resorting to prostitutes in London. Mockler claims that he did so soon after Vivien agreed to marry him.

Prostitutes certainly fascinated Greene throughout his life. He had something like a real love affair with one called "Annette" in the mid-Thirties, and the heroine of one of his last

---

* *The Graham Greene Film Reader: Reviews, Essays, Interviews & Film Stories.* Edited by David Parkinson. New York, Applause Books, 1994.

novels, Clara, in *The Honorary Consul*, is a member of the oldest profession. He made a point of patronizing the brothels in every foreign country he visited, if only as a non-participating observer. But that he indulged this taste at the very outset of his marriage was hardly a good omen for its future. Although Greene certainly cared for Vivien, dedicated books to her, and sent her affectionate messages on many occasions, he spent much of his married life deliberately living away from her and their two children, often in the company of a mistress.

There is some evidence that their sexual relationship was not helped by Catholic teaching on birth control. Greene fully shared Cyril Connolly's belief that "the pram in the hall was the enemy of good art," but Vivien would have been a dutiful daughter of the Church in this respect. According to Mockler, the bedroom of their first flat was divided into two sections by a curtain to assist sexual abstinence. In his conversations with Leopoldo Duran, Greene criticized the Catholic prohibition on artificial contraception with almost monotonous regularity, and I happen to know that he sent my own novel *The British Museum is Falling Down* to Cardinal Heenan, in the forlorn hope that he might find its satirical treatment of this subject instructive.

But sex was not the only point of incompatibility between the Greenes. Graham was a man driven by strange demonic energies, brilliant, moody and self-obsessed, often on the edge of suicidal depression. Vivien in contrast was shy, passive, conventional, "nice" in a quintessentially English way. As Mockler rather obviously but justly observes, "Two such different people, one feels, should never even have considered getting married." Marriage brought them both more misery than happiness, but whereas Greene's imagination thrived on pain and guilt, for Vivien it was just ordinary, unproductive unhappiness. Yet she seems to have been as incapable, or as unwilling, as Greene to make a clean break until long after the marriage had irremediably broken down.

Further uncomfortable light is thrown on this tormented marriage in Sherry's second volume. According to Vivien, it ended sexually just before the beginning of World War Two, but they continued to cohabit intermittently, apparently sharing the same bed, until 1947, though Greene was more often absent from than present in the matrimonial home. From 1935 till the outbreak of war, this was a Queen Anne house on the north side of Clapham Common. At this time Greene was making a precarious living as a freelance writer, supplementing his modest royalties from fiction with literary journalism, travel writing, film-reviewing, and writing screenplays. He worked with manic and reckless energy, driven partly by financial anxiety, but more, one suspects, to escape from the frustrations and conflicts of his personal life. Probably, too, the encroaching shadow of the war, which he, like so many others, thought inevitable, made him feel he had a limited time in which to make his mark on English literature. For a period in 1939 he worked on two books simultaneously, the "Entertainment" *The Confidential Agent* (completed in six weeks) in the mornings and *The Power and the Glory* in the afternoons, using benzedrine to keep going. Finding it impossible to work at home, he had rented a room in Bloomsbury for this purpose. His landlady's daughter, living in the same house, was Dorothy Glover, a former stage dancer turned book illustrator, and by or before the outbreak of war she had become Greene's mistress.

Readers of *The Confidential Agent* may recall that at one particularly exciting part of the story the hero, known as D., fleeing from enemies intent on murdering him, breaks into an unoccupied flat with the name "Glover" beside the doorbell. The interior and its contents "spoke to him of an unmarried ageing woman with few interests." It was a private joke of a kind that Greene frequently inserted into his fiction – a joke between himself and Dorothy, but rather cruelly excluding Vivien, who must have read this passage years before she had any idea of Greene's relationship with a woman called Glover. War broke out, Vivien was dispatched with the children to live more safely, but uncomfortably, first with Greene's parents, and then with friends in Oxford.

Greene himself remained in London, nominally residing in the Clapham house, but in fact spending most of his time with Dorothy. Adultery probably saved his life, because one night when Greene was in Bloomsbury, the Clapham house was destroyed by a German bomb (an ironic escape which found its way in displaced form into *The End of the Affair*). For Greene it was as if the shackles of bourgeois domesticity had been struck from his limbs. Malcolm Muggeridge said that he would "never

forget the expression of utter glee that came across Graham's
face when he told me that his family home had been destroyed." Later, Greene imaginatively finished off the work of the
German bombers in a blackly comic short story called "The
Destructors". Vivien for her part was devastated by the loss,
and henceforward dedicated herself to collecting period dolls'
houses. At times the Greene marriage resembled a psycho-
drama written in collaboration by Strindberg and Ibsen. But
Vivien's description of her first encounter with Dorothy Glover,
when she dropped in at Graham's London flat unexpectedly
one day after the war, reads more like something by Noël
Coward:

> I don't think we went much further than the hall, and we
> were just chatting. He was a bit uneasy and presently a small
> stoutish woman in blue glasses, like a character in a Victorian
> novel, came up the stairs. She was quite small and roly-poly,
> and she came up and was taken aback and said, "Oh!
> Graham, I came to ask if I could borrow your telephone – I
> wanted to telephone my furrier." At once I thought, "Fancy
> climbing three flights of stairs to borrow a telephone and
> then to telephone your furrier at about 6.45." He introduced
> us, and I made a getaway. He was taking her out to dinner
> obviously, and this ridiculous story about a furrier.

Dorothy was in her fifties by that time, but even when she was
younger her attraction for Greene was something of a mystery
to his friends. She was short, stocky, and, to judge by the only
photograph of her in the Sherry volume, had a face like a frog.
But she was loyal, discreet, and plucky. Greene particularly
admired her cool courage in the London Blitz, when he was
working in Central London by day and acting as a firewatcher
by night, fitting in dalliance with Dorothy in his off-duty hours.
(An official was once scandalized to see them necking in the
corner of an air-raid shelter. "But that is Mr Greene," said the
chief warden, "one of our best wardens, and his nice wife.")

2

It is something of a commonplace that many young men of
Greene's generation and class, brought up on the heroic,
imperialistic adventure stories of Kipling, Henty, and Rider

Haggard, and educated in the patriotic ethos of the British public schools, felt to some extent cheated or guilty because they were just too young to fight in the Great War, and sought to compensate for this and "prove themselves" by adventurous foreign travel and/or participation in the Spanish Civil War. Greene's dangerous and uncomfortable journeys through Liberia and Mexico, recorded in *Journey Without Maps* and *The Lawless Roads* respectively, conform to the pattern. If he didn't (after a halfhearted and abortive attempt to contact the Basques) get involved in the Spanish war it was because he was ideologically divided about it. Most Catholics at that time sided with Franco because he was defending the Church against Republican persecution, but Greene disliked fascist dictatorships. His novels and Entertainments of the Thirties express a sympathy for the exploited and underprivileged that was thoroughly compatible with the left-wing political views fashionable in literary and intellectual circles at the time, but he was not a socialist. As he wrote in *Journey Without Maps*, "I find myself always torn between two beliefs: the belief that life should be better than it is, and the belief that when it appears better it is really worse." He was one of the very few writers of note who declined to answer the famous questionnaire *Authors Take Sides on the Spanish War* (1937).

Given this background, it might have been expected that Greene, like his fellow Catholic convert and friend Evelyn Waugh, would eagerly seek active service in World War Two, especially after the Nazi-Soviet Pact, when (in the words of Waugh's Guy Crouchback) "the enemy at last was plain in view" (i.e., the double-headed monster of fascist and Communist tyranny). Greene records in *Ways of Escape* that he did indeed volunteer for the infantry, and was accepted, but asked for six months' deferment to finish *The Power and the Glory*. However, as Sherry and Mockler observe, the dates don't fit: Greene had already finished his novel before his interview with the recruiting board. Sherry charitably supposes he wanted more time to accumulate literary earnings for his family, but it seems more likely that, while enjoying the Henty-like gesture of volunteering for the infantry, Greene had a pretty good idea of how irksome regimental life and military discipline would be to such an anarchic character as himself (something Waugh had to discover from painful experience), and postponed his induction in the hope that something more exciting and less restrictive would turn up.

He tried to interest the authorities in a scheme to appoint "official writers to the Forces" – on the lines of the well-established War Artists programme. That would have suited him perfectly: an opportunity to experience combat at first hand, while retaining the personal liberty of a freelance writer (much later he was to establish such a rôle for himself in South-East Asia). But he had no success with his idea, and his experience of action was confined to the Home Front in the London Blitz – which, to tell the truth, was more exciting and dangerous than anything experienced by most servicemen at the time. Greene enjoyed waking to the sound of broken glass being swept up in the street, realizing one had survived another night of dicing with death, and even took a kind of dark satisfaction in the destruction of the city's fabric, which he saw as the nemesis of a rotten civilization.

Some two months before he was due to be called up into the army, Greene accepted (or sought – some wisps of smoke screen still hang about this episode) a post in the Ministry of Information. As Sherry observes, this was a somewhat surprising move, because it was not long since he had jeered at Stephen Spender for accepting just such a safe bureaucratic job. The inconsistency did not inhibit Greene from satirizing the Ministry of Information in his story "Men at Work," but there is perhaps an element of self-accusation in this little gem of understated irony, which Mockler rightly singles out for praise. As the Battle of Britain rages, and Europe is flattened under the Nazi jackboot, the central character, Skate, has to chair a Book Committee meeting, the agenda for which reads:

1. Arising from the Minutes.
2. Pamphlet in Welsh on German labour conditions.
3. Facilities for Wilkinson to visit the A.T.S.
4. Objections to proposed Bone pamphlet.
5. Suggestions for a leaflet from Meat Marketing Board.
6. The problem of India.

Someone comes in with news of the latest German air raids.

"We must really get Bone's pamphlet out," Hill said.

Skate suddenly, to his surprise, said savagely, "That'll show them," and then sat down in humble collapse as though he had been caught out in treachery.

Later, when the committee has dispersed, Skate goes to the window.

Far up in the pale enormous sky little white lines, like the phosphorescent spoor of snails, showed where men were going home after work.

It is good to be reminded, as the dust-sheets are twitched from Greene's sometimes discreditable private life, that there were few modern writers who could construct a sentence as precise and beautifully weighted as that. And it is interesting, though not surprising, to learn from Leopoldo Duran that it was Greene's habit to read aloud his work in progress, because "he attached great importance to the cadence of a sentence."

Greene was sacked, uncomplainingly, from the Ministry of Information in some bureaucratic purge after serving for about six months. Shortly afterwards he became literary editor of the *Spectator*, but this was hardly a significant contribution to the war effort. So far, Greene had not had a distinguished war. Then, in 1941, he was recruited for the British Secret Service by his younger sister Elisabeth.

"By nature he was the perfect spy," Sherry observes. Shelden says: "It is impossible to make sense of Greene's life until one acknowledges the extent of his devotion to spying." Spying indeed ran in the family. Greene's uncle, Sir William Graham Greene, was one of the chief architects of the Naval Intelligence department of the Admiralty; his older brother Herbert, the black sheep of the family, spied for the Japanese in England, and for unidentified clients in Spain; Elisabeth, as well as working for MI6, married one of its most senior officers, Rodney Dennys.

Shelden claims, on the basis of memoirs by Graham Greene's contemporaries at Berkhamsted School, that his father encouraged the boys to spy on each other and to report irregular behaviour, especially anything pertaining to masturbation and homosexuality. When still an undergraduate, Greene obtained a free trip from the German embassy in return for writing newspaper articles sympathetic to German protests against French occupation of parts of the Ruhr, while at the same time offering to purvey information to the French government. Shelden plausibly suggests that it can hardly have been coincidental that Greene took a "holiday" in Estonia in 1934, just as a political coup occurred in neighbouring Latvia, where he changed planes. And it seems certain that his trip to Liberia, which he presented in *The Lawless Roads* as a quixotic, metaphysically motivated journey into the heart of darkness, was sponsored by the Anti-slavery Society, which was anxious to gather evidence against the Liberian government and its ruthless military commander, Colonel T. Elwood Davis. Greene's recruitment to the British SIS was in a sense a call he had been waiting for all his life.

His initial experience in this role was, however, bathetic. His training was a farce – he was hopeless at drill, and kept falling off the motorbike he was taught to ride. And his first posting, to Sierra Leone, West Africa, was in one of the least important theatres of war. His only duty of any practical consequence was the tedious and rather demeaning one of searching neutral ships for contraband. His own enterprising and entirely characteristic scheme to elicit information from Vichy officers in neighbouring Senegal by setting up mobile brothels staffed by prostitute-agents was not implemented (though it received surprisingly serious consideration in London).

In Freetown Greene lived alone in an uncomfortable, badly situated bungalow, regarded with equal suspicion by the colonial ex-pats and his African neighbours (who called him in their own language "the bad man"). Nevertheless he developed a deep affection for West Africa, which he called "the soup-sweet land." Perhaps it was, in the memorable words of *The Heart of the Matter*, "the loyalty we all feel to unhappiness, the sense that that is where we really belong." Sierra Leone, and Freetown in particular, were of course to provide the setting for that novel, which made him internationally famous, and Sherry's meticulous research reveals that there was a real-life source for practically every character and incident in it. That, however, was all in the future. The book he actually wrote in

Freetown was *The Ministry of Fear*, one of his best Entertainments, set in wartime London.

In 1943 he was recalled to London and assigned to the Portuguese desk in Section V of MI6. ("It did not seem to matter," Shelden laconically comments, "that he knew practically nothing about the country and could neither read nor speak the language.") His superior was a man who had been recruited to the secret service at the same time as Greene. His name was Kim Philby. The two men became friends.

Portugal was a place of critical importance to Allied intelligence operations, for much of the misinformation with which they confused German speculation about the planned invasion of France passed through this neutral country (in particular through a spy code-named Garbo, whose inventive lies later inspired the character of Wormold in *Our Man in Havana*). Another stream of information that passed through Portugal in the opposite direction concerned the German resistance to Hitler, and its leaders' tentative soundings of Allied governments about the prospects for a negotiated peace, should Hitler be assassinated. This would have been of particular interest to Greene because his cousin Barbara, who had improbably accompanied him on his safari through Liberia (and who wrote her own book about the trip), was living in Germany, married to a Catholic aristocrat sympathetic to the resistance. They were extremely fortunate to survive the ruthless purge that followed the July 1944 plot.

It is known that Philby discouraged contacts with the anti-Hitler party in Germany, because a negotiated peace would be against Soviet interests in a postwar European settlement. He was also at this time probably passing to the Russians the highly secret intelligence gathered through Ultra, the code-breaking operation at Bletchley, though this was expressly forbidden for fear that the Nazis would be alerted to the existence of Ultra in this way. As Mockler usefully explains, other members of MI6 besides Philby were unhappy about withholding vital, life-saving information from an ally, and at least one also defied the rules. How much did Greene know about these matters? Both Sherry and Shelden agree that his surprising resignation from MI6 in May 1944 suggests that he at least suspected something about Philby's activities as a double agent. This was just about the most exciting time of the entire war for the Secret Service, with the opening of a Second Front in Europe imminent, and growing evidence of resistance to Hitler in Germany. Why did Greene choose to leave at this crucial moment, and to take instead a footling job, in something called the Political Warfare Executive, of exactly the kind he had satirized in "Men at Work"? (His first duty was to edit a literary magazine to be distributed by parachute in Occupied France to bring the French up to date on world literature.)

Greene's own story was that he had perceived that Philby was manoeuvring for promotion in MI6, and that this would entail his own appointment as Philby's successor over the head of a more deserving colleague, and that he wanted no part of such office intrigues. But again the dates don't quite fit. It wasn't until six months later that Philby obtained the job he coveted: head of counterintelligence operations against Soviet Russia. There was no reason for Greene to have acted so precipitately on such grounds. Both Sherry and Shelden believe that Greene must have realized that Philby was a Soviet mole, and decided to get out before (to use E.M. Forster's celebrated formula) he was obliged to choose between betraying his friend and betraying his country. Greene never admitted to this motive, but when Sherry asked him what he would have done if he had known Philby was a traitor, he answered that he "might have allowed [him] 24 hours to flee as a friend, then reported him."

This was far from being the end of Greene's connections with the Secret Service or with Philby. At the time, however, Greene seemed in a hurry to return to civilian life and concerns. He rather surprisingly became a publisher, accepting a directorship with the well-established firm of Eyre & Spottiswoode. He seems to have felt that he was played out as a creative writer (he had written nothing in 1943–1944) and he was looking for a congenial alternative with financial security. By all accounts he was an effective and businesslike publisher, who invigorated the Eyre & Spottiswoode list by acquiring foreign writers he admired, like Mauriac and Narayan; but in the end his temperament proved too mercurial for the job. Colleagues could just about tolerate his penchant for practical jokes and hoaxes (e.g., inventing a missing manuscript and impersonating the indignant author in letters and phone calls), but when he lost Anthony Powell from the list by constantly delaying the publication of Powell's biography of John Aubrey, and describing it to the author's face as "a bloody boring book," he was obliged to resign. The details of this affair are disputed, but the outcome was fortunate for English letters, for Greene then entered on what was to be one of the most creative periods of his life, in the course of which he produced the novels *The Heart of the Matter* and *The End of the Affair*, the films *The Third Man* and *The Fallen Idol*, and the stage play *The Living Room*.

By the early 1950s he was arguably the most famous and highly esteemed living English novelist, with a huge following in other countries all round the world. It was also a period of intense emotional and sexual turmoil, dominated by the great love of his life, Catherine Walston. It has been known for some time that she was the "C" to whom *The End of the Affair* was dedicated, and the model for its heroine, Sarah. But the extraordinary story of the real affair, as told by Sherry and Shelden, would seem hardly credible in a work of fiction.

3

When Catherine Walston entered Greene's life, in September 1946, he was still involved in a cooling relationship with Dorothy Glover in London, while maintaining and occasionally visiting Vivien and his children in the house he had bought in Oxford. Vivien knew about Dorothy by now, and about other, more casual, relationships, but stifled her resentment, perhaps for the sake of the children, perhaps because she hoped the marriage might yet be saved. Greene for his part seems to have been unable to make a clean break with either of these women. Scobie's misery and guilt in *The Heart of the Matter*, torn between the claims of his unhappy wife, Louise, and the pathetic young war widow, Helen, who becomes his mistress, pretty clearly reflected Greene's sense of his own plight at this time. Perhaps that was why he could never bear to reread this novel in later life, and always expressed dislike for it. He was two-thirds of the way through writing it when he met Catherine Walston.

She was half-English by birth, American by nationality and upbringing, the wife of a rich English landowner, Harry Walston, who later became a Labour peer. She had the looks of a film star and was given to wilful and eccentric behaviour. Theirs was an "open marriage", and she had had several affairs, apparently condoned by Walston, before she met Greene. He, however, knew nothing about her when he received a letter from her saying that she had decided to become a Catholic as a result of reading his books. Shortly afterward, she rang up Vivien and asked if Greene would act as her sponsor or godfather on her reception into the Church. This must count as the most original seduction gambit in the history of reader-author relations. Greene was amused, and sent the ever-willing Vivien to attend the ceremony in his stead.

An extraordinary photograph of this occasion survives, and is reproduced by Sherry, in which a rather dowdy Vivien is looking askance at the poised and glamorous Catherine with an expression that mingles puzzlement with dislike, as if already trying to estimate the trouble this woman is going to cause her. When Greene gathered from Vivien what a remarkable person his new godchild was, he arranged to give her lunch in London. After the meal she insisted on showing him her stately home in East Anglia, and when he demurred because of the difficulty of returning to Oxford the same day, nonchalantly offered to fly him home in a hired plane – which she did. Such a combination of wealth, impulsiveness and beauty was irresistible to Greene. He fell in love with Catherine, and they commenced a great affair in which agony and ecstasy were fairly evenly balanced. Vivien confided to Sherry many years later what it felt like from her point of view. "I think she was out to get him and got him. I think it was a quite straightforward grab. . . It was just as if you got into a railway carriage with somebody you knew very well and they got the tickets and sat down to read and presently they got up and simply opened the door of the carriage and heaved you out."

A strikingly paradoxical feature of the affair was that the religious faith the lovers shared, and which had brought them together, condemned adultery as a very grave sin. Both Greene and Catherine seemed to be able to live with this contradiction, and even to derive a strange spiritual exaltation from it. In his letters to Catherine, Greene often mentioned that he had been a much more fervent Catholic, and far more regular in attendance at mass, since meeting her than he was before. "I'm a

much better Catholic in mortal sin! or at least I'm more aware
of it." This spiritual balancing act was achieved by dint of a
rather magical attitude toward confession and a rather liberal
interpretation of the "firm purpose of amendment," which
moral theologians deem necessary for the sacrament of penance
to be valid.

The point is vividly illustrated in a story Vivien told Sherry
(and Shelden, with some slight variation of details) about
returning to her house in Oxford one evening in April 1947 to
find Greene there with Catherine. They were on their way back
to London from a stay in Catherine's cottage on Achill island,
off the West Coast of Ireland; and Vivien guessed then, if she
had not guessed before, that they were lovers. Greene explained
that Catherine had a bad back and suggested that she should
stay the night in Oxford.

> And I said, for something to say, "I see it is your name day
> tomorrow. I am going to Mass anyway, it's only just round
> the corner." She said, "Oh, I'll come with you" and she
> came and she had Communion next to me. Some later time,
> I brought this up . . . and he said . . . "Oh we both went to
> confession before we came here." But they went straight on
> to London to live together and that was sort of sickening.

Sherry notes that Vivien was wrong in this last particular: at this
time Greene was still living with Dorothy Glover during the
week.

Vivien's self-restraint finally gave way when she read a love
letter from Greene to Catherine which had been wrongly
addressed and returned to the Oxford house. It must have
reminded her poignantly of his two thousand love letters to
herself in years gone by. She had a showdown with Greene, as a
result of which he left her. She remembers the date because it
was the wedding day of the future Queen Elizabeth II.

Greene, however, had still to make the break with Dorothy.
As if determined to wring the maximum amount of pain out of
it, he planned to take her on holiday in Marrakesh, and there to
give her a letter explaining that he was in love with somebody
else and that they must part (it is not clear whether he intended
to watch her read the letter or creep away into the desert at that
point). Dorothy, however, discovered the affair independently

in the spring of 1948, just before the projected vacation. Bizarrely, they went ahead with the trip and, as might have been predicted, had a thoroughly miserable time. Only then, in May 1948, did Greene finally move out of the flat he shared with Dorothy in Gordon Square. In the same month *The Heart of the Matter*, with its epigraph from Péguy, "*Le pécheur est au coeur même de chrétienté* . . ." ("The sinner is at the very heart of Christianity"), was published and made Greene famous.

Greene's affair with Catherine was a rich, decadent mixture of sex and spirituality. He wrote to her once that he wanted to lie in bed with her, reading Saint John of the Cross. In another letter he expressed in transparent code a wish to bugger her and in another there is a suggestion of experiments in sadomasochism: "My dear, the important cigarette burn has completely gone. It must be renewed." The relationship inspired the most erotically explicit and intensely religious of Greene's novels (also the most formally perfect), *The End of the Affair* (1951). Greene referred to it familiarly in his correspondence with Catherine as "the great sex novel." Evidently it was even more explicit in early drafts. "A few 'narrow loin' cuts do make an enormous difference," he wrote to Catherine in November 1950. (The allusion, which Sherry does not identify, is to a much derided passage in Evelyn Waugh's *Brideshead Revisited*: "now on the rough water, as I was made free of her narrow loins. . . .")

The publication of *The End of the Affair* was to have a considerable impact on the real-life affair. Up to that time, Harry Walston seemed to be a complaisant husband, and to tolerate his wife's frequent absences from home in Greene's company. But when the novel was published he was pained to find himself very obviously portrayed as the cuckolded civil servant, though with typical playfulness Greene gave the character his own baptismal first name, Henry. Walston now demanded that the relationship must end. There followed much heart-searching, big emotional scenes, rows and reconciliations and more rows. Harry was heard sobbing in his room all one night. Greene himself frequently claimed in his letters to Catherine to be weeping over their separation – though they continued to meet occasionally in various parts of the world. He

was always begging her to leave her husband, and forever trying
to square the theological circle in which they were trapped: as
practising Catholics they could neither divorce their respective
spouses and marry again, nor cohabit without being married.
For example:

> Whenever we settled for any length of time, we would have
> two rooms *available*, so that at any time without ceasing to
> live together & love each other, you could go to Communion
> (we would break down again & again, but that's neither here
> nor there).

When Catherine made the counter-proposal that they should
continue as platonic lovers (an ironic reprise of Greene's
courtship of Vivien), Greene rejected it with a quotation from
his favourite poet, Browning: "Better sin the whole sin sure that
God observes."

Greene destroyed all Catherine's letters to himself, so we get
a rather one-sided picture of their relationship, but a letter from
her to her sister, quoted by Sherry, gives us an idea of her view
of him:

> Graham's misery is as real as an illness . . . He has no work,
> no family, no friends whom he has any responsibility for, and
> every hour of the day he has nothing to plan for or no one to
> consider but himself, and for a melancholic by nature, this is
> a terrible breeding ground, and all I do, really, is to make
> things worse in the long run by my own fears of abandoning
> him.

Eventually the affair petered out, rather than ended in any
decisive or dramatic way, in the early Sixties, as Greene realized
that Catherine was never going to leave her husband and family
and devote herself exclusively to him. By 1966 he had taken
another mistress, Yvonne Cloetta, who was to remain his
companion for the rest of his life. The remainder of Catherine's
was rather melancholy. Drink and illness ravaged her beauty
and she refused to let Greene see her when she was dying of
cancer in 1978. After her death Greene and Walston became
good friends again, an outcome eerily anticipated in *The End of
the Affair*.

For obvious reasons, literary biography tends to focus on the parallels between its subject's life and work, but sometimes the discrepancies can be just as interesting and revealing. In *The Quiet American*, for instance, Greene shackled his hero, Fowler, with an estranged wife who, because she is a devout Anglican, refuses to divorce him, thus preventing him from marrying his Vietnamese mistress; but in real life Greene declined the offers of the devout Catholic Vivien to divorce after his affair with Catherine Walston had effectively ended their marriage of twenty-one years, and he never even legalized their separation. Why was this? Perhaps in spite of his fervent pleas to Catherine to leave her husband, he subconsciously feared another permanently binding relationship, and perpetuated his dead but valid marriage to Vivien as a defence.

Even while he was involved with Catherine he had adventures with other women; for example, Jocelyn Rickards, a handsome young Australian who specialized in glamorous literary conquests in postwar London – her other lovers included A. J. Ayer and John Osborne. Sherry passes over this affair quickly and discreetly, but Shelden gets a good deal of mileage out of it. It was by Jocelyn Rickards's own account a short but passionate and exuberant affair in which Greene indulged his penchant for having sex in public places (in parks, railway carriages, etc.). He evidently derived a thrill from the risk of discovery. Shelden also reports a friend's remark that Greene and Catherine had sex behind every high altar in Italy – but that sounds like a piece of conversational hyperbole.

4

It is time to consider the extraordinarily hostile spirit of Shelden's book. (The jacket of the British edition carries a photographic portrait that makes him look, very appropriately, like a brutal interrogator from one of Greene's own novels.) One has to say first, though, that of the four biographies under review, Shelden's is the best written: its style is vigorous and lucid, its narrative structure is clear and gripping, and it is packed with interesting insights and discoveries, as well as dubious speculations. Sherry's work, when completed, will be the definitive biography of record, and it is already a remarkable and heroic achievement. But there are times, especially in the second volume, when the shape and rhythm of Greene's life are blurred and smothered by the plethora of information, and by its thematic (rather than chronological) organization. Shelden, because he was not allowed to quote from the letters and other private papers, is obliged to paraphrase, and thus manages to deal with the whole life in one volume, which is more satisfying for the reader.

He is also the best literary critic of this bunch (or should one say "a clutch" of biographers?) – sharp and observant on, for instance, the echoes and allusions to Conrad, Pound, and T.S. Eliot in Greene's work. He is the first critic I have encountered who seems to have worked out how Pinkie's gang murders Hale at the beginning of *Brighton Rock* (by choking him on a stick of the eponymous candy, which melts and leaves no trace). He makes some fascinating connections between Harston House in Cambridgeshire, which belonged to Greene's uncle, Sir William Graham Greene, and is where the novelist spent several summer holidays in childhood (it is surprisingly not discussed in Sherry's first volume), and the rather baffling story of Greene's later years called "Under the Garden".

Nevertheless Shelden's book is fuelled by a virulent hatred of its subject, which makes one wonder if there is not some source for it in Shelden's own life. In a revised introductory chapter, written for the American edition, Shelden claims that he embarked on his biography as a devoted admirer of the novelist, and changed his opinion of him as a result of his researches. One is reminded of Oscar Wilde's observation: "Every great man nowadays has his disciples, and it is always Judas who writes the biography."

Shelden's case against Greene is that his work is driven by hatred and malice and other negative feelings which his admiring readers have failed to recognize and acknowledge. "They do not hear – or do not want to hear – the anti-Semitism, the anti-Catholicism, the misogyny, or the many jokes made at their expense." He frequently protests that he is not seeking to disparage Greene's literary achievement in this way. "The weakness of the man cannot overshadow the merits of his art"; "Greene's genius is marred by a wide streak of malice . . . but it is not a valid reason for dismissing his novels as works of art." But it is hard to see how one could continue to admire Greene's novels while accepting Shelden's reading of them as expressing, or releasing, the nastiest elements he claims to have discovered in Greene's character and behaviour. This, for instance, is what he says about *Brighton Rock*:

> The unpleasant truth is that the author regards us as easy victims. . . . we want to be liked, and we want to like others. We want to trust Greene, we want to feel sorry for Pinkie, we want to think the world is not such a bad place after all. And while our smiling faces are busy looking for goodness and wisdom and purpose, Pinkie and Greene are cursing us for being Jews or Catholics, for being fat or crippled, for being old or female.

Brighton Rock is certainly a novel that disturbs and challenges received ideas about good and evil, right and wrong: but fortunately the relationship between its "implied author" and protagonist is much more subtle and complex than the simple identification asserted here. Shelden, however, suggests that to admire the novels we have to either misread them or revel vicariously (and masochistically) in an essentially diabolic vision of the world.

If he himself is evidently quite comfortable with the second option it may be because he claims a perverse kinship between the novelist and the biographer. This is particularly marked in the British edition. For example, after discussing the libel action that followed Greene's review in October 1937 of a Shirley Temple movie, a review described in court as "gratuitous indecency" (Greene suggested that the juvenile star was being marketed as a stimulus to jaded sexual appetites), Shelden airily admits to having indulged in "an occasional wild surmise and gratuitous indecency" himself. He comments that Greene "was ruthless in his willingness to use friends and family for copy," and adds, "no wonder he was often tempted to write biography, an art that demands a shameless devotion to voyeurism." Again, invoking a famous metaphor of Greene's for the writer's temperament, he writes, "It is the 'splinter of ice' in the novelist's – or biographer's – heart that enables him to plunder other lives for material." When he speculates archly on the kind of biography of Greene the character Parkinson, the loathsome journalist in *A Burnt-out Case*, might have written – "digging up all the dirt and burying even his best work under the pile" – he anticipates but does not deflect a possible criticism of his own project.

Undoubtedly there is an element of truth in many of Shelden's accusations, but they are exaggerated, or tendentiously expressed, or developed in unjustified ways. There is no doubt, for instance, that Greene's early novels betray a kind of prejudice against Jews that would be unacceptable today – but then so did the work of many English writers of his generation. It is perverse to judge this strain in his work from a post-Holocaust position in history. And Greene's Jewish characters are far from being anti-Semitic caricatures. Myatt in *Stamboul Train*, for instance, is drawn with considerable subtlety and not without sympathy and understanding. Though he is morally flawed, he shows more human feeling than most of the other characters. The charge of misogyny is another anachronistic invocation of political correctness that doesn't help define the real limitations of Greene's characterization of women. As to what Shelden strangely calls Greene's anti-Catholicism, it was precisely his refusal to act as a literary propagandist for the Church or its members that made his religious novels interesting and valuable, to Catholics and non-Catholics alike.

Shelden's index in the British edition has a long, lip-smacking list of entries under "Greene, sex" including: "anal sex, flagellation, incest theme, interest in male love, possible actual homosexuality, masochism, paedophilia, prostitutes and brothels." The evidence for paedophilia, perhaps the most "unspeakable" of these alleged proclivities, is all gossip and unwarranted extrapolation. For instance, Greene reacted with what Shelden regards as suspicious heat to Richard Aldington's hostile biography of Greene's Capri neighbour Norman Douglas, who certainly was a pederast. But Greene was always prone to take up the cudgels in this furious, impulsive way, especially on behalf of anyone he knew and liked. A man called Scoppa who used to deliver telegrams to Greene's villa on Anacapri was surprised to find Italian boys staying there, and was told by unidentified people in the town that they were for sexual purposes. This was early in Greene's occupation of the villa, at a time when Catherine used to come and stay with him, sometimes bringing her sons. Could these have been the boys

Scoppa saw? Is it in any case likely that Greene would have been interested in this kind of sex while engaged in a passionate heterosexual love affair?

"From beginning to end the subject of homosexuality is an intrinsic part of Greene's work," Shelden claims. "His male characters are forever searching for some elusive bond with another male." But those two sentences are not logically connected. Shelden has confused homoerotic attraction and desire (which there is no evidence that Greene ever felt or indulged) with the formation of intensely emotional friendships between boys, and between men, which was the inevitable concomitant of a segregated educational system like that of the British public schools and (as regards college life) universities in Greene's day. Shelden is obliged, invidiously, to endorse the crass reaction of the film producer David O. Selznick to the script of *The Third Man*, when Greene and Carol Reed first showed it to him. The occasion was drolly recalled by Greene in *Ways of Escape* and the passage is reprinted in *The Graham Greene Film Reader*:

> "It won't do, boys," he said, "it won't do. It's sheer buggery."
>
> "Buggery?"
>
> "It's what you learn in your English schools."
>
> "I don't understand."
>
> "This guy comes to Vienna looking for his friend. He finds his friend's dead. Right? Why doesn't he go home then?"
>
> After all the months of writing, his destructive view of the whole venture left me speechless. He shook his grey head at me. "It's just buggery, boys."
>
> I began weakly to argue. I said, "But this character – he has a motive of revenge. He has been beaten up by a military policeman." I played a last card. "Within twenty-four hours he's in love with Harry Lime's girl."
>
> Selznick shook his head sadly. "Why didn't he go home before that?"

Fortunately Selznick changed his mind or forgot his objections, which the film makers quietly ignored. The rest is cinematic history.

5

Mention of *The Third Man* brings us back to the subject of Philby and the whole question of Greene's relations with the Secret Intelligence Service. When Philby, like Burgess and Maclean before him, defected to Russia in 1963, narrowly escaping arrest for treason, Greene wrote a newspaper article observing jocularly that he had invented the phrase "The Third Man" long before anyone could have imagined that it would one day apply to his old friend. But the real joke, hidden from most of his readers, was that the character of Harry Lime was based on and inspired by Kim Philby – or so Shelden very persuasively argues (he has the edge on Sherry in this matter). A crucial episode in Philby's initiation into politics took place in Vienna before the war; and the equivocal attitude of Holly Martins to Harry Lime, divided between moral disapproval of his criminal activities and the claims of friendship and personal liking, exactly mirrors what we know about Greene's relationship with Philby in their MI6 days. Shelden justly observes: "Greene never betrayed his friend Philby, but he spent the rest of his life thinking about the dilemma. He returned to it again in *The Human Factor*, and even sent the manuscript to Philby in Moscow, asking his opinion of the novel."

The story of *The Human Factor* concerns a Soviet mole in the British Secret Service, married to a black South African woman, who reveals to the Russians a secret treaty between the Western powers and the South African government to prevent South African gold mines from falling into Soviet hands. Shortly after the novel was published, the existence of such a treaty became public knowledge. Leopoldo Duran cites this as an example of Greene's uncanny powers of political clairvoyance, but it is possible that he got the idea through his contacts with the Secret Service. For these did not cease with his resignation from MI6 in 1944. Shelden claims to have received confirmation, in a "briefing" by the British Cabinet Office, that throughout the postwar period, up till the early 1980s, Greene's trips to foreign countries were sometimes sponsored or subsidized by SIS and that he regularly reported back to its officers even if he was not a paid agent. After carefully considering the evidence, Norman Sherry concludes that, as the French authorities always suspected, Greene was acting as a British spy in Indochina during the French war against Ho Chi Minh, though he represented himself as a journalist and a novelist looking for material.

When Philby published his memoirs in 1968, Greene contributed an admiring introduction which caused a good deal of offence in England. He was accused of defending a traitor who had the blood of many British and Allied agents on his hands. The parallel Greene drew between Philby's covert pro-Soviet activities and the undercover actions of recusant Catholics in Elizabethan times was denounced as sophistry. Perhaps in *The Human Factor* (1978) Greene sought to give the part of the mole a more sympathetic face by associating him with an irreproachably moral cause – opposition to the regime responsible for apartheid. But if Greene was collaborating with SIS all through the cold war period, then perhaps his public espousal of Philby's cause was an ingenious cover which made Greene *persona grata* in Soviet Russia and gave him access to the great defector. Perhaps Greene was extracting information from Philby on his visits to Russia, perhaps he was part of a plot to "turn" Philby again, perhaps Philby had already turned. Here we enter the bewildering labyrinth of mirrors that is the world of modern espionage, in which anything is possible.

To Shelden, Greene's continuing contact with SIS belied his pretensions, in later life, to be the friend of "international socialism", and for some British reviewers (e.g., Philip Norman in the *Independent on Sunday*) it has been the most disillusioning revelation of the new biographies. On the other hand, if you never approved of "international socialism", you might think his putative undercover intelligence work was to his credit. It was always Evelyn Waugh's belief, for instance, that Greene was "a secret agent on our side and all his buttering up of the Russians is 'cover'." In many ways this is an attractive explanation of Greene's puzzling behaviour. To publicly endorse Philby's treachery, bringing down obloquy on his own head, as a means of serving his country secretly would have been a gesture worthy of the heroes of the patriotic adventure stories Greene was brought up on. But it is a little too neat a theory, and doesn't explain why Greene was troubled in his conscience about Philby until the very last hours of his life.

According to an article by Ron Rosenbaum in the *New York Times Magazine* (10 July 1994), Norman Sherry wrote to

Greene when he was on his deathbed in Switzerland, asking him if there was any truth in a suggestion, which he, Sherry, had encountered in the course of his researches, that Philby was a double-double agent, posing as a defector, but in fact passing information back to British SIS. Greene was sufficiently disturbed by this inquiry to send for all his papers referring to Philby, as if he wanted to reexamine the question of Philby's motivation for himself. A tantalizing detail in Leopoldo Duran's account of visiting Greene on his deathbed – "Amanda [Greene's niece] mentioned something to him to do with the Secret Service which had been worrying him in recent days" – is presumably a reference to this matter. Duran comments: "Although he had difficulty articulating the words, he was completely conscious when he replied." Perhaps, since it was not spoken under the seal of confession, Duran will one day reveal what the reply was.

My own opinion, for what it is worth, is that Greene's political views were confused and contradictory, and that his postwar involvement with the Secret Service was essentially personal and opportunistic in motivation. We know that he was addicted to hoaxes, practical joking, and social deceptions of various kinds, and we know that from a precociously early age he dabbled in the business of spying not for any ideological reason but for the sheer hell of it, and for the pleasure of seeing the world at somebody else's expense. Undoubtedly it tickled him to move around the globe, hobnobbing with selected political leaders, observing wars and revolutions and political intrigues at first hand. It was, in the pro writer's familiar phrase, all material.

His stance on the cold war was always idiosyncratic. Its guiding principle was an anti-Americanism that went back to his days as a film critic before World War Two. In review after review he made it clear how much he detested Hollywood and everything it had done to the art of the cinema. In finding Shirley Temple movies sexually titillating in the magazine *Night and Day* he went too far for Hollywood, and the studios punished him for his temerity by suing him and the magazine for libel. *Night and Day* collapsed and Greene was heavily fined. He did not forget or forgive that episode.

Greene made a shrewd and prophetic analysis of the folly of

the US involvement in Southeast Asia in *The Quiet American* (1955), but he had been generally sympathetic to the anti-Communist campaign of the French colonialist forces in his journalism a few years earlier. He was quite capable of singing the praises of communism just because it affronted American opinion, while secretly supplying British Intelligence with information gathered on his travels behind the Iron Curtain. His anti-Americanism also led him into a rather undiscriminating endorsement of revolutionary and populist movements and their leaders in Central America – Castro, Trujillo, Torrijos, the Sandinistas – whose morals and methods were often dubious and brutal. Shelden makes some very telling points against Greene's dabbling in Central American politics, which he sees as both duplicitous and irresponsible. It will be interesting to see if Sherry can cast any redeeming light on this phase of Greene's life in the third volume of his biography.

Sherry and Shelden are the heavyweights in this biographical competition, and will probably be slugging it out for some time to come. Anthony Mockler is a journalist and military historian, a Catholic by education. He knew Greene's daughter in youth, and has travelled widely, often along the same routes as the novelist. On the face of it he is well qualified for his task, yet his book comes across as curiously amateur in tone. He appeals intermittently for help from other students of Greene's life, like a contributor to some arcane hobby-journal. He is, understandably, still sore at having had his original biography spiked by legal action, and, like Shelden, is severely restricted in his freedom to quote by the executors of the Greene estate. Nevertheless he has gleaned from the available evidence a few interesting details overlooked or underestimated by his fellow biographers.

The oddest of the books under review is Leopoldo Duran's memoir. He first met Greene in the early 1970s, after Duran presented the novelist with a copy of his doctoral dissertation, completed at London University. One day Greene rang him up and invited him to lunch at the Ritz. Duran seems never to have recovered from the dazzlement of this occasion, and it was indeed a surprising and uncharacteristic gesture by Greene, who tended to dodge his admirers, especially clerical ones. Nor was Duran, on the face of it, the kind of priest to whom Greene's imagination had been drawn in his fiction. He comes across as thoroughly conventional in character and views, indeed distinctly right-wing in political and theological matters. He is an unrepentant admirer of Franco, which perhaps accounts for otherwise unexplained difficulties in his academic career. He alludes darkly to a student boycott of his classes, and to his failure to obtain the promotion his publications on Greene might have been expected to bring him (the novelist, so he tells us, was very shocked by this instance of academic injustice).

Duran has a Pooterish way with an anecdote which makes his book often very funny, if unintentionally so. For instance, he was once invited to give a lecture on Greene at Complutense University. Greene personally helped him to revise his text, but when Duran turned up to deliver it, nobody came. Not a single soul.

> Later, when I phoned Graham to tell him what had happened, the line seemed to have gone dead. I thought that we had been cut off. But it was not that; he was thinking.

One would love to know what he was thinking.

Nearly every summer Greene would spend a week or two with Duran, being driven about the Spanish countryside, mainly in the northwest of the country, with a hamper of food and a good deal of wine in the trunk, talking and drinking. Greene called these excursions "picnics". Their conversations, of which Duran kept a detailed record, were often about religious questions, and especially about Catholic teaching on sex.

> Graham and I used to relate our most intimate experiences to each other. He never tired of hearing me speak about girls I used to know and his eyes would sometimes moisten when we spoke about such matters.

Were they perhaps tears of laughter Greene was suppressing? Certainly he recognized the priest's potential as a comic character by portraying him (with Duran's slightly coy collusion) as the eponymous hero of *Monsignor Quixote* (1982), a curious and not entirely successful book, like an extended private joke. Duran's memoir is furnished with numerous snapshots in which Greene is invariably scowling at the lens as if consumed with impatience and ill-temper, but he clearly found the Spanish priest's transparent sincerity soothing to his spirit, and asked to see him when he was dying. Duran administered the last sacraments.

6

Mockler's book ends with a brief section entitled, "What do I think of Graham Greene?" The question is rather plonkingly formulated, but it is one that every reader of Greene's novels is bound to ask himself or herself on emerging from this welter of new biographical information and speculation. I have additional, personal reasons for addressing it. The work of Graham Greene was more closely entwined with my own pursuit of a literary career than that of any other contemporary writer, and although I met him only a few times, and corresponded with him at long intervals, those contacts were of special interest and importance to me.

In the late nineteen-forties and early nineteen-fifties, when I was a sixth-former and undergraduate with literary aspirations, Greene was at the height of his fame, widely regarded as the most interesting and gifted living English novelist. Of his generation, only Evelyn Waugh was a serious competitor for this accolade, and many critics thought Waugh's work had declined since (some said, with) *Brideshead Revisited* (1944), whereas *The Heart of the Matter* (1948) and *The End of the Affair* (1951) were two of Greene's best novels by any standard. I read both writers with avid interest and enormous pleasure, and learned much about the craft of fiction from both of them. It was important to me that they were both converts to Roman Catholicism, and wrote about Catholic themes, because I was myself a Catholic by baptism and education. Not that the parochial, lower-middle-class, predominantly Irish Catholic subculture I knew had much in common with Waugh's papist aristocrats and socialites, or with Greene's Catholic criminals, exotic whiskey-priests and adulterous expats. The point was that these two writers had made Catholicism, from a literary point of view, interesting, glamorous and prestigious. There

were no Anglican novelists, or Methodist novelists, thus identified, on the contemporary literary scene, but there was, it
seemed, such a creature as a Catholic novelist.

Greene, in particular, suggested that it was possible to be all
the things that an artistically inclined adolescent dreamed of
being – rebellious, bohemian, shocking to the bourgeoisie –
while writing within a framework of Catholic faith and practice.
My own early novels transposed some characteristically Greeneian themes – belief and unbelief, transgression and guilt – into a
less luridly lit, more suburban milieu, but not without some
stylistic echoes. My first published novel, *The Picturegoers*
(1960), had a minor character called Harry who, in his fantasy
life at least, somewhat resembles Pinkie in *Brighton Rock*, and
Kingsley Amis, in a generally favourable review of the novel,
noted "two or three lapses into pea-Greene simile – 'the fellow
carried his failure before him like a monstrance.' "

I started writing *The Picturegoers* as a lance-corporal clerk in
the Royal Tank Regiment, while doing two years of National
Service between my BA and my Masters degree at University
College London. The London MA in those days was a two-year
research degree, and I chose as my topic, "The Catholic Novel
in England from the Oxford Movement to the Present Day."
Greene was the subject of the concluding and climactic chapter
of a monstrously long thesis (there turned out to be far more
Catholic novels buried in the stacks of the British Museum than
I or anyone else had ever dreamed of). My approach to the
Catholic novel was initially thematic, showing how fiction was
used to mediate a changing and developing Catholic "world
view"; but as the work proceeded I became more interested in
questions of fictional form. A close analysis of Graham Greene's
technique certainly seemed the best way to defend him against
his academic detractors, of whom I encountered quite a few.
Greene was always more popular with non-academic critics and
readers than with academic ones. The two most influential
schools of criticism at that time were: the American New
Criticism, which took the lyric poem as the highest form of
literature, and was therefore biased in favour of the modernist
symbolist novel, against the traditional realistic novel; and the
school of Leavis, which was more sympathetic to realism, but

only if the writer was "on the side of life", and belonged to a Great Tradition of secularized English Puritanism. Greene's work, which spoke eloquently in favour of death, and fused together the romantic adventure story, the modern crime thriller and the French Catholic novel of sin, salvation and "mystical substitution" exemplified by Bernanos and Mauriac, did not satisfy the criteria of either of these schools of criticism, and was predictably rubbished in the academic critical journals that were their mouthpieces.

I saw Greene at that time as a novelist who, in spite of his evident compassion for suffering and oppressed humanity, had an essentially anti-humanist, anti-materialistic view of the human condition, encapsulated in T.S. Eliot's aphorism in his essay on Baudelaire, "it is better in a paradoxical way to do evil, than to do nothing; at least we exist" – echoed with a new twist in *The Heart of the Matter*: "only the man of goodwill carries in his heart this capacity for damnation." But this abstract message, if one may so crudely describe it, was invested with a vivid and persuasive concreteness in Greene's fiction, and given a different thematic emphasis in each of his novels. I identified in each novel a key-word or word-cluster, usually some abstraction like "trust" in the *Confidential Agent*, "pity" in *The Heart of the Matter*, "love and hate" in *The End of the Affair*, which recurred again and again and had an almost subliminal effect in organizing and focusing the reader's response to the always engrossing story and sharply evoked milieu. Out of this exercise grew a rather more sophisticated interest in literary style which I explored in my first academic critical book, *Language of Fiction* (1966). In that same year I published a revised and expanded version of my thesis-chapter on Greene as a pamphlet in the Columbia Essays on Modern Writers series.

I had in the meantime published two more novels: *Ginger, You're Barmy* (1962), a novel about National Service which, as I realized some years after writing it, was structurally modelled on *The Quiet American* in its use of first-person narration and time-shift; and *The British Museum is Falling Down* (1965), my first explicitly comic novel, which included a series of parodies, one of which was of Greene. This was an act of homage rather than satire, but I felt a certain trepidation when I decided to send Greene a copy of the novel in 1966, along with the newly published Columbia pamphlet, and with a covering letter expressing my long-standing interest in and admiration for his work. It was the first time I had ventured to write to him. I received a reply that gave me enormous pleasure. He thanked me for the pamphlet but said that he didn't much enjoy reading criticism of his own work (a feeling I have come to recognize and share); *The British Museum* was a different matter. "I have enjoyed it immensely. It's very funny and very important at the present time." Greene urged me to send a copy of the book to Cardinal Heenan, and, when in my reply I demurred (I thought it would seem rather arrogant, and in any case I couldn't in those days afford to give away free copies of my books), he promised to do so himself. Shortly afterwards the novel was accepted for publication in America by Holt Rinehart, and they asked me, as publishers of little-known writers do, to suggest some prominent writers whom they might approach for a quote to put on the dustjacket. Rather nervously I asked Greene if we might quote his letter, and he generously agreed, as he has done for other writers on numerous occasions. Needless to say, this was a priceless endorsement as far as I was concerned.

From then onwards I always sent Greene a copy of my latest novel, when it was published, and always received a kind acknowledgement from the Residence des Fleurs in Antibes. But we did not meet until 1975, when a group of academic admirers, headed by Miriam Allott (co-author with her husband Kenneth of the first book-length study of Greene) and my friend Ian Gregor, (a Catholic academic with a longstanding interest in Greene's work) invited him to a dinner to celebrate his seventieth year and the production of his play, *The Return of A. J. Raffles*, which brought him to London at that time.

The dinner was held in a restaurant in North London near Miriam Allott's flat, where we foregathered. Greene seemed shy and rather ill-at-ease, and we were somewhat constrained by our inability to enthuse about the play, which we had seen earlier in the day at a matinée, and which was not his most distinguished piece for the theatre. He gradually relaxed and told a number of entertaining anecdotes which we received with a proper sense of privilege, and were somewhat disconcerted to read almost verbatim in an interview published the next morning in a Sunday newspaper. I don't think Greene was playing one of his practical jokes on us, but merely being economical with the social effort required by the occasion. In later life he submitted, like most well-known writers, to the media exposure that now routinely accompanies the publication of novels, but his interviews were more than usually repetitive, as though he was keeping to a carefully prepared and memorized script, which concealed more than it revealed.

In the following year, the British Council wrote to say that Greene had agreed to record a taped interview in a series they were producing aimed at foreign students of contemporary English literature, and that he had either suggested or approved the choice of myself as interviewer. I accepted the invitation with alacrity, and a London rendezvous was arranged for the recording on a Saturday morning in March. I made some notes about the occasion, which Greene's presence seemed to imbue with his own characteristic mixture of seediness and irony.

The address of the recording studio was in Dorset Square. I arrived early, but found Greene already there, peering into the window of a newsagent's shop with his clear, slightly protuberant blue eyes. He wore a shaggy black belted overcoat and was bareheaded, his grey hair fluffy like a baby's on his balding scalp. We recalled the driver of the minicab we had shared after the dinner of the previous year – a talkative Iranian who insisted in joining in our conversation and claimed acquaintance with one of the academics present at the dinner, Professor Molly Mahood, perhaps mistaking her Irish name for a Persian one. "Almost the high-spot of the evening," Greene remarked laconically, and confessed that he had been ill-at-ease during the dinner, confronted with so many strange faces, and not having properly identified each of them at the introductions stage of the evening.

We found the studio in an extremely dilapidated basement. I resisted the temptation to allude to the title of his story, "The Basement Room," but everything about the place seemed characteristic of Greeneland. On the ground floor of the house a long dining-table was visible through the window, elaborately laid for dinner, with candles in candlesticks, though it was only ten thirty in the morning. The door at the bottom of the area steps was opened, after some delay, by the British Council producer, a man called Lidderdale, who led us along a damp, dirty, and cluttered passage to the crummiest and most cramped recording studio I have ever been in. The table on which the microphones stood was covered with dirty brown baize, scorched with cigarette burns and apparently slashed with razor blades.

There were brief, slightly embarrassed introductions to the technicians. Then, with cups of black instant coffee before us, we recorded about an hour's conversation. Greene was rather uncommunicative at first, tending to answer my carefully prepared questions disconcertingly with a simple yes or no. He gradually warmed up, and although I don't think he said anything he hadn't said before, Lidderdale pronounced himself pleased with the result. Afterwards, somewhat to my surprise, he paid us both in cash, thirty pounds each, with notes taken from his own wallet, and we signed rather improvised-looking receipts. Greene proposed taking me for a drink, and Lidderdale recommended the buffet of the nearby Marylebone station because of its Ruddles' draught beer, then a novelty. Eventually he decided to accompany us.

Greene was pleased by the bar, and expressed great satisfaction at having discovered it. He said he thought it would make a good rendezvous for meeting his brother Hugh, who was a keen beer-drinker. Greene spoke of an imminent trip he planned to make to Greece with Hugh, and Lidderdale, a Byzantine enthusiast, recommended some interesting sites accessible only by mule. Greene said he was getting too old to ride a mule, and recalled a very long mule ride in Mexico. I asked him about his trip to Liberia, recorded in *Journey Without Maps*, and what had happened to the cousin who accompanied him. He said she was still alive and living in Europe after a rather adventurous life during the war. He recalled that he had invited her to accompany him to Liberia when rather drunk at a family wedding, and had been disconcerted when she accepted and insisted on going through with it against the advice of the family.

The sound recordist and Lidderdale's secretary joined us. We had more drinks, switching from Ruddles to gin and tonic, and got slightly drunk. When Greene came back from the bar with another round of g & t's, I remarked that it would make a hole in his fee. He grinned and said, "Can you think of a better kind of hole to make in it?" We talked about films, especially the projected film of *The Honorary Consul*. Afterwards, just before we all parted outside the buffet, Greene asked what was the furthest destination you could travel to from Marylebone station. It seemed a revealing and characteristic question from one of the great literary travellers of our time.

Over the years that followed, our correspondence became a little more frequent, and we got on to first-name terms. When I sent him a copy of *How Far Can You Go?* he responded with some generous praise which he again allowed my publishers to quote (I made it clear that he would not be bothered again with such requests), and added the following comment: "One thing puzzled me. I have never encountered the kind of Catholic types that you portray, perhaps because I belong to a much earlier period. I thought that the idea that contraception was wrong and a belief in hell vanished before the war. I seem to have mixed with a rather different sort of Catholic perhaps by being so much abroad." This seemed to me slightly at odds with the eschatological perspective of his own novels up to at least *The Heart of the Matter* (1948), and with his insistence on sending Cardinal Heenan a copy of *The British Museum is Falling Down*, but it was of course perfectly true that the Catholic Church he had joined was very different from the one I described, especially in its post-Vatican II manifestations: vernacular liturgy, guitar-accompanied folk hymns, sponsored walks for CAFOD, house masses, Marriage Encounter weekends and charismatic prayer-groups.

It was obvious from Greene's novels and *obiter dicta*, from *A Burnt-Out Case* (1961) onwards, that his own faith was changing, and drying up. Whereas he used to describe himself as a "novelist who happened to be a Catholic," he now referred to himself as "a Catholic agnostic". In an interview he drew a distinction between Belief, which he no longer possessed, and Faith, which he did, though it sounded more like a wistful kind of Hope that the whole Christian myth might improbably turn out to be true after all. I am, I suppose, a kind of Catholic agnostic, or agnostic Catholic, myself, but it still seems to me that Greene's most powerful and enduring novels are those that

were based on an uncompromisingly incarnational and eschatological Christian theology to which neither of us, in the period
of our acquaintance, subscribed any longer.

In May 1985, my wife and I had a short holiday in the South
of France, and I took up a longstanding invitation to visit
Greene at his home in Antibes when a convenient opportunity
arose. He gave us drinks in his modestly proportioned flat
overlooking the Marina, and showed us the damage inflicted on
his front door by the local criminal *milieu* that was trying to
intimidate him (the full story was told in his pamphlet, *J'Accuse:
the dark side of Nice* [1982]). He took us to lunch in the old
quarter by the harbour, and talked freely and sometimes
indiscreetly over the fish soup and grilled sole. His appetite for
life and for literature seemed undimmed. He told us with some
satisfaction that he had survived an operation for cancer of the
bowel in his seventies, and that he had just thought of a way of
going on with a novel abandoned some years before. He seemed
to derive a mischievous glee from the tribulations poor Norman
Sherry had suffered in trying to retrace his subject's every step. I
came to the conclusion that Greene's frequently expressed
indifference to death and his cult of failure as a sign of
existential authenticity were in part propitiatory or defensive
gestures against hubris, that secretly he greatly enjoyed his
celebrity and longevity.

I was writing some notes of our conversation a day or two
later, sitting at the rim of a hotel swimming pool somewhere in
Provence, when a small whirlwind, *le petit mistral* as they call it
in that region, suddenly descended on the peaceful scene,
whipped the water into waves, overturned the tables and
umbrellas, and sucked my manuscript pages hundreds of feet
into the air. Open-mouthed with astonishment, I watched them
swirling across the landscape and then fluttering down into a
distant olive-grove. My wife and I drove after them and
recovered a few of the sheets, crumpled and dusty, but still
legible. Later I developed the incident into a story, "Hotel des
Boobs", in which a writer is similarly surprised in the middle of
composing a story about the women sunbathing topless round
his hotel pool. I think Greene might have been amused by the
story's genesis, but I never told him about it, in case the
admission that I had made notes of our conversation should

jeopardize our relationship, though he must have guessed that nearly everyone who met him did the same.

I have only warm memories of Graham Greene, which the revelations of his biographers have done nothing to shake, though they have perhaps mitigated any regret that I didn't know him better. (His relations with other writers were generally happiest when conducted at long distance; he and Anthony Burgess, for instance, fell out when they became near neighbours on the Côte d'Azur.) For many admirers of Greene's writing, however, the exposure of his private life has been as dismaying as it was for fans of Philip Larkin when his letters, and Andrew Motion's biography, were published not long before. This is an understandable, but illogical reaction. Revelations about a writer's life should not affect our independently-formed critical assessment of his work. They may, however, confirm or explain reservations about it.

The biographies certainly haven't changed my opinion that the novels and Entertainments Greene wrote in the thirties and forties, up to and including *The End of the Affair*, were the work of a major writer, without which the map of modern literary history would look significantly different. But I cannot dissent from Shelden's verdict that his work in the latter phase of his career was increasingly disappointing, and here perhaps the biographical facts are relevant. In a postscript to my Columbia pamphlet on Greene written in 1976, I concluded:

> The epigraph to *The Honorary Consul*, from Thomas Hardy, expresses accurately enough his present view of the world: "All things merge into one another – good into evil, generosity into justice, religion into politics . . ." but his most successful work was based on the clash of antithetical ideas rather than this hazy, ambiguous flow of one idea into another.

The new information about Greene's equivocal and perhaps duplicitous dealings with the SIS in the cold war period does help to crystallize certain doubts about the novels of the later period – *The Comedians, Travels with my Aunt, The Honorary Consul* and *The Human Factor*. Never less than technically accomplished, these novels are in the end curiously unsatisfying because they pick up large political and philosophical issues only to drop them unresolved. Reading Sherry and Shelden one is led to the conclusion that Greene had no coherent and consistent world-view, and that he used his often-repeated insistence on the necessary disloyalty of the artist to ideological systems as a screen for his own lack of one. This wouldn't have mattered perhaps if he hadn't addressed himself so directly to such subjects in the later novels.

But the oddities and extravagances of Greene's private life, his often selfish and callous behaviour in personal relations, as revealed by his biographers, do not in any way retrospectively invalidate the emotional and spiritual insights of his best work. The moral discrepancy between the real-life writer and the "implied author" of these works is not a scandal but a manifestation of the principle famously enunciated by T.S. Eliot, the separation of the man who suffers from the mind that creates. Greene certainly suffered, and it is hard to understand why Sherry is so puzzled by "the paradox . . . that this author, thought by many to be the greatest novelist of his generation, and also the most successful . . . should yet suffer from a despair that was beyond success, beyond money." The temperament that Greene possessed, or that possessed him, is usually beyond rational explanation. To observers it looks like a kind of illness, but fortunately for Greene – and for us – he found a palliative, if not a cure. "Writing is a form of therapy," he wrote; "sometimes I wonder how all those who do not write, compose or paint can manage to escape the madness, the melancholia, the panic fear which is inherent in the human situation." May he rest in the peace that lies beyond biography.

POSTSCRIPT

After the publication of the first version of this article in the New York Review of Books, *the following correspondence*[*] *between Michael Shelden and myself was published in that journal (21 September 1995) under the heading* "Greene & Anti-Semitism."

To the Editors:

In "The Lives of Graham Greene" [*NYR* 22 June] David Lodge does a clever job of defending Greene against various charges raised in my biography. His brief discussion of Greene's anti-Semitism is especially interesting. Instead of offering readers specific evidence for their consideration, he launches a vague attack against me as a "perverse" critic whose book uses "exaggerated" accusations to harm a good reputation. According to Lodge, the anti-Semitism in the early novels is simply the "kind of prejudice" found in "most English writers" of Greene's generation.

If Lodge is right, then there must have been many English novelists in the 1930s whose books ridiculed "Jewesses" as "little bitches" or whose essays condemned the cowardice of "large fat foreign" Jews. These are Greene's phrases, and, unfortunately, they are not isolated examples. I invite Lodge to name one English novelist whose published work of the 1930s contains remarks similar to the following quotations from Greene:

"That Semitic expression . . . above the hooked nose of being open to the commercial chance" (*Journey Without Maps*); "He had been a Jew once, but a hairdresser and a surgeon had altered that" (*Brighton Rock*); "She deserved something better than a man named Furtstein. . . . The domed Semitic forehead, the dark eyes over the rather gaudy tie" (*The Confidential Agent*); "How the financial crisis has improved English films! They have lost their tasteless Semitic opulence and are becoming – English" (the *Spectator*, 7 April 1939).

As this last quotation indicates, Greene tried to stir up antagonism toward the "alien" community of Jewish immigrants and refugees in England. In 1936 he used the *Spectator* to frighten readers with the image of "the dark alien executive tipping his cigar ash behind the glass partition in Wardour Street." Greene was well aware of the growing threat to Jews in Europe – his brother was the Berlin correspondent of the *Daily Telegraph* – yet his attacks continued even after the awful events of *Kristallnacht*.

This evidence, and much more, is presented in my biography, but Lodge does not refer to any of it. Clearly, it would undermine his attempt to make my argument look "exaggerated". Moreover, it would destroy his effort to create sympathy for Greene as a victim of my "virulent hatred". The only evidence he offers is Greene's portrait of Myatt in *Stamboul Train*, which he contends is not an anti-Semitic caricature. This is an odd view, to say the least. The truth is that Greene's novel presents Myatt as a "short and stout and nasal" businessman who cares for nothing but money. When Myatt makes a mercenary marriage, the narrative says that he wanted to "set up his tent and increase his tribe." Surely Lodge – a widely acclaimed critic as well as novelist – cannot really believe that Myatt is convincing proof that "Greene's Jewish characters are far from being anti-Semitic caricatures."

Although I greatly admire many of the literary qualities in Greene's best books, I cannot put a good spin on his anti-Semitism. It is worse than anything in T.S. Eliot or Evelyn Waugh, and David Lodge should be willing to confront that fact, even though his "warm memories" of Greene may suffer as a result. In any case, criticizing me will do nothing to make the unpleasant evidence go away.

Michael Shelden
Department of English, Indiana State University

David Lodge *replies*:

I wrote in my article: "There is no doubt . . . that Greene's early novels betray a kind of prejudice against Jews that would be unacceptable today – but then so did the work of most English writers of his generation. It is perverse to judge this strain in his work from a post-Holocaust position in history." Probably I should have said "many" rather than "most".* Greene was certainly not unique in this respect; and I still stand by my second sentence.

I don't have the time at my disposal to comb through the fiction of the 1930s to match Mr Shelden's gathering of allegedly anti-Semitic quotations from Greene's work, but in any case merely listing such phrases torn from their context proves nothing. The first reference in Mr Shelden's letter, for instance, claims that Greene "ridiculed 'Jewesses' as 'little bitches'." The passage in question occurs in *Brighton Rock* and describes Pinkie Brown, the teenager gangster who is the novel's central character, waiting in the lounge of a luxury hotel for an appointment with Colleoni, the leader of a much more powerful rival gang:

> A little Jewess sniffed at him bitchily and then talked him over with another little Jewess on a settee. Mr Colleoni came across an acre of deep carpet from the Louis Seize Writing Room, walking on tiptoe in glacé shoes.
>
> He was a small Jew with a neat round belly; he wore a grey double-breasted waistcoat, and his eyes gleamed like raisins. His hair was thin and grey. The little bitches on the settee stopped talking as he passed and concentrated. He clinked very gently as he moved: it was the only sound.

---

* This change has been made in the article as reprinted here.

The description is focalized through Pinkie's warped, resentful, demonic sensibility, and the word "bitch" primarily expresses his anxiety about his own sexuality, and his conflicted feelings about women. At the end of the novel, he leaves a message for Rose, the young Catholic girl who loves him, using the same word: "God damn you, you little bitch, why can't you go home and let me be?" Arguably the rhetorical effect of the earlier passage also draws on social and cultural prejudices and stereotypes concerning Jews which were common in English society before World War II, but to label it as anti-Semitic ridicule is crudely reductive.

It would be tedious to analyse every one of Mr Shelden's quotations in the same way, but his interpretation of those drawn from the *Spectator*, where Greene wrote in his own person, calls for comment. Greene was devoted to the cinema as an art form and as a critic waged constant war against the vulgarization and commercialization of the medium by Hollywood and its British equivalent. Since many of the leading figures in the industry were Jews, he was able to exploit British suspicion of foreigners in general and Jews in particular to reinforce a specific cultural argument. This was certainly not to his credit, but it is deeply misleading to suggest that he was trying to "stir up antagonism toward the 'alien' community of Jewish immigrants and refugees in England" *in toto*. There is no evidence that Greene was an anti-Semite in the sense of holding that Jews were an undesirable and destabilizing presence in the state who should be denied full civil rights (as for instance Hilaire Belloc and G.K. Chesterton maintained).

As to the character of Myatt, it is absurd to describe him as caring for nothing but money. In the first section of *Stamboul Train*, for instance, he is shown acting as a Good Samaritan to two other characters. When the political refugee Czinner wakes from a doze in the restaurant car:

> something in the sudden change from sleep to a more accustomed anxiety, something in the well-meaning clothes betrayed by the shabby mackintosh, touched Myatt to pity. He presumed on their earlier encounter.
> "You've found a compartment all right?"

"Yes."

Myatt said impulsively: "I thought perhaps you were finding it hard to rest. I have some aspirin in my bag. Can I lend you a few tablets?"

Later Myatt gives the chorus girl Coral, who has fainted, his first-class berth, standing in the cold corridor himself so that she can sleep; and although they later become lovers, this is not presented as a seduction gambit. These are hardly the actions of "an anti-Semitic caricature". Indeed, no truly anti-Semitic novelist would have made the imaginative effort to adopt the point of view of a Jewish character and to render his experience (including the experience of being snubbed by gentiles) from within.

Lucky Jim Revisited

Lucky Jim was first published by Victor Gollancz in January 1954. It went through ten impressions in that year, and reached its twentieth by 1957. I myself read it for the first time in the summer of 1955, a long-postponed treat after finishing my BA course in English literature at University College, London, where the syllabus stopped well short of contemporary British fiction. I consumed it with exquisite pleasure, and read each succeeding novel by Kingsley Amis as soon as I could borrow it from the public library. (New fiction was beyond my means in those days, and paperback publication lagged years behind the hardback. The first paperback edition of *Lucky Jim* did not appear until 1959, tied to the Boulting Brothers' disappointing film of the novel.)

In 1963 I published one of the first academic articles on Amis's work, subsequently incorporated in my *Language of Fiction* (1966). Since then I have taken down *Lucky Jim* from my bookshelves on many occasions, and skimmed through it or dipped into it for the purposes of teaching or quotation, but it is some time since I reread it carefully from cover to cover. Doing so for the purposes of writing this introduction* I found it to be a rather different book from the one I remembered, and from

* To the Penguin Twentieth Century Classics edition of *Lucky Jim* (1992).

the one that is described in most surveys of post-war British fiction. It is not so much that I – we – misread the book in earlier years, as that we seem to have screened out some of the elements of which it is composed.

"The novel that changed a generation," declares the blurb on the back of the 1981 Penguin edition. "In his hilarious send-up of academic life, Kingsley Amis poked devastating fun at a very British way of life, and gave post-war fiction a new and enduring figure to laugh and laugh at." As far as it goes, this is a perfectly accurate description: *Lucky Jim* is indeed a classic comic novel, a seminal campus novel, and a novel which seized and expressed the mood of those who came of age in the 1950s. But there is more to it than that. *Lucky Jim* is not, for instance, as *continuously* funny as one remembers it being, or as its legend might lead new readers to expect. There are many passages in it where we are not invited to chuckle, or even smile; passages, usually to do with the hero's sentimental education, that are surprisingly serious in tone and import. More about this in a moment. First let us pay due tribute to its comedy.

This derives from two sources, situation and style, and while the comedy of situation is inseparable from the style, the reverse is not always true: the style can provoke laughter on its own. Both, however, depend on Amis's flawless sense of timing: the way he controls the development of an action, or a sentence, to create that combination of surprise and logicality that is the heart of comedy. Comedy of situation is exemplified by such memorable scenes as Jim's accident with the bed-clothing at the Welches' and his efforts to conceal the damage, his attempts to deceive Mrs Welch and her son Bertrand on the telephone by disguising his voice, his hijacking of the Barclays' taxi after the College Ball, and his drunken lecture on "Merrie England". All these episodes involve the violation of a polite code of manners and contain an element of farce; they belong to a tradition of British comic writing which goes back through Waugh, Wodehouse, Dickens and Fielding to Restoration and Elizabethan comedy.

The comedy generated by Amis's style was more original, and introduced a distinctively new tone into English fiction. The style is scrupulously precise, but eschews traditional "elegance". It is educated but classless. While deploying a wide

vocabulary it avoids all the traditional devices of humorous
literary prose – jocular periphrasis, mock-heroic literary allusion, urbane detachment. It owes something to the "ordinary
language" philosophy that dominated Oxford when Amis was a
student there. It is a style continually challenged and qualified
by its own honesty, full of unexpected reversals and undermin-
ings of stock phrases and stock responses, bringing a bracing
freshness to the satirical observation of everyday life. The italics
in the following quotations from the opening pages are mine:

> He'd found his professor standing, *surprisingly enough*, in
> front of the Recent Additions shelf in the College Library . . .

> To look at, *but not only to look at*, they resembled some kind
> of variety act . . .

> He and Welch might well be talking about history. At
> moments like this Dixon *came near to* wishing they really
> were.

> ". . . and the resulting confusion . . . my word . . ."
>   *Quickly deciding on his own word*, Dixon said it to him-
> self . . .

> "Don't laugh at me if I say I think the Board did a better
> job than they knew when they appointed you." *He hadn't
> wanted to laugh then, nor did he want to now.* What would she
> be wearing this evening? He *could just about bring himself* to
> praise *anything but* the green Paisley frock in combination
> with the low-heeled, quasi-velvet shoes.

> "In considering this strangely neglected topic," it began.
> *This what neglected topic? This strangely what topic? This
> strangely neglected what?*

The last quotation is Jim's private interrogation of his own
scholarly article, on the publication of which his professional
future depends.

Lucky Jim was the first British campus novel (as distinct from
the Varsity novel, about the goings-on of young people at
Oxbridge) – the first to take as its central character a lecturer at
a provincial university, and to find a rich seam of comic and

narrative material in that small world. According to Amis himself, the original inspiration for the novel was a glimpse of the Senior Common Room at what was then University College, Leicester, in 1948, when he was visiting Philip Larkin, who was a librarian there:

> I looked around a couple of times and said to myself, "Christ, somebody ought to do something with this." Not that it was awful – well, only a bit; it was strange and sort of *developed*, a whole mode of existence no one had got on to from outside.

Thus is the genesis of *Lucky Jim* recalled in Amis's *Memoirs* (1991); but he put the story about Leicester into circulation a long time before, perhaps to deflect attention from University College, Swansea, where he taught from 1949 to 1961, as a possible source for the novel. In any event, *Lucky Jim* certainly started something, a distinctively British version of a kind of novel that had hitherto been a peculiarly American phenomenon. My own novels of university life, and those of Malcolm Bradbury, Howard Jacobson, Andrew Davies *et al.*, are deeply indebted to its example. Jim Dixon's anxiety about his professional future, his dependence on the patronage of a senior colleague whom he despises, is a recurrent feature of the genre, and in Professor Welch ("No other professor in Great Britain, he thought, set such store by being called Professor") Amis drew an immortal portrait of the absent-mindedness, vanity, eccentricity and practical incompetence that academic institutions seem to tolerate and even to encourage in their senior staff (or at least did before the buzz-word "Management" began to echo through the groves of academe in the 1980s).

But academic politics in the broader sense, intellectual competition and intrigue, taboo sexual relations between staff and students, and the social and educational dynamics of the seminar and tutorial, which are the stuff of most campus novels, British and American, have little or no place in *Lucky Jim*. Its university setting functions primarily as the epitome of a stuffy, provincial bourgeois world into which the hero is promoted by education, and against whose values and codes he rebels, at first inwardly and at last outwardly. The longest and most important piece of continuous action in the novel, extending over six chapters and some fifty pages, centres on a ball, a device for bringing characters together that goes back as far as the eighteenth-century novel, and one which might equally well have been associated with some other hierarchical institution, such as a bank or a business.

This brings us to the question of *Lucky Jim*'s historical and sociological significance. In 1954 it was acclaimed as marking the arrival of a new literary generation, the writers of the 1950s, sometimes referred to as "The Movement" or "The Angry Young Men". These were two distinct but overlapping categories. "The Movement" was a school of poetry, of which Philip Larkin was the acknowledged leader, and to which Amis himself belonged, along with other academics like John Wain, Donald Davie and D. J. Enright. The anthology that launched them was Robert Conquest's *New Lines* (1956), and they consciously set themselves to displace the declamatory, surrealistic, densely metaphorical poetry of Dylan Thomas and his associates with verse that was well-formed, comprehensible, dry, witty, colloquial and down-to-earth. Several of them besides Amis also wrote novels that cultivated the same qualities. Philip Larkin, for instance, whom Amis met and befriended as a student at Oxford, had published *Jill* in 1946 and *Girl in Winter* in 1947, though without making much impression on the reading public. The first of these novels anticipated *Lucky Jim* in having a hero of humble origins ill-at-ease in a university milieu. Amis showed Larkin an early draft of *Lucky Jim* around 1950, took his advice about cutting out superfluous characters (see *Memoirs*) and dedicated the finished novel to him.

"The Angry Young Men" was a journalistic term, originally put into circulation by a leading article in the *Spectator*, used to group together a number of authors and/or their fictional heroes, who appeared on the literary and theatrical scenes in the mid-to-late 1950s, vigorously expressing their discontent with life in contemporary Britain. They included John Osborne/ Jimmy Porter (*Look Back in Anger*), Alan Sillitoe/Arthur Seaton (*Saturday Night and Sunday Morning*), John Braine/Joe Lampton (*Room at the Top*) and Kingsley Amis/Jim Dixon. The category was soon stretched to include any interesting new young writer who came along – for example, Colin Wilson, whose existentialist tract *The Outsider* had nothing whatsoever in common with the above-named works. Amis himself explicitly repudiated the label of Angry Young Man, but it stuck to him as such things tend to do.

Although these writers "arrived" in the 1950s, their education and careers had in many cases been delayed or interrupted by the Second World War, and their formative years were really the 1940s. If one looks carefully at the text of *Lucky Jim* it becomes clear that it is a novel *about* the 1940s, and distinctly under the shadow of the war. Jim's oppressively keen student Mitchie is an ex-serviceman "who'd commanded a tank troop at Anzio when Dixon was an RAF corporal in Western Scotland". Jim keeps his lecture notes in an old RAF file, and visualizes the streets and squares of London by "remembering a weekend leave during the war". Even Welch, in an unwonted display of compassion, remarks that "It's only to be expected, after a war" that young men should find it difficult to settle into a job.

No dates are specifically mentioned in the text. It cannot be set later than 1951 since a Labour government is in power. Bertrand's remark about their inability to "pour water on troubled oil" may be a reference to the Persian Oil Crisis of that year. (In his *Memoirs*, Amis attributes this witticism to Dylan Thomas, and accuses him of having rehearsed it in order to impress a bar-room audience of university staff and students at Swansea.) In that case the action would be taking place in the summer term of 1951, but we know that Amis was working on the novel earlier than that. The point is that although it was published when the Tory government elected in 1951 was well into its stride, encouraging consumerism and free enterprise, the atmosphere of the novel itself is clearly that of socialist, "austerity" Britain in the 1940s, when a young university lecturer might plausibly possess only three pairs of trousers, live in a lodging house, surrendering his ration book to his landlady, not even dream of owning a car, and keep anxious count of his cigarette consumption, not on health grounds, but financial ones.

By the same token, the lifestyle of the Welches has a quality of the pre-war bourgeoisie. They live in a house that boasts a *music-room*, and have *maidservants*. (This degree of affluence, untypical of a professor of history at a provincial university, is explained by attributing a private income to Mrs Welch.) The two Welch sons, the "bearded pacifist painting" Bertrand and the "effeminate writing" Michel, seem in many ways hangovers from pre-war Bohemia. Indeed Bertrand's pacificism is hardly consistent with the Toryism he expounds in his political arguments with Jim. For his part, Jim's socialism is not ideologically sophisticated: "If one man's got ten buns and another's got two, and a bun has got to be given up by one of them, then surely you take it from the man with ten buns." It is not entirely surprising that once progressive politics became trendy, as they did in the 1960s, Kingsley Amis and his heroes turned against them (see his 1967 essay, "Why Lucky Jim Turned Right"); indeed, in Jim's tacit agreement with Beesley on the decline of educational standards one can already see a premonition of the slogan, "More will mean worse", that Amis later applied to the expansion of universities. The left-wing stance of *Lucky Jim*, in short, is an emotional, intuitive matter, more concerned with class and manners than with politics as such.

The received wisdom of the 1940s was that the Second World War, the "People's War", the landslide victory of the Labour Party in the General Election of 1945, and the establishment of the Welfare State, with free secondary and tertiary education, had genuinely democratized British society, and got rid of its class divisions and inequalities for good. But to many young people who grew up in the post-war period, and benefited from the 1944 Education Act, it seemed that the old pre-war upper classes still maintained their privileged position because they commanded the social and cultural high ground. For myself and many others, it was doing National Service in the peacetime army that opened one's eyes to this fact. For Jim Dixon, it was taking up a university post at a time when provincial universities were all mini-Oxbridges, aping and largely staffed by graduates of the ancient universities.

Jim is ill-at-ease and out of place in the university because he does not at heart subscribe to its social and cultural values, preferring pop music to Mozart, pubs to drawing-rooms, non-academic company to academic. Looking into the face of a not particularly attractive barmaid while fetching a drink for Margaret, "he thought how much he liked her and had in common with her, and how much she'd like and have in common with him if she only knew him." He feels a fraud as a teacher. His students "waste my time and I waste theirs". Why did he take up this uncongenial profession in the first place? He gives a revealing answer when Beesley asks him this very question: "feeling I'd be no use in a school and so on." When he loses his university job, however, Jim resignedly prepares to take up schoolteaching (at his own school) as if there were no alternative. A huge proportion of first-generation humanities graduates in the 1940s and 50s went into educational careers not because they had a vocational call, but because entry to the other liberal professions – administrative civil service, the foreign service, law, publishing, etc. – was still controlled by the public-school-Oxbridge-old-boy network. They were the ideal readers of *Lucky Jim*.

Nowhere is Jim's scorn for the protocol and pieties of the academic life expressed more pungently than in his private commentary (already quoted in part) on the scholarly article he is hoping to publish.

> Dixon had read, or begun to read, dozens like it, but his own seemed worse than most in its air of being convinced of its own usefulness and significance. "In considering this strangely neglected topic," it began. This what neglected topic? This strangely what topic? This strangely neglected what? His thinking all this without having defiled and set fire to the typescript only made him appear to himself as more of a hypocrite and fool. "Let's see," he echoed Welch in a pretended effort of memory: "oh yes; *The Economic Effect of the Developments in Shipbuilding Techniques, 1450 to 1485.*"

The note of self-accusation in this passage is crucially important. For most of the novel's action, Jim's rebellion against bourgeois values and institutions is purely mental, or physically expressed only through the pulling of grotesque faces when he thinks he is unobserved. His desire to take violent action against those who oppress him is discharged in harmless private fantasies of a childish nature (though no less funny for that) – plunging Welch feet-first into a toilet bowl, beating him about the head and shoulders with a bottle, pushing a bead up Margaret's nose, etc. After one such fantasy, Jim sadly reflects that, "He'd never be able to tell Welch what he wanted to tell him, any more than he'd ever be able to do the same with Margaret." The first occasion on which Jim's inner and outer speech exactly coincide comes after he fights Bertrand and succeeds in knocking him down.

> The bloody old towser-faced boot-faced totem-pole on a crap reservation, Dixon thought. "You bloody old towser-faced boot-faced totem-pole on a crap reservation," he said.

After this, Jim's fortunes begin to improve, in spite of deceptive appearances to the contrary. In his drunken lecture on Merrie England he again expresses, albeit involuntarily, his true self; and though he gets the sack in consequence, this turns out to be a liberation. Shortly afterwards he is liberated from his emotional bondage to Margaret. He is rewarded with the job, and the girl, of his dreams.

Several critics have perceived a fairy-tale buried in the deep structure of *Lucky Jim*, in which Jim is the Frog Prince, Christine the Princess, Gore-Urquhart the Fairy Godmother, and Margaret the Witch. But Jim's relationship with the two women is more subtle and complex than that analogy suggests. It is the most serious strand in the novel, and is pursued with particular attention in the chapters leading up to Jim's fight with Bertrand. The character of Christine, admittedly, rarely rises above her archetype, the blonde, beautiful, virginal yet voluptuous object of male desire, and the conversations between her and Jim are often embarrassingly banal. The dark, skinny, neurotic Margaret is much more interesting. Her claim on Jim's emotional loyalty is analogous to the university's claim on his professional allegiance. Just as he goes through the motions of being a university teacher knowing he is in bad faith, but unable to do anything about it, so he feels bound to go through the motions of being Margaret's partner, even though he has no desire, and hardly any affection, for her. When he finally brings himself to tell her this, candidly, in Chapter 16, she throws a fit of hysterics, then apologizes: "You were absolutely right, saying what you did. Much better to clear the air like that. I just behaved like a perfect idiot." This would seem to release Jim honourably from any further responsibility for Margaret, freeing him to pursue the promising intimacy he established with

Christine on the night of the Ball. Yet he remains perversely in Margaret's thrall. Shortly afterwards Bertrand angrily accuses him of trying to entice Christine away from himself. Jim stands up to this bullying; but when Christine and Margaret come into the room this passage of highly significant introspection occurs:

> He looked at Margaret and an intolerable weight fell upon him.
>
> He knew now what he'd been trying to conceal from himself ever since the previous morning [Margaret's hysterics], what the row with Bertrand had made him temporarily disbelieve: he and Christine would not, after all, be able to eat tea together the following afternoon. If he was going to eat that meal with any female apart from Miss Cutler [his landlady], it would be not Christine, but Margaret. He remembered a character in a modern novel Beesley had lent him who was always feeling pity moving in him like sickness, or some such jargon. The parallel was apt: he felt very ill.

It is part of Jim's loathing for all high-cultural affectation that he will never admit, even to himself, to remembering the names of the books and authors he has read. But there is little doubt that he is recalling here Graham Greene's *The Heart of the Matter* (1948). The closest parallel to the simile cited by Jim actually occurs in Greene's *Brighton Rock* (1938), where "a prick of desire disturbed him [Pinkie Brown] like a sickness." But it is in *The Heart of the Matter* that the hero is dominated and finally destroyed by the emotion of pity. The word "pity" occurs scores of times in the text, often in similes like the one half-remembered by Jim Dixon (e.g., "pity smouldered like decay at his heart"). When he was a B.Litt. student at Oxford, between 1947 and 1949, Amis was commissioned, rather improbably, by an Argentinian university to write a book on Graham Greene. The project came to nothing, and one may infer Amis's opinion of his potential publisher by the fact that the academic charlatan, "L. S. Caton", who plagiarizes Jim's article, disappears to a chair in Argentina. But it is certain that Amis would have been reading extensively in Greene, and would have read *The Heart of the Matter* on its publication with particular attention, when his own first novel was in gestation.

It is hard to think of two modern novelists who have less in common than Kingsley Amis and "Grim Grin" (as Greene's name is travestied in Amis's *I Like It Here*). But that of course is the point. In the late 1940s Greene was probably the most highly esteemed living British novelist; the success of *The Heart of the Matter* put a seal on his reputation. He was precisely the kind of figure that a young aspiring writer might measure himself against and try to displace, or at least differ from. *Lucky Jim* is a comic inversion of the tragic *The Heart of the Matter*. Amis's hero acquires happiness and good fortune by throwing off the pity and guilt that destroys Greene's Scobie. (It is worth noting perhaps that though, like most critics, I refer to Amis's hero affectionately and familiarly as "Jim", he is actually referred to throughout the text by his surname, as is Greene's.) Many phrases describing Scobie's feelings towards his shrewish wife would apply equally well to Jim's feelings towards Margaret: "pity and responsibility reached the intensity of a passion"; "the terrible impotent feeling of responsibility and pity"; "he was bound by the pathos of her unattractiveness". Even that quintessentially Greeneian sentence, "He felt the loyalty we all feel to unhappiness, the sense that that is where we really belong," seems applicable to Jim, as he resumes his joyless association with Margaret. Margaret herself is surprisingly honest, even generous, in this scene, heightening the perversity of Jim's renunciation of Christine:

"You'd have much more fun with her than you ever had with me."

"That's as may be. The point is that I've got to stick to you . . ."

"I don't hold with these renunciations. You're throwing her away for a scruple. That's the action of a fool."

This time, a minute or two went by before either spoke. Dixon felt that his role in this conversation, as indeed in the whole of his relations with Margaret, had been directed by something outside himself and yet not directly present in her. He felt more than ever before that what he said and did arose not out of any willing on his part, nor even out of boredom, but out of a kind of sense of situation. And where did that sense come from if, as it seemed, he took no share in willing it?

It comes, of course, from Jim's conscience, from a kind of pale, secularized version of the self-sacrificing Christian ethic that is overdeveloped in Greene's Scobie, and a fear of transgressing its imperatives. As Jim says later to Christine, "I'm sticking to Margaret because I haven't got the guts to turn her loose and let her look after herself, so I do that instead of doing what I really want to do, because I'm afraid to."

What happens subsequently is that Jim is freed from his self-imposed loyalty to unhappiness by two developments in the plot. First, he is liberated from an unsatisfying career in education by Gore-Urquhart's offer of a job as his private secretary – a post doubly desirable because it entails living in London, where Jim longs to be, and because it is coveted by Bertrand. It is, however, worth no more in salary than Jim's university lectureship, and will be less secure than school-teaching, so Jim's ready acceptance is a sign of a new willingness to accept risk in his life. Secondly, he is redeemed from his emotional thralldom to Margaret by discovering, via Catchpole, that she faked the suicide attempt that originally bound him to her in a relationship of guilt and pity. Whereas Scobie's inability to reconcile the responsibilities he feels towards his wife, his mistress and God, leads to his suicide, the discovery that Margaret had no intention of committing suicide releases Jim from his paralysis. What he has always believed – that nice things are nicer than nasty ones – he now at last acts upon. "For the first time in his life he felt that it was no use trying to save those who fundamentally would rather not be saved." He determines to back his luck – and Christine's:

> Christine's more normal, i.e. less unworkable, character no doubt resulted, in part at any rate, from having been lucky with her face and figure. But that was simply that. To write things down as luck wasn't the same as writing them off as non-existent or in some way beneath consideration. Christine was still nicer and prettier than Margaret, and all the deductions that could be drawn from the fact should be drawn: there was no end to the ways in which nice things are nicer than nasty ones.

Is this contrast drawn between the two women sexist? Of course it is! So was most fiction written by men in the 1950s, or indeed at any other time, judged by 1990s standards of what is Politically Correct. The real objection to the characterization of Margaret is not that she is portrayed as hysterical, deceitful and sexually frigid, for it would be absurd to pretend that such women have never existed, but that the behaviour in which she manifests these traits is in one important respect rather implausible. I refer to her double deception of Jim and Catchpole over her faked suicide attempt, entailing the forging of a doctor's prescription. Like the sudden intervention of Gore-Urquhart with his job-offer, this discovery works in narrative terms only because it occurs in a comic novel, because we want to believe in it, because we want the hero to be released from his enchantment and find happiness. Margaret's story is potentially tragic, but it is not told here (it was to be told many times, and powerfully, by women novelists).

Perhaps the ethical pragmatism finally embraced by Jim Dixon can only be sustained if the subject enjoys good luck. "Nice things are nicer than nasty ones" is not much of a consolation for or defence against disease, madness, addiction, depression and death. As Kingsley Amis allowed these nasty things to impinge more and more on the world of his later novels they became progressively darker, to the disappointment of many readers of *Lucky Jim*, but also deeper.

Sex, Creativity and Biography: The Young D.H. Lawrence

There were several million facts of Lawrence's short life and long work, of which Dubin might master a sufficient quantity. He'd weave them together and say what they meant – that was the daring thing. You assimilated another man's experience and tried to arrange it into "thoughtful centrality" – Samuel Johnson's expression. In order to do that honestly well, you had to anchor yourself in a place of perspective; you had as a strategy to imagine you were the one you were writing about, even though it meant laying illusion on illusion: pretend that he, Dubin, who knew himself passing well, knew, or might know, the life of D.H. Lawrence . . . Though the evidence pertains to Lawrence, the miner's son, how can it escape the taint, the subjectivity, the existence of Willie Dubin, Charlie-the-waiter's son, via the contaminated language he chooses to put down as he eases his boy ever so gently into an imagined life? My life joining his with reservations. But the joining – the marriage? – has to be, or you can't stay on the vicarious track of his past or whatever 'truth' you think you're tracking . . . There is no life that can be recaptured wholly; as it was. Which is to say that all biography is ultimately fiction.

So muses William Dubin, the fictional biographer of D.H.

Lawrence whose midlife crisis is recounted in Bernard Malamud's *Dubin's Lives* (1979). It's a passage that focuses many of the anxieties – professional, ethical, psychological – of the modern biographer: the obsessive and almost perverse nature of the enterprise; the felt need to try to "become" the subject of one's work, and the impossibility of succeeding; the straining to be comprehensive while knowing that selectivity is inevitable; the desire to give the biographical narrative unity and shapeliness, and the recognition that this is inevitably to deform the "truth".

Dubin's conclusion that "all biography is ultimately fiction" is one with which most contemporary theorists of literature would concur. It is a post-structuralist commonplace that language constructs the reality it seems merely to refer to; therefore all texts are fictions (some more useful than others), whether they acknowledge it or not. Even in the groves of academe, however, a distinction between empirical and fictional narrative stubbornly persists. Granted that any interpretation is partial, subjective, and open to revision – therefore a kind of "fiction" – nevertheless there is a difference, many would argue, between facts that are recovered by historical research, and "facts" that are invented by the creative imagination. This distinction is the foundation of literary biography, which is constantly occupied in showing the process by which the first type of fact was turned into the second. Modern theory, in contrast, is suspicious or dismissive of the idea that a writer is the unique origin of the meanings of the texts he or she inscribes. Literary biography thus constitutes the most theoretically conservative branch of academic literary scholarship today. By the same token, it is the one that remains most accessible to the "general reader".

One respect in which modern biography resembles fiction that has nothing to do with these theoretical arguments, but partly explains why it is so popular, is its fascination with its subjects' sexual lives. In the eighteenth and nineteenth centuries the novel was the literary genre above all others to which readers turned for the representation of sexuality. Biography restricted itself to the public lives of its subjects – or, insofar as it dealt with their private lives, did not intrude into the bedroom.

George Eliot's second spouse and first biographer, John Cross, transcribing her account of how she came to write fiction ("one morning as I was lying in bed, thinking what should be the subject of my first story, my thoughts merged themselves into a dreamy doze") cut out the words "as I was lying in bed" because the context made clear that she was in bed with George Lewes. A modern biographer, noting that the occasion was in effect their honeymoon, would be more likely to draw a connection between the burgeoning of George Eliot's fictional imagination and her sexual fulfilment.

Sex and creativity are two subjects of inexhaustible interest in our culture. What are other people's sexual lives really like? And how do writers convert their experience, especially their emotional and erotic experience, into literary fiction? Once readers turned to novels for an answer to the first question, and could only speculate about the second. Modern literary biography attempts to answer both, and its demonstrated power to recuperate facts that one would have thought irrecoverable is impressive. (If, gentle reader, you don't wish the most private moments of your life to become the object of interested scrutiny by future generations, you would do well not to become a great writer, or have anything to do with one.)

In no modern writer are sexuality and creativity more deeply and intricately connected than in D.H. Lawrence. In other respects too he is an ideal subject for the modern literary biographer. He lived at a time when people still communicated extensively by letter, especially when they travelled abroad, as Lawrence constantly did; and letters are the biographer's primary source of information about the subject's inner and private life. One justification for producing a new full-scale biography of D.H. Lawrence now is that much of his correspondence has only recently come to light, in the magnificent edition of the Letters published by Cambridge University Press under the general editorship of James Boulton. (To give some idea of the copiousness of Lawrence's correspondence: the latest volume contains 768 items written between March 1927 and November 1928, and runs to over 600 pages. Surprisingly few of these items are trivial or fail to throw some light on the writer.) At the same time Cambridge University Press has been publishing a scholarly edition of the Works, making available new textual and biographical information – notably a novel, *Mr Noon* (1984), half of which was previously unknown, which casts a vivid illumination on the early days of Lawrence's union with Frieda Weekley.

Contemplating the awesome task of assimilating all this new material (plus the formidable mass already in existence in the form of memoirs and recorded recollections of Lawrence, and his own autobiographical writings) and distilling it into a biographical narrative, the executors of the Lawrence estate and Cambridge University Press evidently came to the conclusion that it was too great a task to be given to one person, and decided to split the undertaking into three parts, each commissioned from a different writer. The first volume, by John Worthen, covers the years from Lawrence's birth in 1885 to 1912, just before the publication of *Sons and Lovers*.[*] The second and third volumes, by Mark Kinkead-Weekes and David Ellis respectively, will cover the middle and late period of the author's life.

This is an interesting experiment, for which there is not, I believe, an exact precedent. It entails, obviously, abandoning William Dubin's attempt vicariously to inhabit Lawrence's life by an act of imaginative empathy. "Can three people, however closely they work together, be sufficiently in harmony to capture Lawrence's identity?" the Cambridge biographers ask in their joint preface, only to dismiss the question as resting on dubious assumptions. They invoke Lawrence's rejection of "the old stable ego of the character" in his own fiction, and give a nod toward poststructuralist theory: "three different voices to tell Lawrence's story . . . give the lie, by their very difference, to the idea that any single view, however detailed and comprehensive, could be 'definitive'; any pattern of interpretation *the* pattern." Their method, however, to judge by the first volume, will be scrupulously, conservatively empirical; and the fact that they are all British male academics is likely to give the composite biography more unity of tone and consistency of interpretation than if one of them had been, say, an American feminist.

[*] *D.H. Lawrence: The Early Years 1885–1912* by John Worthen. Cambridge University Press, 1991.

(Another biography of Lawrence, incidentally, is in preparation by Brenda Maddox, the biographer of Nora Joyce.)*

Not that feminists will find much to complain of in John Worthen's volume, which is notable for its thoughtful and fair-minded discussion of Lawrence's relationships with women. In other respects, too, it is a fine achievement. It is a work of impeccable scholarship, and comes provided with an impressive apparatus of notes, appendices, chronological tables, family trees, an exemplary index, and complete lists of Lawrence's prose and verse writings in the relevant period, making it an invaluable resource for serious students of Lawrence; but it is also written in a lucid, unpretentious style which lay readers will find accessible and enjoyable. In particular, Worthen seems to me to have perfectly judged the proportion of literary criticism to biographical narrative. In other words, there is not too much of the former. Many academic biographers seem to think they must give us an exhaustive critique of each of their subject's major works, whereas the fact is that, once embarked on the story of a life, we do not want to be detained by a critical essay, however good it is.

As well as creativity and sex, the early life of D.H. Lawrence has one other ingredient that makes it of consuming interest: namely, class. Lawrence, the son of a coal miner, born and brought up in the small mining village of Eastwood, Nottinghamshire, was the only indisputably major English writer of this century who came from the working class. Not surprisingly, Worthen spends a good deal of time examining and analysing the precise nature of Lawrence's social background, and how he drew on it, modified it, and variously interpreted it in his work. Lawrence himself liked to give the impression that while his father was working-class, his mother was middle-class, and he defined the conflict between the Morels in *Sons and Lovers* in these terms. Worthen argues that Lawrence overstated the social gap between his parents. Lydia Beardsall's father was only a skilled artisan, an engineering "fitter", which was not a middle-class occupation. A serious accident when Lydia was nineteen rendered him unable to work, and the resulting

---

* This was published in 1994 under the title, *The Married Man: A Life of D.H. Lawrence.*

poverty anchored the family still more firmly in the working class.

One of the incidental revelations of Worthen's biography is the dangerousness and precariousness of the British industrial worker's life in the late nineteenth and early twentieth centuries. Between 1868 and 1919, for instance, a miner was killed every six hours, seriously injured every two hours, and injured badly enough to need a week off work every two or three minutes. Arthur Lawrence (the novelist's father) was injured several times, once suffering a compound fracture of the right leg which left him with a limp for the rest of his life. Miners could earn relatively high wages when they were fit and strong, but as the years took their inevitable toll they were shunted into less arduous and less rewarding jobs, or laid off altogether. Thus families in mining communities had built into them something of the harsh generational struggle of the Freudian primitive tribe, in that the sons sooner or later challenged, because of their greater earning ability, the authority and status of the father. This led to a locally celebrated tragedy in the family of Arthur Lawrence's brother Walter, who, unemployed and goaded beyond endurance by the contempt of one of his sons when the latter returned home from the pit, threw a tool at him, and killed the young man. This incident must have made a deep impression on David Herbert Lawrence, then a schoolboy, and probably influenced his portrayal of the violent behaviour of Mr Morel in *Sons and Lovers*.

When Lydia Beardsall married Arthur Lawrence, however, he was a strong, handsome young man, earning good money as a "mining contractor" (a rather grand local term for the leader of a small team of underground workers). Worthen suggests that she married him because of his virile charm and because he offered her an escape from the cramping poverty of her own family, then spent the rest of her life rather unfairly complaining because he did not share her own aspirations to gentility. Lydia Lawrence believed in self-improvement through education, self-discipline, and thrift. She had a genuine, if conventional taste for literature, and was prepared to tackle anything her son put in her way (he described her reading a translation of Flaubert's *A Sentimental Education* in 1910 "with a look of severe disapproval"). She took a leading role in the local branch of the

Women's Co-operative Guild. Within her limited means she furnished her house in a style perceptibly more elegant than that of her neighbours. Realizing that her husband had no sympathy with her values and aspirations (his leisure time was spent in the masculine camaraderie of the public house) she projected them onto her gifted sons: William Ernest (known in the family by the second of these names, but in *Sons and Lovers* by the first), who died suddenly of blood poisoning at the age of twenty-three; and then David Herbert ("Bert").

As a rather weakly child, of sensitive temperament and artistic gifts. D.H. Lawrence identified with his mother and feared his father ("Now we are going to be very happy while Father is away," he is reported to have said as the unfortunate Arthur Lawrence was taken off to hospital after an accident at the pit). After her death in 1910 he came to see this close relationship with his mother as unhealthy, retarding and obstructing his sexual development, especially when Frieda explained Freud's theory of the Oedipus complex to him, and his final revision of *Sons and Lovers* reflects this shift of interpretation. Near the end of his life he became more sympathethic toward his father, criticised his mother's genteel cultural values, and celebrated the physical, masculine world of the colliers as a kind of organic community:

> The pit did not mechanize men. On the contrary . . . the miners worked underground as a sort of intimate community, they knew each other practically naked, and with curious close intimacy . . . ("Nottingham and the Mining Countryside")

In Worthen's opinion, this was a mythologizing of the pit that owed more to Lawrence's "religion" of blood and instinct than it did to observation or experience.

Indeed, if this volume has a thesis or overarching interpretative theme, it is that D.H. Lawrence's literary and personal development was achieved at the cost of a certain distortion and neglect of his regional and working-class roots. Worthen praises very highly Lawrence's early plays like *The Collier's Friday Night* and *The Daughter-in-Law*, with their earthy humour and finely rendered dialect speech, and regrets that Lawrence did not pursue this vein more extensively in his fiction. He shows how

Lawrence began to acquire middle-class attitudes and values when he moved from Eastwood to the outer London suburb of Croydon in 1908, to take up a post as a schoolteacher while trying at the same time to launch himself as a writer through contacts in the London literary world like Ford Madox Hueffer (Ford Madox Ford).

"It was in Croydon that Lawrence started to grapple with his awareness of his own strangely ambivalent situation, belonging as he did both to the working class and to the educated middle class," writes Worthen; and he shows with great subtlety the reflection of this ambivalence in the uncertain tone and attitude of the narrative voice in the short stories that Lawrence wrote at this period. On the most famous of these pieces, "An Odour of Chrysanthemums," he comments: "Having in the first part of the story written an incomparable account of the tensions in the lives of ordinary people in the mining community . . . he turned its ending in the 1909 and 1910 versions of the story into a lugubrious moral epistle about drunkenness and death."

D.H. Lawrence did not become a middle-class Englishman. Instead he became a bohemian, a traveller, an exile, like so many great modern artists. But more than once Worthen wistfully wonders what kind of writer he would have been if he had stayed in England. What drew or drove Lawrence away from England was primarily sex, incarnated in Frieda von Richthofen. What might have detained him was a permanent union with one of the several English women with whom he was emotionally involved before he met her. The elopement of Lawrence and Frieda is one of the great love stories of literary history, and does not suffer in the retelling. But it came as the climax to seven years' overlapping relationships between D.H. Lawrence and other women, which Worthen disentangles and examines with commendable clarity and tact.

Like many sensitive, physically delicate, intellectually precocious and mother-dominated boys, Lawrence seems to have remained sexually innocent and inexperienced beyond the average age for his social class, still ignorant of "the facts of life" at the age of fourteen or fifteen, according to the testimony of one contemporary. It was for this reason that he was able to conduct an emotionally intense but physically chaste relationship with Jessie Chambers, the daughter of a large family of tenant farmers in the countryside near Eastwood, with whom he spent most of his spare time in his youth, as a schoolboy, then a clerk in a surgical support factory, then a trainee schoolteacher. It was to Jessie, herself training to be a schoolteacher, that he confided his ambitions to be a writer, and whom he used as critic, counsellor, and collaborator. It was Jessie who launched him into print by sending a sheaf of his poems to Ford Madox Hueffer's *English Review*. But Lawrence did not appear to see how odd and potentially exploitative this relationship had become until members of his family, and especially his mother, who had never approved of Jessie's hold over her son, told him that he must either court her in the normal way or sever the relationship. Lawrence refused to do either, telling Jessie with cruel candour that he did not find her sexually desirable, but that he valued her friendship. Crushed, but helplessly in love with Lawrence, Jessie lived for several years in an emotional limbo, while Lawrence looked for sexual fulfilment elsewhere, often making Jessie the confidante of his relationships with other women.

When he moved to Croydon he courted for a time a young woman called Agnes Holt. It seems likely that he broke off the relationship when she refused to have sex with him, because shortly afterward, in a sudden reversal of attitude, he asked Jessie to do so. As Worthen drily remarks, "he was turning to the one woman in England likely to say 'yes'." But before Jessie gave herself to him in body as well as soul he had been pursuing another London acquaintance, Helen Corke, a much more liberated young woman than either Jessie or Agnes, who had her own literary ambitions. This relationship, or Lawrence's fantasies about it (for there is no evidence that Helen Corke ever slept with him) are reflected in "The Saga of Siegmund", which later became *The Trespasser*. Lawrence concealed from Jessie the full extent of his interest in Helen Corke, though he introduced the two women to each other, just as he had introduced Jessie to Agnes Holt in 1909. In August 1910, Lawrence terminated the sexual relationship between himself and Jessie (it had been a furtive, infrequent business, which brought little joy to either of them). A few months later, in December of the same year, with his mother dying, he impulsively proposed to Louie Burrows, whom he had met when they were both training to be teachers in Nottingham.

This engagement seems a classic instance of a man snatching at life in the midst of death; and by betrothing himself to someone of whom his mother would have approved Lawrence was perhaps avoiding any sense of disloyalty to her. Louie Burrows was lively and good-looking, but essentially a sensible, conventional young woman with sensible, conventional expectations. She believed in "saving up" for marriage in the sexual as well as the financial sense. Lawrence never cared about possessions or, at that time, about financial security, while, as he clearly hinted in his letters to Louie, he was impatient to consummate his desire:

> I cannot slowly gather flowers as I saunter. I wish to heaven I could. I cut straight through like a knife to what I want. I cannot, cannot slowly enjoy watching the rose open: I can't help it Louie, I can't. I am really dangerous in my fixed mad aim. I love my rose, and no other: and when I have her I shall want no other. But when I have her not, I have nothing.

Louie, however, held on to her principles, and her virginity. Some time in the latter half of 1911 Lawrence relieved his sexual frustration by beginning a covert affair with Alice Dax (the Clara of *Sons and Lovers*), a married woman who lived in Eastwood. In November, he fell ill with pneumonia, and took leave from his teaching post (he was never to return to it) to convalesce, first on the Isle of Wight, and then at the family home in Eastwood. In February 1912 he broke off his engagement to Louie, to her hurt bewilderment. Worthen reprints the rather heartless letter (to Edward Garnett) in which Lawrence describes a meeting in London at which Louie made a last effort at reconciliation:

> She had decided beforehand that she had made herself too cheap to me, therefore she thought she would become all at once expensive and desirable. Consequently she offended me at every verse end – thank God. If she'd been wistful, tender and passionate, I should have been a goner. . . . I took her to a café, and over tea and toast, told her for the fourth time.

When she began to giggle, I asked her coolly for the joke: when she began to cry, I wanted a cup of tea.

Fifty years later Louie Burrows read that letter in Harry T. Moore's edition of *The Collected Letters* (1962) and was sufficiently moved, and hurt, to emend and annotate her copy. She crossed out the words, "when she began to cry," and wrote in the margin, "I was simply dumb with misery." She added: "I said Is there another girl He said Yes, if you'd call her a girl." It is at moments like this that biography gives us access to intimate human experience that we would have thought long buried with the participants.

Later, Louie assumed that Lawrence had been referring on that occasion to Frieda Weekley, whom she always blamed for "seducing" Lawrence away from her; but in fact he was referring to Alice Dax, for he and Frieda had not yet met. Ernest Weekley, Professor of Modern Languages at Nottingham University, invited Lawrence to call on him and his wife one Sunday in March of that year. Alice Dax remembered Lawrence describing, shortly afterward, the impression Frieda had made on him; she was immediately convinced that their own relationship would come to an abrupt end. She was right.

Though the story of Lawrence's and Frieda's elopement is well known, it is worth recalling just how astonishing, reckless, and scandalous an action it was, especially for that time and place. Frieda Weekley was six years older than Lawrence, the mother of three children, the first of whom had been born when he was still at high school. She had a devoted husband and a comfortable house with the servants that went with an upper-middle-class life-style in those days. Yet within three months of meeting him, she had sacrificed security, respectability, and her beloved children in order to run away with a penniless, physically delicate ex-schoolteacher with no prospects apart from those offered by a promising first novel (*The White Peacock*) and a handful of poems and stories. That she did so is testimony to the strength of Lawrence's will, and his personal magnetism. But it could not have happened if Frieda had been the totally respectable bourgeois housewife she outwardly appeared to be.

She came from a cultured aristocratic German family whose attitude to sexual morality was worlds away from that of the burghers of Nottingham. Her sister Else, married to the economist Edgar Jaffe, had a liaison with the Austrian psychoanalyst Otto Gross, and bore him a son, without separating from her husband. On visits home to Germany in 1907–1908 Frieda herself had a passionate affair with Gross, and enthusiastically embraced his ideas about free love and the supreme value of sexual fulfilment. (Martin Green has written very well about this matrix of ideas and personalities in his book *The Von Richthofen Sisters: The Triumphant and Tragic Modes of Love* [1974], a work surprisingly not mentioned by Worthen.)

Frieda was erotically unfulfilled by the rather stiff and conventional Weekley, who was fourteen years her senior, and there is evidence that she was discreetly unfaithful to him in Nottingham, as well as on trips to Germany. Even by today's standards, Frieda's indifference to sexual fidelity seems pretty startling. While she and Lawrence were walking over the Alps from Bavaria into Italy just weeks after their elopement, for instance, she had a tumble in the hay with a casual acquaintance, Harold Hobson, a friend of David Garnett's, when Lawrence and Garnett happened to be absent for a few hours (the episode is recorded in both the *Letters* and *Mr Noon*).

Frieda and Lawrence found an opportunity to make love very soon after their first meeting. No doubt she thought that she could have an exciting clandestine affair with this ardent and fascinating young man without disturbing the even tenor of her marriage, but she reckoned without his willpower. In comparison with the timid or repressed English girls he had known, her uninhibited and generous sexuality must have been a heady experience, but the attraction was deeper than that. "There are plenty of well-shaped women in England or in Germany who would love me enough in a licentious fashion," he wrote, a few weeks later. "But I don't want them. They are *not* life to me: they would brutalize me. This woman mates my soul."

The tragicomedy of the elopement and Frieda's estrangement from Weekley can be pieced together from the letters and the relevant sections of *Mr Noon*. Frieda went to visit her family in May, secretly accompanied by Lawrence. When he turned up at her parents' house in Metz, her relatives were horrified at the potentially ruinous consequences and tried to persuade her to sever the relationship, or at least conduct it discreetly. Telegrams and anger began to flow between Nottingham and Metz as rumours of scandal reached England. Lawrence retreated temporarily to another town; Frieda dithered and seems to have consoled or distracted herself with another brief affair, with a German officer. Lawrence forced the issue by informing Weekley that he and Frieda were lovers. As Worthen comments, "In the hectic muddle and confusion of these days, Lawrence had one single advantage: he was the only person who knew what he wanted." What he wanted was Frieda, and he got her. But the price she paid was heavy: custody of her children was inevitably awarded to Weekley when he divorced her the following year. "Lawrence never found a way of coping with her misery," Worthen comments. And he had left behind in England at least three other women with broken hearts: Jessie Chambers, Louie Burrows, and Alice Dax.

Jessie perhaps had most to complain of, for she had been used by Lawrence over the longest period, and faced further pain and humiliation when *Sons and Lovers*, finally revised under the influence of Frieda, was published in 1913. ("The Miriam part of the novel is a slander, a fearful treachery," she claimed.) She derived some solace or satisfaction from publishing her own account of their relationship (*D.H. Lawrence: a personal record*) anonymously in 1935. Louie Burrows remained devoted to Lawrence and did not marry until she was fifty-three. "Her family always regarded her life as having been ruined by Lawrence," Worthen reports. As to Alice Dax, she seems to have been a remarkable woman. She was devastated when Lawrence left her, trapped in an unsatisfying marriage, ill, and pregnant; but on reading Frieda's memoir *Not I, But The Wind . . .* (1934) many years later she wrote her a magnanimous and poignant letter:

> I had always been glad that he met you. . . . I was never *meet* for him. What he liked was not the me I *was* but the me I might-have-been – the potential me which would never have struggled to life but for his help and influence. I thank him always for my life though I knew it cost him pains and

disappointments . . . we were never, except for one short
memorable hour, whole; it was from that one hour that I
began to see the light of life.

To be fair to Lawrence, he did suffer occasional qualms of
conscience about his treatment of these women, especially
Jessie. In 1910 he confessed to a correspondent that he had
behaved "rather disgracefully" to her when he broke off their
relationship, and had "muddled my love affairs most ridicu-
lously and maddeningly." When in 1913 Jessie sent him an
account of their relationship in the form of a novel (which she
subsequently destroyed), it made him "so miserable I had
hardly the energy to walk out of the house for two days." He did
not scruple, however, to use his intimate knowledge of these
women in his fiction and poetry. As Worthen comments,
"writing and understanding were always more important to
Lawrence than personal loyalty." Though he was a maverick
modernist who had little sympathy for the aesthetic formalism
of Eliot and Joyce, he did subscribe, like them, to the doctrine
of creative "impersonality". In a remarkable letter to Gordon
Campbell in 1915 he tried to express his "feeling that one is not
only a little individual living a little individual life, but that one
is in oneself the whole of mankind . . . Not *me* – the little vain,
personal D.H. Lawrence – but that unnameable me which is
not vain nor personal, but strong, and glad, and ultimately sure,
but so blind, so groping, so tongue-tied, so staggering." The
transcendence of self which he strove to achieve, he tended to
demand of others, whether they liked it or not.

By conscious intention Lawrence put women and their plight
at the centre of much of his mature fiction – to "do my work for
women better than the suffrage," as he put it to a correspondent
in December 1912. But as Worthen points out, under the
influence of his union with Frieda he tended to present the
liberation of women exclusively in utopian sexual terms. "Lawrence's passionate writing about the liberation of women
through the active realization of their own sexuality would
ignore the continuing predicaments – and solutions – of women
like Alice Dax and Louie Burrows and Jessie Chambers" –
intelligent and progressive women who for one reason or
another could not, like him, uproot themselves from their

deeply conservative social milieu, but were obliged to reach a compromise with it. As Worthen concludes his biography he seems to stand spiritually with these women on the English shore, looking wistfully and with a certain disapproval as Lawrence and Frieda journey blithely into their bohemian exile.

Henry Green:
A Writer's Writer's Writer

Henry Green occupies a special but somewhat puzzling place in the history of modern English fiction. That his real name was Henry Yorke is symbolic of the general elusiveness of his literary identity. He seems to stand to one side of his fictional *oeuvre*, smiling enigmatically and challenging us to put a label, and a value, on it. He has been called a "writer's writer", and even, according to Terry Southern, "a writer's writer's writer". W.H. Auden, Eudora Welty, V.S. Pritchett, Rebecca West and John Updike have all described him, at various times and in various ways, as the finest novelist of his generation, yet he never enjoyed either the commercial success or the literary fame of contemporaries such as Evelyn Waugh, Graham Greene and Christopher Isherwood.

He was neither shrewd nor lucky in the development of his literary career. After a precocious and promising debut, *Blindness* (1926), begun while he was still at school, he wrote a brilliant novel about working-class life, *Living* (1929), several years before such subject-matter became fashionable, and then took ten years to write his next, *Party Going* (1939) – a work whose concern with a group of narcissistic socialites setting off on a Continental holiday seemed rather frivolous in the encroaching shadows of World War II. In the 1940s he became more productive, and more widely read (*Loving* [1945] even appeared briefly on the US best-seller lists), but just as he was beginning to attract serious critical attention, interest was diverted by a new wave of British writers, the so-called Angry Young Men, with whose coarse, iconoclastic energies he had little affinity. Whether it was coincidence or cause and effect, his creativity seemed to suddenly dry up at this time. The latter part of his life, from the publication of his last novel, *Doting*, in 1952, to his death in 1973, was a sad story of increasing reclusiveness, alcoholism and melancholia. His novels went out of print, and his name virtually disappeared from the canon of modern British fiction.

In the last decade or so there has been a determined effort by Green's admirers to remedy this state of affairs, by reissuing his novels and writing about them. Now Henry's grandson has put together a volume of his uncollected (and in some cases previously unpublished) writings, with an appreciative introduction by John Updike.* It is a curious, fascinating hotchpotch of gems and barrel-scrapings, which will be of intense interest to Henry Green's fans, though it is unlikely to make any new ones, except by sending readers to the novels. It is chronologically arranged, and includes juvenilia, bits of autobiography, short stories, prose poems, fragments of unfinished novels and stories, book reviews, texts of radio broadcasts, the script of a television play commissioned in the 1950s but never produced, an interview with Terry Southern reprinted from the *Paris Review*, the first chapter of a projected autobiographical work about Green's wartime experiences in the fire service, and a brief memoir by his son, Sebastian. Since there is as yet no proper biography of Green, and the autobiographical *Pack My Bag* (1940) conceals as much as it charmingly reveals, this volume is particularly interesting for the light it throws upon his life and family background.

From the description "writer's writer's writer" you might guess, if you knew nothing else about Henry Green, that he was a fastidious and innovative stylist rather than a great storyteller, that he was totally absorbed by the practice of his art, and that he led the literary life. Only the first of these inferences would be correct. For most of his adult life Green worked as managing

---

* *Surviving: The Uncollected Writings of Henry Green*, edited by Michael Yorke.

director of the family engineering business, and he had little time or energy (and, it would seem, little enthusiasm) for literary parties and literary politics. He was not, by all accounts, a particularly effective or efficient man of business, but his experience of commerce and industry – unique, to my knowledge, among English literary novelists of the twentieth century – left its mark on his fiction and gave it a rare social range.

Henry Yorke was born (in 1905) into a family of landed gentry with an impressive pedigree but no great wealth. His father, Vincent, was a Cambridge classics don whose favourite bedtime reading was Homer. When Vincent married Maud Evelyn Wyndham, daughter of the second Baron Leconfield, the family bought for him a semi-bankrupt engineering company, which included a foundry in Birmingham called H. Pontifex and Sons. Vincent built up the business with some success and used it as an entrée to the City of London, where he acquired several lucrative directorships. The pastoral and patrician lifestyle of the family estate, Forthampton Court, Gloucestershire, where young Henry grew up and spent his vacations from Eton and Oxford, invisibly supported by the capitalist exploitation of industrial labour in grey and grimy Birmingham, might be seen by a Marxist historian as an epitome of the social and economic structure of Britain in the early twentieth century. A fragment of dialogue found among Henry's papers, and probably written when he was nineteen, throws an amusing and sardonic light on family life at Forthampton Court, and incidentally demonstrates the future novelist's precocious understanding of the conversational games people play.

After dinner, VINCENT *reads the paper*
VINCENT *(reading)* In 1920 there were 4000 less dogs
    born in England than in 1924.
Silence
VINCENT I won't speak again.
MAUD Henry, did I ring for coffee?
VINCENT You did dear, I'm sorry.
MAUD Ring again Henry will you? No, dear boy, not that
    bell, it doesn't ring. I'm afraid something must have
    gone wrong with it.

HENRY *rings*
Silence
MAUD Billy, did you write to Hepworth about the kitchen
range?
VINCENT Yes dear, I sent the letter off directly you told
me. I do my best.
MAUD The cook is in despair, Vincent. I do not know
what to do about it, and this brute of a man Hepworth
will not send anyone to mend the range. He can be up
to no good in Birmingham, Vincent. What does he do
all day? Playing about with the typists instead of doing
the work?
VINCENT (*reading*) In Somerset two boys were drowned in
a river.

It reads like a collaboration between Noël Coward and Ivy
Compton-Burnett, and is nearly as good as either.

"Hepworth" was presumably the general manager of the
Birmingham factory, and Henry soon had an opportunity to
discover what he, and the rest of the employees, were "up to".
After reading English at Oxford for two years without much
enthusiasm (he did not get on with his tutor, C.S. Lewis, or
with the syllabus, which stopped at 1830 in those days and
included a great deal of Anglo-Saxon), Henry left the university
without a degree, and went to work at the Birmingham factory,
starting as an apprentice, and living in workmen's lodgings.

The idea was, of course, that he should learn about the
business from the shop floor up, preparatory to eventually
taking it over – a familiar pattern in family-owned companies.
But perhaps few "boss's sons" undergoing this initiation went
so far as to live like their fellow workers outside the factory
gates, and it would be interesting to know whether this was
Henry's own choice. Whatever his motivation, in these two
years (between 1927 and 1929) he acquired a great respect and
affection for the Birmingham factory workers, and a knowledge
of their manners, speech habits, working practices and domestic
lives that enabled him to write *Living*, arguably the best British
novel about the industrial working class published in the
twentieth century.

Most fiction about industrial life recoils in horror from the dirt, danger, and dehumanizing monotony of factory work, and pities those condemned to it. Green did not glamorize or sentimentalize such work, but he understood how men can take a pride in it, how they use humour and comradeship to make its material conditions tolerable, and how they become in due course psychologically and metabolically dependent upon its rhythms and intervals. One of the most moving parts of *Living* is the portrait of Mr Craigan, coming with difficulty to terms with retirement:

> Mr Craigan had gone to work when he was nine and every day he had worked through most of daylight till now, when he was going to get old age pension. So you will hear men who have worked like this talk of monotony of their lives, but when they grow to be old they are more glad to have work and this monotony has grown so great that they have forgotten it. Like on a train which goes through night smoothly and at an even pace – so monotony of noise made by the wheels bumping over joints between the rails becomes rhythm – so this monotony of hours grows to be the habit and regulation on which we grow old. And as women who have had nits in their hair over a long period collapse when these are killed, feeling so badly removal of that violent irritation which has become stimulus for them, so when men who have worked these regular hours are now deprived of work, so, often, their lives come to be like puddles on the beach where tide no longer reaches.

When the time came for Henry to take over the management of the company, he moved to London to work at its head office in George Street. Sebastian Yorke attributes the long interval between his second and third novels to the stresses and distractions of his new responsibilities, but perhaps Henry also missed the stimulus of the factory floor and the Birmingham back streets. Significantly, the most productive phase of Green's literary career seems to have been started off by his joining the London Fire Service in World War II, an experience which had much the same impact on him as his two years in the Birmingham factory. The prose sketches from this period in *Surviving* are reminiscent of *Living* in the way they relish the demotic speech and manners of the fire station, and take pride in the hard, dangerous work of firefighting.

Although he was never political in the fashionable left-wing style of many of his contemporaries, Green was a natural democrat, who welcomed any opportunity to break down the rigidities of the British class system. As a writer he was equally committed to breaking down the rigidities of English literary prose; indeed, for him the two enterprises were inseparable. Writing in 1941 on C.M. Doughty, the author of *Arabia Deserta* (1888), whose idiosyncratic, deliberately difficult prose style he greatly admired, he asked rhetorically:

> Now that we are at war, is not the advantage for writers, and for those who read them, that they will be forced, by the need they have to fight, to go out into territories, *it may well be at home*, which they would never otherwise have visited, and that they will be forced, by way of their own selves, towards a style which, by the impact of a life strange to them and by their honest acceptance of this, will be pure as Doughty's was, so that they will reach each one his own style that shall be his monument? (Italics mine.)

The first public manifestation of this principle in Green's fiction was the almost total elimination of articles from the narrative discourse in *Living*. For example, on the first page:

> Two o'clock. Thousands came back from dinner along streets . . .
>
> Thousands came back to factories they worked in from their dinners . . .
>
> Noise of lathes working began again in this factory. Hundreds went along road outside, men and girls. Some turned in to Dupret factory.
>
> Some had stayed in iron foundry shop in this factory for dinner. They sat round brazier in a circle.

When, many years later, Terry Southern asked Green why he had adopted this technique, the novelist replied: "I wanted to make that book as taut and spare as possible, to fit the proletarian life I was then leading. So I hit on leaving out the articles." This comment is, however, a somewhat misleading oversimplification. We discover from *Surviving* that Green was experimenting with the omission of articles long before writing *Living* and to entirely different effect. The new volume includes a remarkable unpublished prose fantasy about a giant, called "Monsta Monstrous", thought to have been written circa 1923, which begins as follows:

> Giant fell from sky into the sea and made great splash and great wave went out on all sides from where he had fallen and damaged many towns where land met the sea. But he first swam then waded, and soon came to coast of Wales . . .

This suggests that Green's experiments with prose are not to be explained simply in terms of expressive form, but as the result of a much more radical project to defamiliarize the world by defamiliarizing the literary medium in which it is conventionally represented. In his own, idiosyncratic, largely unassisted, and disarmingly amateurish way, Green was a theorist, who continued the modernist preoccupation with formal innovation in a period (the Thirties and Forties) generally unsympathetic to aesthetic experimentalism, and discovered for himself some of the fundamental principles of modern linguistics. This comes out particularly strikingly in two BBC radio talks, which he delivered in 1950 and 1951, entitled "A Novelist to His Readers, I & II", which are among the most fascinating items in *Surviving*.

Artists, according to Green, "are all meaning to create a life which is not. That is to say, a life which does not eat, procreate, or drink, but which can live in people who are alive." Art is "non-representational" in the sense that it is not identical with reality and cannot be mistaken for it.

> But, if it exists to create life, of a kind, in the reader – as far as words are concerned, what is the best way in which this can be done? Of course, by dialogue. And why? Because we do not write letters any more, we ring up on the telephone instead. The communication between human beings has now come to be almost entirely conducted by conversation.

(This is a somewhat simplistic argument. In fact Green had another, more substantial reason for privileging dialogue over narrative which we shall come to in a moment.) But, he immediately points out, conversation in novels is still nonrepresentational, "not an exact record of the way people talk", because meaning in actual conversations is dependent on *context*, that is to say on all kinds of unspoken information shared by the interlocutors concerning the world in general and their personal relationships in particular. In the terminology of Mikhail Bakhtin, all speech is dialogic in a double sense: an utterance may echo, allude to, anticipate, and engage with many other actual or virtual speech acts besides the one it is ostensibly responding to. Green gives an example almost certainly drawn from his own experience:

> Supposing a husband and wife live opposite a pub: at nine-thirty any evening when both are at home, he may say, "I think I'll go over now." She will probably answer, "Oh," and there may or may not be a wealth of meaning in that exclamation. And his reply to her will probably be, "Yes." After twenty years of married life any couple will talk in a kind of telegraphese of their own which is useless to the novelist.

One solution to this problem, not approved by Henry Green, is for the novelist to gloss the enigmatic utterances of his characters in the narrative discourse. He parodies this technique as follows:

> "How soon d'you suppose they'll chuck you out?"
> Olga, as she asked her husband this question, wore the look of a wounded animal, her lips were curled back from her teeth in a grimace and the tone of voice she used betrayed all those years a woman can give by proxy to the sawdust, the mirrors and the stale smell of beer of public bars.

Green's objection to this kind of thing is that the novelist is claiming a privileged insight into his characters' motives to which he is not entitled:

> Do we know, in life, what other people are really like? I very much doubt it. We certainly do not know what other people are thinking and feeling. How then can the novelist be so sure?

His own preferred solution is a stylized kind of dialogic fiction in which the speech of the characters is made slightly more explicit than in "real life" and presented with the minimum of authorial comment and interpretation. Green rewrites his own example as follows:

> At last he looked at the clock, laid the newspaper aside, and getting out of his armchair, wandered to the door. "I think I'll go over the way now for a drink," he said, his finger on the handle.
> "Will you be long?" she asked, and put her book down. He seemed to hesitate.
> "Why don't you come too?" he suggested.
> "I don't think I will. Not tonight. I'm not sure. I may," and she gave him a small smile.
> "Well, which is it to be?" he insisted, and did not smile back.
> "I needn't say now, need I? If I feel like it I'll come over later," she replied, picking her book up again.

This is the style of the late novels, like *Nothing* (1950) and *Doting* (1952). They are subtle, exquisite, and often very funny anatomies of human behaviour, but inevitably court the description "slight". One can't help feeling that Henry Green had by this time painted himself into an aesthetic corner by his dogmatic limitation of the scope of narrative discourse in the novel. He was not of course alone in his preference for staying on the surface of human speech and behaviour, eschewing both the authorial omniscience of the classic novel and the psychological subjectivism of the modernist novel: it is to be observed in the work of his contemporaries, Waugh, Powell, Isherwood, Ivy Compton-Burnett. But in Green's case it entailed sacrificing one of his own great strengths as a writer, his power of lyrical description. *Living* and *Party Going* contain memorable prose epiphanies, and one of the fragments collected in *Surviving* shows that the gift had not deserted him much later in life. It is the opening section of a projected autobiographical work about Green's wartime experiences in the fire service, published in the *London Magazine* in 1960. Green and his wife were on holiday in Connemara at the time of the Munich crisis, staying in a hotel full of anxious British officers' wives whose husbands had been recalled to duty.

My wife sea bathed, we sat about, but every night at nine there was the relentless wireless. Always, each day, news worse than the last . . .

We used to walk out with sandwiches to get away from the lounge where these women were already in wait for each evening and nine o'clock. And almost as soon as we were out of the grounds the coast was deserted, or so we thought. Enormous crescent beaches curved one after the other as wandering forward we shrimped in sea anemone garlanded, limpid emerald pools. Each one of these led to another and so in turn round the next jutted point of sand over which waves broke in shawl after shawl after shawl of whey-coloured lace, advancing, receding, hissing into a silence where no sea birds were.

It was at one of these divisions between one creamy beach and another that we saw a seal come out of the pewter sea as far as black shoulders, in its mouth a flapping sole so bright the fish was like a shaft of white light, violently vibrating.

This is descriptive writing of a high order, evoking the concrete details of the scene with piercing sensuousness but without obviously straining for effect. Evidently Green felt less constrained in using the authorial voice in autobiography than in fiction, but by this time he seemed to have lost the energy, or the will, to persevere with either form. The wartime memoir was never completed, and the last piece in *Surviving* is a pathetic fragment of self-description, dated 1963, which contains the poignant observation: "Green can write novels, but his present difficulty is to know quite how to do it." This is the worst curse that can fall upon a writer, and the final impression left by this book is therefore a somewhat gloomy one. Nevertheless it contains many delightful reminders of what an exceptionally gifted and truly original writer Henry Green was.

Joyce's Choices

This is the text of a public lecture given at University College Dublin, in a series of biannual lectures on James Joyce sponsored by the makers of Bailey's Irish Cream. What Joyce (whose favourite tipple was a dry Swiss white wine he referred to as "archduchess's urine") would have made of the intensely sweet and viscous liqueur one can only imagine, but if it had existed in his lifetime it would certainly have found its way into *Finnegans Wake* (as "Jamesy's Irish dream", perhaps). It was Augustine Martin, Head of the Department of Anglo-Irish Literature at UCD, who had the bright idea of asking Bailey's to sponsor the lectures, which they did so munificently that I thought the fee mentioned in Gus's letter of invitation must be a misprint. The idea of the series, he explained, was to invite well-known writers with a critical/scholarly string to their bow, and to encourage them to talk about Joyce's influence on their own work. Consequently there is a little overlap between this piece and an earlier essay, "My Joyce" (published in *Write On*). I gave my lecture in February 1995, in the old Physics Theatre of UCD where Stephen Dedalus discusses the word "tundish" with the Dean of Studies in *A Portrait of the Artist as a Young Man.* Sadly, Gus Martin died, suddenly and much too early in life, later the same year.

It is a very great honour to be invited to speak on the life and work of James Joyce in the city that was the inspiration and setting of every book he wrote. The last and only previous occasion on which I did so was at the James Joyce Symposium of 1982, the centenary of his birth, when I gave a paper on "Joyce and Bakhtin" – one of the first attempts by an English-speaking critic, I think I can claim, to bring those two names into conjunction. It was a memorable conference, not so much for its official sessions as for what might be called its fringe events. Many of my audience will remember that on 16 June, Bloomsday, and well into the following day, the entire text of *Ulysses* was read on a local Dublin radio station for some thirty-six hours, without censorship or interruption. As you walked down the street you heard the immortal words coming out of open windows, or from car radios, or from the transistors carried by people on the pavements, and when you returned from a lecture or seminar to your hotel room and switched on the bedside radio, it was still continuing. During the same day actors impersonating the various characters of *Ulysses*, dressed in period costume, appeared at appropriate times and places in the city, and in the middle of the afternoon the great Vice-regal procession in the chapter known as "The Wandering Rocks" was re-enacted. That imaginative piece of street theatre gave me the idea for the performance of scenes from *The Waste Land* on the streets of Lausanne (where T.S. Eliot wrote his poem) in my novel *Small World* – a novel which I first conceived at the previous James Joyce Symposium of 1979 in Zurich (the only real conference among all the fictitious ones described in its pages).

Although I have taught courses and written scholarly essays about him, James Joyce has always been a writer of more than academic interest to me. He was a formative influence in my youth, when my own ambitions to be a writer were germinating, and he continued to be a model and inspiration as my literary career developed. Traces of his influence, or incidental acts of homage to his achievement, can be found in most of my novels. He is, of all modern writers, the one I revere the most. This may seem a surprising assertion, given that most of my fiction belongs to a very English tradition of the realistic novel of manners, social satire and ethical dilemma – the tradition of Henry Fielding, Jane Austen and Charles Dickens, to name a few canonical names – against which Joyce reacted, at a very early stage of his career, in favour of a kind of fiction that was experimental, cosmopolitan and increasingly non-realistic. But the paradox is only superficial. Every writer of fiction can learn from Joyce, whatever style or mode they favour, and there were particular personal reasons why I was susceptible to his influence.

Although I am English by nationality, and a Londoner by birth and upbringing, my mother was half Irish. Her father was a Cork man called Murphy, who ran a series of pubs in south-east London frequented by famous boxers of the day. As he died when I was in infancy I have no recollection of him, but family tradition made him seem a little like Mr Joyce senior, or his fictional counterpart, Simon Dedalus: he was a popular and sociable man who got into ruinous business difficulties in later life, causing a sad decline in his wife and children's lifestyle. My maternal grandmother was Belgian, and Catholic like her husband. My mother was therefore a Catholic, and as my father has no particular religious affiliation I was brought up and educated as a Catholic.

Ours was not a typical Catholic home – I was an only child for one thing – but in my schooling and participation in parochial life, I moved in a world of behaviour and ideas which was not all that different from the world described in Joyce's fiction. The Catholic church has been so volatile and pluralistic in the last few decades, following the Second Vatican Council, that we are apt to forget how stable and unchanging it was in the preceding hundred years or so. In liturgy, theology, morality and manners, the "ghetto" Catholicism of my suburban London parish in the 1940s and 50s was not vastly different from the milieu in which James Joyce grew up. Certainly, when

I read *A Portrait of the Artist as a Young Man* in late adolescence, I felt an immediate thrill of recognition.

Perhaps this was partly because Joyce's persona in the novel, Stephen Dedalus, seems more like an only child than the member of a large and gregarious family. That was the intended effect of Joyce's drastic reorganization and condensation of the material he had represented more fully and conventionally in his first attempt at an autobiographical novel, *Stephen Hero*. As we know from the fragment of this work that has survived, Stephen's relationship with his siblings, particularly with his young brother Maurice (the fictional persona of Joyce's brother Stanislaus), was much more fully and realistically rendered in *Stephen Hero*. In *A Portrait*, the family life of the hero is drastically reduced and flattened into a kind of vague backcloth, in order to focus attention on his inner thoughts and feelings. There is some loss of human interest entailed in this procedure, but also a great gain in intensity. *Stephen Hero* was a conventional expansive autobiographical novel like Samuel Butler's *The Way of All Flesh* or D.H. Lawrence's *Sons and Lovers*, in which the hero's development is situated in a fully rendered social and familial world. *A Portrait* boldly presents its hero as a kind of Christ-figure, whose siblings are almost as vague and undifferentiated as the brethren of Jesus in the Gospels.

Perhaps another reason why I identified readily with the character of Stephen Dedalus was that like him and his creator I had been separated from my home and parents at an early age, though for a much shorter period. At the time of the Blitz in World War Two, I was briefly a boarder at a convent school in the country, where the atmosphere of physical austerity and religious discipline was not unlike that of the Jesuit school at Clongowes where Joyce was sent at the age of six. The experience is represented in my novel *Out of the Shelter*, the early part of which was written in conscious imitation of *A Portrait of the Artist as a Young Man*, using a simple, naïve third-person narrative discourse to imitate the expanding consciousness of a sensitive, timid, questioning child.

After the war, I attended a Catholic grammar school in South London run by the De La Salle Brothers, a teaching order similar to the Christian Brothers who taught Joyce very briefly in Dublin, after he left Clongowes and before the Jesuits offered to take him on as a day-pupil at Belvedere College, without fees. As we know from *A Portrait*, the Joyce family rather snobbishly despised the Christian Brothers and their schools (" – Christian brothers be damned! said Mr Dedalus. Is it with Paddy Stink and Micky Mud? No, let him stick to the jesuits in God's name since he began with them. They'll be of service to him in after years. Those are the fellows that can get you a position.") I'm sure Joyce had a better education than I did, but there was a good deal of similarity in ethos and routine between our respective schools. We too had annual "retreats", and though the sermons were not quite as frightening as those delivered in *A Portrait*, I was very familiar with the eschatological terror with which the Catholic Church exercised control over its members in those days before the Second Vatican Council.

Like Stephen Dedalus, I grew to despise the philistinism and repressiveness of Anglo-Irish Catholicism – but unlike him I did not feel it necessary to renounce my religious allegiance, as he did, on escaping from the discipline of school. Our situations were different in that he inhabited a Catholic culture, I a Catholic subculture. "When the soul of a man is born in this country," Stephen famously tells his friend Davin, "there are nets flung at it to hold it back from flight. You talk to me of nationality, language, religion. I shall try to fly by those nets." There were no nets threatening me. To escape the Catholic ghetto it was necessary only to walk out of it as soon as one achieved adulthood, and join the materialistic, pluralistic, secular world that surrounded it. But precisely because it was so easy, such a choice seemed rather pointless. It was more interesting to challenge the secular world with the ideological apparatus of a Catholic education and upbringing. To be a Catholic in secular, liberal humanist England was to be a nonconformist, a critic, a rebel even – precisely what Stephen Dedalus was, what most artists had fancied themselves to be since the Romantic Movement. Catholicism and Anglo-Catholicism were rather fashionable in the literary world of the Forties and Fifties. Graham Greene, Evelyn Waugh and T.S. Eliot were names to conjure with. Thus, while Joyce/Stephen prepared themselves in their student years to make a break with Church, country and family, I confirmed my allegiance to these things as an undergraduate at University College London.

Indeed, I found my Catholic education and background stood me in very good stead when it came to studying medieval literature – or the work of James Joyce.

In my third year I read *Ulysses* for the first time. It was undoubtedly the most exciting and rewarding experience of my literary education. Three things about the book particularly impressed me, as I suppose they impress most readers. The first was the extraordinary mimetic power of the language in the early, stream-of-consciousness chapters, language which describes everything, from the most trivial and commonplace sensations to the most complex and private thoughts, so exactly, so definitively, that you feel you never perceived the nature of reality so clearly before. I choose, from a thousand possible examples, Stephen's observation on Sandymount strand of a dog, belonging to a pair of cocklepickers, discovering the carcase of another dog washed up by the sea. The syntax and rhythm of the sentences imitate the dog's movements as exactly as the vocabulary describes them:

> Unheeded he kept by them as they came towards the drier sand, a rag of wolfstongue redpanting from his jaws. His speckled body ambled ahead of them and then loped off at a calf's gallop. The carcass lay on his path. He stopped, sniffed, stalked round it, brother, nosing closer, went round it, sniffing rapidly like a dog all over the dead dog's bedraggled fell. Dogskull, dogsniff, eyes on the ground, moves to one great goal. Ah, poor dogsbody. Here lies dogsbody's body.

The second feature that impressed me was Joyce's use of Homer's *Odyssey* as a kind of skeleton or scaffolding for his story of a day in Dublin in 1904, setting up echoes and cross-references – ironic, parodic and sometimes poignant – between the deeds of the ancient Greek heroes and the ordinary lives of ordinary people in a twentieth-century city. (For example, the allusions to the metamorphoses of Proteus, the god of the sea, in the description of the dog in the passage just quoted: "wolfstongue . . . calf's gallop . . .") This was what T.S. Eliot called Joyce's "mythical method . . . making the modern world possible for art" – a method he used himself in *The Waste Land,* with its manipulation of parallels between the quest for meaning in a post-Christian age and the Grail legend.

And the third feature that impressed me was the mutation of the verbal style of the narrative in the later chapters, so that the language of the novel simultaneously reflects both the world and some particular type of discourse about the world – the inflated rhetoric of journalism in "Aeolus", for instance, or the boozy bluster and racy anecdotal chatter of a Dublin bar in "Cyclops", or what Joyce himself called the "namby-pamby jammy marmaladey drawersy (alto la!) style with effects of incense, mariolatry, masturbation, stewed cockles, painter's palette, chit chat, circumlocution, etc. etc.," culled from cheap women's magazines for Gertie MacDowell in "Nausicaa".

What I learned from *Ulysses*, though it took some time for the lesson fully to sink in, or to manifest itself in my own writing, was that a novel can do more than one thing at once – indeed, that it *must* do so. It should tell us more than one story, in more than one style. The first of my novels to be consciously written "polyphonically" (in Mikhail Bakhtin's terminology) was *The British Museum is Falling Down*, in which the mental stress of the hero, a young married Catholic graduate student suffering from a losing streak at Vatican Roulette, a.k.a. the rhythm method of birth control, is reflected in and licenses a series of parodies of the modern novelists whom he is studying. The last parody, attributed to the hero's wife, is an imitation or pastiche of Molly Bloom's soliloquy – and an act of homage rather than a parody. In writing the chapters of *Changing Places* in different narrative modes (present tense, past tense, letters, documents, screen-play, etc.); in basing a story of amorous and competitive scholars jetting from one international conference circuit to another in *Small World* on the coincidence-ridden and inter-laced narratives of chivalric romance like the *Morte D'Arthur* and *Orlando Furioso*; in making the relationship between Vic Wilcox and Robyn Penrose in *Nice Work* ironically re-enact the plots of the Victorian industrial novels on which Robyn is an academic authority – in using such fictional devices I have, like many other modern novelists, followed humbly and gratefully in Joyce's footsteps. But long before I had written any of these novels, Joyce had become for me a kind of posthumous master, a guiding spirit, a model and an exemplar of the dedicated writer, the writer as perfectionist.

There is a story well known to all students of Joyce, that one day in Zurich, when he was writing *Ulysses*, he met his friend Frank Budgen in the street and told him he had been working all day and had produced only two sentences. "You have been seeking the right words?" asked Budgen "No," replied Joyce, "I have the words already. What I am seeking is the perfect order of words in the sentences I have." This little anecdote epitomizes Joyce's approach to his craft: total commitment, infinite patience, utter confidence in his own judgement. He constructed his entire literary career on the principle by which he composed those sentences. Each book was perfect of its kind, each one was different from the one before, each a more ambitious exploration of the possibilities of language. He spent seven years writing *Ulysses* and seventeen writing *Finnegans Wake*. He had the courage and self-critical objectivity to abandon *Stephen Hero* when he had written over a thousand pages of manuscript; and he had the fortitude and faith in himself to survive some of the bitterest frustrations and disappointments in his early career that any young writer has ever had to undergo. The vacillations and broken promises of English and Irish publishers, the arguments and threats of prosecution over alleged obscenity and libel, caused seemingly endless delays in the publication of *Dubliners* and *A Portrait*. His masterpiece, *Ulysses*, was for years branded as a dirty book, banned and pirated in English-speaking countries, and its author consequently denied the royalties that were his due. Even when his literary reputation was secure, and he was relieved of financial need, mainly by the generosity of Harriet Shaw Weaver, he had to live with the knowledge that almost everybody, including his closest friends and admirers, regarded the work of the last two decades of his life as a gigantic literary folly. Now *Finnegans Wake* is firmly established in the literary canon. There is a whole scholarly industry dedicated to its explication and annotation. It is in many ways the exemplary text of modern critical theory, a book which anticipated and embodied the tenets of post-structuralism, deconstruction, Lacanian psychoanalysis and Bakhtin's poetics of the novel. Joyce did not live to see the critical vindication of *Finnegans*

Wake, but it would not have surprised him. "I have written something to keep the professors busy for the next hundred years," he said of *Ulysses,* but it could have been said with even more truth of *Finnegans Wake.*

The more we contemplate the life and work of James Joyce, the more plain it becomes that he was a man of extraordinary determination and self-confidence. There is an increasing body of evidence that writers – artists of any kind, but especially writers – have an above-average susceptibility to depressive and manic-depressive mental illness, and are more likely to commit suicide than any comparable professional group. This does not seem to have been true of Joyce, however. When he was depressed or in despair there was nothing neurotic about it. He invariably had good reason to be depressed or in despair: for instance, poverty and rejection in his early life; in later life, the banning of *Ulysses,* his painful and debilitating eye trouble, and the distressing mental illness of his daughter Lucia. He does not seem to have suffered the inexplicable and crippling *Angst* of the true melancholic, nor to have ever suffered from what is called writer's block. Often the periods of his life most marked by material difficulties were his most fertile as a writer.

If Joyce had a neurosis, it was paranoia. Leon Edel has called him the great Injustice Collector. He sometimes exaggerated or fantasized injuries committed against him by others – most notably perhaps when he uncritically accepted the claim of his friend Cosgrave that he had enjoyed sexual favours from Nora Barnacle at the time when Joyce was courting her. That disclosure was made some years after the alleged event, on one of Joyce's last visits to Ireland, but it threw him into extravagant paroxysms of jealousy, which he vented in letters home to Nora in Trieste. Some of Joyce's biographers have wondered whether this emotion wasn't almost deliberately whipped up by Joyce so that he could draw on it for his fiction. Nora complained later in their marriage that "Jim wants me to go with other men so that he will have something to write about." She never did and Joyce would have been devastated if she had actually done so. Though their relationship had its ups and downs, and their sexual life was certainly peculiar and rather prematurely terminated, the union of Joyce and Nora proved strong and durable.

In his choice of a partner, Joyce showed the same decisiveness and consistency as he showed in his choice of vocation.

I have called this lecture "Joyce's Choices" because it seems to me useful to look at his writing in terms of the choices or decisions which determined its development. Some of these were aesthetic choices, and some were life choices, but the two were always interrelated. These are some of the key choices Joyce made and stuck to with extraordinary steadfastness: to renounce the Catholic faith in which he was brought up; to become an artist, rather than a priest, or a doctor or a lawyer; to live for most of his life in exile from Ireland, never returning to it after the age of thirty; to write in the English language, or his own polyglot mutation of it, and to turn his back on the revival of Gaelic and the Irish Literary Movement at the turn of the century; to concentrate as a writer on prose fiction as opposed to verse or drama; and to form a permanent and monogamous if for many years irregular relationship with a woman of humble background, limited education, and such scant interest in literature that she never read *Ulysses*.

It is instructive to compare and contrast Joyce in this respect with Søren Kierkegaard, the great philosopher of existential choice, and a lifelong sufferer from depression – or what he called "melancholy". His first major work, *Either/Or* (1843), was, as its title suggests, all about choice. It consists of letters, essays and other documents written by two men called A and B. A is a clever but cynical young bachelor, a prey to melancholy, whose aesthetic philosophy of life renders all choice ultimately meaningless. The other persona, B, is a judge, a pillar of society, and a happily married man. He represents the ethical as against the aesthetic philosophy of life. He writes two long letters to his friend A, urging the necessity of choice, if it is only the choice of despair, because, "when one has truly chosen despair one has fully chosen what despair chooses, namely oneself in one's eternal validity." Kierkegaard himself, however, had the greatest difficulty in exercising choice in his personal life. When he was twenty-one he met and fell in love with a young girl called Regine. In due course the couple became engaged, but almost at once Kierkegaard began to doubt the wisdom of his decision, and convinced himself that because of his character and temperament he could never make Regine happy. After about a year he broke off the engagement, in spite of the appeals of Regine and her father. He fled Copenhagen for Berlin, where he wrote *Either/Or* as a kind of indirect apology, explanation and expiation for his conduct towards Regine. He tried to convince himself that he had acted rightly, but he secretly hoped that somehow, through no will of his own, the broken engagement would be mended and Regine would be restored to him. He was therefore dismayed when he returned to Copenhagen a year later and discovered that Regine had got engaged to another man. He pretended that this outcome was what he had wanted all along, but in fact he never ceased to love Regine, or to mourn her loss. Though he was never able to speak to her again, he dedicated most of his books to her and made her his sole legatee.

What a contrast there is between this story of high-flown sentiment, elected celibacy and self-lacerating indecision, and Joyce's courtship of Nora Barnacle. They met on a Dublin street, the threadbare, jobless ex-student and the bonny, down-to-earth chambermaid from Galway, and were immediately attracted to each other. After one failed attempt to make a date, Joyce walked her out one evening down to the seashore, where, to his surprise and delight, she relieved his sexual arousal in the simplest, safest way, by unbuttoning the fly of his trousers and slipping her hand inside. (Joyce commemorated the date by making it "Bloomsday".) A few weeks later the couple eloped together in defiance of religious precept, social convention and commonsense prudence. It was because Nora had the same courage and resolution as himself that Joyce loved her. He wrote to her at the time of their elopement, significantly using the verb "to choose":

> The fact that you can choose to stand beside me in this way in my hazardous life fills me with great pride and joy.

In his story "Eveline" he indicated just how difficult such a choice was for a young Irish woman of that time and place, and how easily the challenge might be failed. He returned to the subject again in his play *Exiles*, which is transparently based on the history of Joyce's elopement with Nora and his retrospective jealousy of her relationship with Cosgrave. The play is obsessed with the question of choice: was Bertha really free to choose to run away with Richard? Will she choose to accept Robert's invitation to have an affair with him? Will Richard choose the safety of a university post rather than the insecure life of a writer?

The union between Joyce and Nora was not legalized for many years, but to outsiders it looked very much like a respectable bourgeois marriage and it lasted until Joyce's death in 1941. As a couple they were known for their disapproval of the sexual promiscuity that was commonplace in the artistic circles in which they moved in Paris. As Joyce used to complain when the Irish literary establishment branded him as an immoral writer, "I am more virtuous than all that lot – I, who am a real monogamist and have never loved but once in my life." The real difference between Joyce and Kierkegaard is not between their views on sexual fidelity, which were in fact quite similar, but between Joyce's confidence in his choice of partner and Kierkegaard's neurotic agonizing over his. Ultimately, Kierkegaard did not find the calm rationality of B an adequate answer to the nihilism of A. In his later work choice is defined in existential religious terms as both "absurd", as A saw it, and necessary, as B saw it – a leap of faith into the void, a total surrender to God in which man realizes his freedom. Later atheistic existentialist philosophers like Sartre would define such choice in terms of political *engagement*. One must progress, Kierkegaard thought, from the aesthetic to the ethical to the religious. But for Joyce, the aesthetic *was* the religious, and although he struck some Fenian attitudes in early life, his views and his writing became steadily apolitical as he matured.

When Stephen Dedalus is a pupil at Belvedere College, the Jesuits seek to draw him into their religious community, encouraging him to think that he has a vocation for the priesthood. Though he is tempted for a while, he rejects the idea and, after his vision of the young girl wading on the seashore, dedicates himself to the life of art in "an outburst of profane joy."

> Her image had passed into his soul for ever, and no word had broken the holy silence of his ecstasy. Her eyes had called him and his soul had leaped at the call. To live, to err, to fall, to triumph, to recreate life out of life!

There is a deliberate fusion or transference here of connotations of religion and art, the sacred and the profane, Christian and pagan, Christ and Lucifer. Joyce often pushed the analogy between himself as artist and Christ to the point of blasphemy. In *Stephen Hero*, Stephen's preparation for the paper he reads to the Literary Society is compared to Jesus's forty days in the wilderness, and Joyce himself wrote to Nora at a time when things were going badly for him as a writer: "I hope that the day may come when I shall be able to give you the favour of being beside me when I have entered into my kingdom." He also compared himself to Lucifer, especially in reference to his apostasy from the Catholic faith. "I am not afraid to make a mistake," Stephen says to Cranly in *A Portrait*, "even a great mistake, a lifelong mistake, and perhaps as long as eternity too."

Everyone who met the young Joyce was struck by his extraordinary pride, arrogance and self-confidence. "There is a young boy called Joyce who may do something," George Russell wrote to a friend. "He is as proud as Lucifer and writes verses perfect in their technique and sometimes beautiful in quality." To Yeats, Russell wrote, "The first spectre of the new generation has appeared. His name is Joyce. I have suffered from him and I would like you to suffer." When he met Yeats Joyce said, "I see you are too old to be influenced by me."

These senior Irish writers recognized Joyce's talent and were disposed to help him, but Joyce declined to be drawn into the Irish literary movement. This was a crucial and particularly difficult choice on his part; because at this time, at the turn of the century, Irish writing was in an exciting and fertile phase, especially in poetry and drama, with the work of Yeats, Synge, Russell, Lady Gregory and others. Most talented aspiring young writers would have been inclined to join the movement, but Joyce held himself aloof and finally turned his back on it, when he went first to Paris as a student, and then to Trieste as a teacher. He felt that the movement's essential tendency was provincial and regressive. It sought to draw his imagination westward, to the traditional, agrarian, Gaelic-speaking Ireland of Celtic legend, whereas he wanted to connect himself to the European modernist movement in art and ideas. Ibsen, Hauptmann and D'Annunzio were the writers who fired his imagination at this period of his life.

It was partly a question of language, or languages. The Irish literary movement, like the Irish nationalist movement, was ideologically linked to the revival of Gaelic. Joyce did study Gaelic in a desultory way for a year or so, but not with the commitment he brought to learning Italian and Norwegian (which he learned so that he could read Ibsen in the original). He certainly rejected the opinion of his Gaelic teacher, Patrick Pearse, that Irish writers should not write in English. The linguistic question is touched on several times in *A Portrait*. In conversation with the English Jesuit Dean of Studies, Stephen reflects resentfully: "His language, so familiar and so foreign, will always be for me an acquired speech." What the Dean calls a funnel, Stephen calls a tundish. But in the journal extracts at the very end of the novel, Stephen records that he looked up the word, tundish, "and [found] it English and good old blunt English too." In short, Stephen realizes that English doesn't belong to the British. "Damn the dean of studies and his funnel. What did he come here for to teach us his own language or to learn it from us." Stephen recognizes that he can use English as a medium without succumbing to British cultural imperialism. Shortly after there is this entry:

> John Alphonsus Mulrennan has just returned from the west of Ireland . . . He told us he met an old man there in a mountain cabin. Old man had red eyes and short pipe. Old man spoke Irish. Mulrennan spoke Irish. Then old man and Mulrennan spoke English. Mulrennan spoke to him about universe and stars. Old man sat, listened, smoked, spat. Then said:
>
> – Ah, there must be terrible queer creatures at the latter end of the world.
>
> I fear him. I fear his redrimmed horny eyes. It is with him I must struggle all through this night till day come, till he or I lie dead . . .

This powerful image, at once comic and sinister, encapsulates Joyce's intuition that he had to escape from the suffocating embrace of the national cultural movement in order to find his own voice as a writer.

The last of Joyce's choices I want to touch on is his choice of prose fiction as his principal literary form or genre. To those who knew the young Joyce, and even to Joyce himself before 1904, this choice would have seemed by no means inevitable, or even predictable. His earliest serious attempts at literary composition were in lyric verse, and he achieved a high degree of technical accomplishment in this form, as Russell testified. His literary ambitions in his student days were focused on drama. He was a keen theatre-goer, and had some success as an amateur actor. His famous manifesto paper delivered to the UCD Literary Society was called "*Drama* and Life" (*italics mine*). His first paid published work was a precocious essay on Ibsen in the *Fortnightly Review* written while he was a student, and he wrote an Ibsenite play, significantly called *My Brilliant Career*, before he wrote his first novel or short story. He also wrote a verse play at this time, perhaps influenced by Yeats and Lady Gregory. Joyce never entirely lost interest in poetry and drama. He continued to write the occasional poem until late in life, and of course he wrote another Ibsenite play, *Exiles*, at the relatively late date of 1912. But his dedication to prose fiction was settled long before then.

The seminal moment was probably his composition of an essay-cum-character sketch entitled "Portrait of the Artist", in January 1904. It was rejected for publication by a new journal called *Dana* to which he submitted it, but it gave Joyce the idea of writing a full-length autobiographical novel. A month later he had begun *Stephen Hero*. But he had already been writing for a couple of years previously the little prose fragments which he called "epiphanies", defined thus in *Stephen Hero*:

> By an epiphany he meant a sudden spiritual manifestation, whether in the vulgarity of speech or of gesture or in a memorable phase of the mind itself.

These epiphanies were exercises through which Joyce developed his mature symbolist prose style. They encapsulate his idea of the quasi-sacramental nature of the artistic process, the mysterious transsubstantiation of quotidian reality into something permanent and transcendent. The crucial feature of the Joycean epiphany is that it embraces vulgarity as well as the sublime, the spoken as well as the written word. Indeed it is overhearing a few fragments of trivial and banal flirtatious talk between a couple "standing on the steps of one of those brown brick houses which seem the very incarnation of Irish paralysis," that gives Stephen the idea of making a collection of such epiphanies.

> The Young Lady – (drawling discreetly) . . . O, yes . . . I was . . . at the . . . cha . . . pel . . .
> The Young Gentleman – (inaudibly) . . . I . . . (again inaudibly) . . . I . . .
> The Young Lady – (softly) . . . O . . . but . . . you're . . . ve . . . ry . . . wick . . . ed

James Joyce never published a book that had the familiar structure and texture of the classic realist novel. *A Portrait of the Artist as a Young Man*, *Ulysses* and *Finnegans Wake* were all highly original deviations from that tradition, each more boldly experimental than the one before. Even the stories in *Dubliners* were more experimental, more subversive of the traditional well-made short story, than they appear at first sight. If we call Joyce a novelist – and there is no other convenient term to use – it must be in the sense in which Mikhail Bakhtin defined the novel, as a type of narrative which has its roots in classical Menippean satire, in the folk tradition of carnival, and in the great parodying-travestying masters of Renaissance literature, Rabelais and Cervantes. The novel as Bakhtin defines it is both a type of discourse and a frame of mind. As a discourse it is characterized by the interweaving of a variety of different voices and styles, oral and written – what Bakhtin called dialogism or polyphony. As a frame of mind it questions and subverts all totalizing ideological systems by the liberating power of laughter and the celebration of the body – what Bakhtin called the carnivalesque. Joyce's choice of the novel as his preferred literary form coincided with his discovery of the possibilities of a dialogic prose in Bakhtin's sense, a medium which could accommodate both the most artificial rhetoric and the most casual speech, which could be sublime or coarse, fantastic or realistic, according to need – and often within the same paragraph or even sentence.

Ezra Pound and T.S. Eliot were to do something similar in poetry, but Joyce's early experiments in verse were constricted by a very traditional literary decorum. The account in *A Portrait* of Stephen's first attempt at writing a poem is instructive. It is inspired by his romantic pubescent attraction to the young girl, Emma Clery, whom he accompanies home from a party on a tram:

> by dint of brooding on the incident, he thought himself into confidence. During this process all those elements which he deemed common and insignificant fell out of the scene. There remained no trace of the tram itself nor of the trammen nor of the horses: nor did he and she appear vividly. The verses told only of the night and the balmy breeze and the maiden lustre of the moon.

That, one might say, is the limitation of Joyce's own poetry: too much of the roughage of reality has been filtered out of it. In the novel itself we get the tram and the trammen as well as the breeze and the moon.

Something similar is true of Joyce's one surviving work for the theatre: *Exiles*. Though it consists almost entirely of dialogue, it is not "dialogic" in Bakhtin's sense. The characters speak a curiously stilted, overly well-formed, tonally limited prose. They are unnaturally articulate about their feelings, unnaturally disciplined in taking their turn to speak. Joyce's novels have better drama embedded in them. The Christmas dinner scene in *A Portrait*, for instance, is incomparably dramatic in the way it builds up from the formulaic bonhomie of the opening, as the family gathers for the meal, through the trivial bickering and teasing about religion and politics which Mrs Dedalus tries in vain to suppress, to the full-blooded row which ends with Mr Casey shouting, "No God for Ireland!" and Dante screaming "Blasphemer" and almost spitting in his face. And was there ever a better curtain line than Mr Casey's as Dante storms out of the room, slamming the door behind her?

> Mr Casey, freeing his arms from his holders, suddenly bowed his head on his hands with a sob of pain.
> – Poor Parnell! he cried loudly. My dead king!

In short, when he chose prose fiction as his *métier*, Joyce did not forget all he had learned about the music and rhythm of language in poetry or what he had learned about dramatic action and speech from the theatre – but he integrated what he had learned into a more complex and all-embracing literary form.

Most of the choices I have been discussing occurred or came to a head in the year 1904. It was indeed a year of decision for Joyce – when he chose Nora, chose exile, chose the English language, chose prose fiction. He exercised these choices with extraordinary resolution and complete confidence in their rightness. A passage from *Stephen Hero* might have been his motto:

> He was persuaded that no-one served the generation into which he had been born so well as he who offered it, whether in his art or in his life, the gift of certitude.

The Making
of "Anthony Burgess"

Anthony Burgess hardly knew his mother, who died in circumstances as poignant and dramatic as any novelist could invent. His father, waiting to be demobbed from the Army in 1919, came home to Manchester on leave to find his wife and daughter corpses, victims of Spanish flu, while his infant son lay burbling in his cot. The father, Burgess suspects, subconsciously resented his son's survival, and sought to shuffle off parental responsibility on to the widow he married a few years later. She was the busy landlady of a pub where he played the bar piano, with two grown-up daughters of her own, and little time or love to spare for her stepson. There was no Oedipal phase in Burgess's childhood, and he grew up to regret the absence of passion and tenderness in his family relationships – the "emotional coldness that was established then and which, apart from other faults, has marred my work." It is, I suppose, true that, for all their energy and gusto, Anthony Burgess's novels are somewhat lacking in emotional warmth, though it is not a judgement I should have presumed to make. That he has made it himself is typical of his unflinchingly candid autobiography.[*]

It is the first instalment of a two-part project which takes us up to Mr Burgess's decision (for very special, not to say

[*] *Little Wilson and Big God* (Heinemann, 1987).

melodramatic reasons) to become a full-time writer, at the age of forty-two. He conceived the idea of writing it while waiting gloomily for a plane in New York, partly to forestall two other self-nominated biographers, partly because he had just torn up a hundred and seventy pages of a new novel, partly because, as he approached the age of seventy, he was conscious that his life was moving towards its inevitable close (some young people in Minneapolis, a few days earlier, had been surprised to find him still alive). He predicts that the second volume, provisionally entitled *You've Had Your Time*, will bring his literary career to an end ("it started late, but there are many captious critics who think it has gone on too long").

Whether or not this prediction proves correct (I shall personally be surprised and sorry if it does) there is no doubt that novelists are well advised to postpone the writing of their autobiographies for as long as possible. It is somewhat disingenuous of Mr Burgess to pretend that their lives are of little interest; to their readers (of whom Mr Burgess has a considerable number) they are of intense interest. This seems to be a legacy of the Romantic poetic of literature as self-expression, which the critical counter-revolutions of our time (the modernist cult of "impersonality", the post-structuralist declaration of the Death of the Author) have hardly dislodged. The curiosity readers feel about the human source of the novel they hold in their hands is something that the media and the literary marketplace eagerly exploit – through interviews, profiles, meet-the-author events, and so on. Most writers collaborate in these activities, either out of vanity or to sell their books, but usually with a degree of anxiety. They recognize that public interest in themselves is a double-edged tribute, which may demote their work to the status of a mere mask or cover for the "real" person. The most frequent question addressed to authors is, "How far is your work autobiographical?" There are dangers in answering it.

An autobiography is, of course, a kind of fiction, and can conceal as much as it reveals. (Mr Graham Greene, for instance, has published two volumes of autobiography that are masterpieces of self-concealment.) But Anthony Burgess has not followed this path. He has let it all hang out – not only emptied his pockets, but pulled out the linings, revealing, inevitably, some unseemly debris. This autobiography is sub-titled, "Being the First Part of the Confessions of Anthony Burgess", and certainly gives the impression of being a candid and unvarnished account of his life. It is not, to be sure, a spiritual or psychological masterpiece to be compared with the confessions of Augustine and Rousseau, but it is a fascinating and remarkably courageous book, self-critical but not falsely modest. It is also wonderfully entertaining, stuffed with an abundance of marvellous anecdotes. Some of them, inevitably, have already found their way into Burgess's novels.

Faced with two versions of the same story, one historical and one fictional, most people in our culture will tend to regard the former as more "real", hence more meaningful; but the novelist is someone who believes the opposite – otherwise he wouldn't go to the trouble of writing fiction. These fictions, however, have the superficial appearance of the historical, and the novelist works his effect partly by concealing the seams that join what he has experienced to what he has researched or invented. To publish one's autobiography is an invitation to literal-minded readers to unpick the stitching.

Readers of Burgess's recent novel, *The Piano Players*, for instance, will recognize in *Little Wilson and Big God* several incidents, like the death of the mother, that appear virtually unaltered in the novel, and will readily perceive where he has used and where departed from the facts of his own relationship, as a child, with his piano-playing father. The rest of his *oeuvre* is, however, less likely to suffer by cross-checking against the autobiography – partly because it is already settled and estab-lished in our minds as literary fiction, and partly because, taken as a whole, it is above all remarkable for its fertility of invention. Burgess's (in order of composition) fifth novel, *The Right to an Answer*, was, he records here, almost wholly invented. "That I could invent was the final proof, to me, that I had not mistaken my vocation." It took him, however, a long time to discover it.

The name "Anthony Burgess" is itself a fiction, thinly disguis-ing the identity of John Burgess Wilson, who took Anthony as his confirmation name. This is a pious custom of the Roman Catholic Church, in which the young John Wilson was brought up. His father was a Catholic of recusant stock, though somewhat wayward, not to say absent-minded, in his allegiance (he once entered a church with his hat and a cigarette on, under the impression that it was a pub, a more habitual place of resort). His stepmother had married into the Dwyers, a staunchly Catholic family of Manchester Irish who produced George Patrick Dwyer, Bishop of Leeds and later Archbishop of Birmingham. Anthony Burgess (as I will continue to call him, to avoid confusion) attended Catholic schools, and although he subsequently lapsed from the Church this education marked his work almost as indelibly as it did the work of his master, James Joyce. Some slightly impatient asides suggest that he still considers himself a more authentically Catholic writer than literary converts like Evelyn Waugh and Mr Greene.

Burgess's memoirs of a Catholic childhood are vivid and often painfully funny. There was the primary school ruled over by Sister Ignatius, "a sort of Lancashire fishwife got up as a nun. She conducted morning prayers as though crying fresh halibut. Prayers were lengthy and featured the Virgin Mary more than her Son or the great fuming dyspeptic God who raged round his punishment laboratory." Burgess moved on to St Xavier's College, whose headmaster, Brother Martin, "mercurial, capricious, unpredictable and dangerous," bore more than a passing resemblance to that image of God the Father. Boys awaiting corporal punishment were made to stand with their hands above their head at assembly, inducing delirium. Burgess was expelled for insubordination and readmitted after a bribe.

The atmosphere of religious guilt and punishment inevitably coloured the young boy's attitude to sex. He was initiated into its pleasures very early, at the age of ten or eleven, by a succession of servant girls who shared his attic bedroom. One encouraged him to fondle her breasts, another got into bed with him in the middle of a thunderstorm and taught him "what heaven was. A heaven meriting hell: the devil's heaven. I now had to face confession." The scandalized priest beat at the grille with a rolled-up newspaper (he had been covertly reading the racing pages) and demanded the young sinner's name. Burgess had the guts to invoke the anonymity of the confessional. It wasn't long before he was enjoying "a shallow variety of the sin of Sodom" with another nubile maid. At fifteen he picked up a young Protestant girl at the cinema and stretched out naked with her on the floor of her scruffy living-room. A future novelist's eye noted a soiled sanitary towel under a chair. The rapturous "heaven" of a disrobed female body, embraced in squalid surroundings, is a *Leitmotif* of Burgess's erotic life, reaching its apotheosis in the beds of the East: perhaps a metonymic displacement of Catholic guilt about the "dirty" act onto its context. Meanwhile, his sexual apprenticeship proceeded. A matronly WEA lecturer, encountered at the Manchester public library, took the schoolboy Burgess home and instructed him in contraception, sexual technique and the rudiments of dialectical materialism on the rug in front of her gas fire.

This adventurous adolescence was not, however, the prelude to a sexually fulfilled early manhood. At Manchester University, nice girls didn't. Sex was "dirty or impersonal or both" – and in short supply, until Burgess met and fell in love with a student called Llewelen ("Lynne") Jones. She too had been precociously initiated into sex, at the age of 14. Their engagement and subsequent marriage, which lasted till Lynne's death in 1968, was unconventional to say the least, neither party demanding or expecting sexual fidelity from the other. The stormy history of this relationship runs like a dark thread through the rest of the narrative.

Burgess read English at Manchester because he didn't have the Physics qualification required to read Music, his first choice. He had wanted to be a composer ever since he was thirteen, and taught himself to play and transcribe with a little help from his pianist father. Attending Hallé concerts and listening to all kinds of music on the radio, from Schoenberg to Joe Loss, were formative experiences of his early life. It was years before he reluctantly surrendered the ambition to earn his living as a composer, and even so it determined his choice of an alternative vocation: "the novel, the only literary genre for failed symphonists."

The bridge between these two art forms for Burgess was James Joyce. When he announced his disenchantment with Catholicism in the sixth form at St Xavier's (the chaplain said it was a case of little Wilson and big God) a lay master recommended him to read *A Portrait of the Artist as a Young*

Man, perhaps anticipating that the hellfire sermon would frighten him back into conformity, which indeed it did. By the time he went to university, however, Burgess, like Stephen Dedalus, had lapsed again, this time for good. He had also read *Ulysses* and soon acquired *Finnegans Wake*. He took both books with him, and little else, when he was called up into the wartime army.

When he wrote his first novel, *A Vision of Battlements*, he drew on his military service in Gilbraltar but based the narrative on the *Aeneid*, as Joyce had based *Ulysses* on the *Odyssey*. Joyce's "mythical method", Burgess plausibly argues, was not merely scaffolding which could be dismantled once the building was complete, but also a way of adding density and resonance, enhancing the pleasure of the text. Such multilayeredness, which Burgess compares to the vertical scoring of symphonic music, has always been a feature of his fiction, and makes it something of a bridge between modernism and post-modernism. Unlike most British novelists who started publishing in the 1950s, Burgess revered the mythopoeia of the moderns and paid it the tribute of imitation. Later, in works like *A Clockwork Orange* and *M/F*, he showed himself capable of wholly original experiment in language and narrative form, and thus helped lever the British novel out of the neo-realist rut in which the Movement and the Angry Young Men had left it.

Burgess was called up into the Medical Corps and subsequently transferred to the Education Corps, being attached to a number of hospitals, depots and garrisons, far from any combat zone. His experiences seem more like those of a peacetime National Serviceman than of a soldier in the epic struggle for Europe, and I understand now why, reviewing my own novel about National Service, *Ginger, You're Barmy*, some twenty-five years ago, in the *Observer*, Burgess complained that "Mr Lodge spells things out as though there was no British Army before 1956." Curiously enough, a wholly invented episode in my novel, in which two guards ambush a bullying corporal, has an almost exact factual parallel in Burgess's narrative. Like me, he was chiefly struck by the way the Army replicated the worst features of the British class system and the way it set out to make life uncomfortable for anyone with intellectual pretensions. A memorable epiphany (in the Joycean sense) occurs when he stands "in the pounding rain with a bank manager, a senior librarian and an anthropologist with a Durham MA, under a towering heap of human faeces" which they have been instructed to shovel on to a lorry.

During the war Lynne had a fairly important job in the Board of Trade in London, where Burgess visited her frequently on forged leave passes signed with the names of various modern writers (e.g. "Ford Madox Ford, Capt. for Lt. Col."). He began to haunt the literary pubs of Fitzrovia, where Lynne had an *entrée*. While he was in Gibraltar, she "technically committed adultery" with Dylan Thomas, though "to go to bed with Dylan was to offer little more than maternal comfort." In 1944 Lynne was robbed and badly beaten up by a gang of American deserters. The experience seemed to change her personality, and certainly started her on the alcohol addiction that finally killed her. (This brutal assault was the "seed" of *A Clockwork Orange*, written nearly twenty years later.) When Burgess was grudgingly granted leave he found a distant and frigid wife who appeared to be hesitating over which of two brothers she would ditch him for. It seemed to Burgess that he was watching a play whose author he had met at some time in a pub. It was evidently a black comedy, for he was required to impersonate one of his rivals to prevent them all being thrown out of a hotel.

In the event the Burgesses stayed married, in spite of all the infidelities, quarrels, financial crises and vocational frustrations of their life together, first in post-war Britain, where Burgess (having now abandoned musical ambitions for literary ones) eked out a wretched living as a schoolmaster, subsequently in Malaya and Brunei, where he was a college lecturer. Burgess explored the fleshpots of the East and revelled in the sexual vocabulary of Malay, in which the term for orgasm literally means "the structure has gone into an ecstatic trance" and to fall in love is "to allow one's liver to tumble on to or into or towards somebody". Always a natural linguist, he made the other colonials jealous by passing his examinations in Malay in record time. His early novels were published with modest success, but *The Enemy In The Blanket* was threatened with a libel suit and temporarily withdrawn. Most of the time "life at home was hell, black with guilt or loud with hysteria, and the cats were dying of feline enteritis." In Malaya, Lynne took an overdose, leaving a note saying "I can't take it any more." Burgess administered an emetic and brought her round. In Brunei he couldn't take it any more, either, lay down on the floor of his classroom one day and closed his eyes. "Let other agencies take over."

The other agencies sent him back home for exhaustive medical investigation (hilariously exploited in *The Doctor is Sick*). He was diagnosed as having a brain tumour and given a year to live. In a rented flat in Hove he sat down to write as much as he could for the support of his putative widow, little knowing that he would outlive her. Thus ends Part One of the Confessions of Anthony Burgess.

If we did not know that the diagnosis was mistaken, and that Anthony Burgess lived on to become a prolific and distinguished writer with thirty novels and nearly as many non-fiction books to his credit, this narrative, for all its wit and funny stories, would be somewhat depressing, for the life it describes is largely one of failure, frustration and discontent, from which only sex and music offered fleeting moments of escape. Since we *do* know, we can only salute the mysterious process by which negative experience can be turned to positive account in artistic creation – and look forward eagerly to the sequel.

POSTSCRIPT

The second volume of the autobiography duly appeared in 1990. As I predicted, the author went on to write several more works of fiction, including the long narrative poem, *Byrne*, published posthumously in 1995.

I met Anthony Burgess several times in the latter part of his life, and regarded him as a friend. In 1986 he came to Birmingham University to receive an Honorary doctorate, and I kept him company for the few days of his visit. I was struck by his ability to "talk shop" with almost every academic I introduced him to, whatever their discipline. He seemed to have read everything and forgotten nothing. While he was with us he completed a musical composition for brass instruments ensemble which was performed by a section of the Birmingham Symphony Orchestra. He was a Renaissance man, polyglot and polymath, born into an age of specialization where such energy and versatility are suspected and sometimes sneered at.

In the autumn of 1992 I shared a reading/signing event with Anthony at Waterstone's bookshop in South Kensington. He had recently published his impressively knowledgeable book on the English language, *A Mouthful of Air*. Puffing defiantly on a cigarillo, he told me that he had just been diagnosed as having lung cancer, and that the prognosis was not good. In spite of bearing the weight of this bad news, he entertained the audience with a characteristic flow of wit and wisdom. It was a performance typical of the courage and professionalism of the man. He died in November 1993, aged 76.

What Kind of Fiction
Did Nabokov Write?
A Practitioner's View

This paper was written for and presented at a small,
select conference entitled "Nabokov at the
Crossroads of Modernism and Postmodernism",
which took place at the University of Nice in June
1995. I rarely attend academic conferences these
days, but I accepted the invitation to this one, for a
mixture of personal and professional reasons. The
convenor and organizer of the conference, Maurice
Couturier, as well as being Professor of English and
American Literature at the University of Nice, and
the leading Nabokov scholar in France, is also, with
his wife Yvonne, the translator of several of my
novels, including *Small World*, or *Un Tout Petit
Monde*, as it is called in French. Many of the
participants were familiar with this novel, and some
asked me if I was going to write another of the same
kind. I could never quite decide whether they feared
or hoped to figure in it. In reprinting the paper I
have left in the introductory remarks which belong to
the occasion on which it was delivered, because they
bear on the general theme of this book.

When Maurice Couturier invited me to participate in a conference entitled "Nabokov at the crossroads of Modernism and
Postmodernism", I was inevitably reminded of the title essay of
one of my books of criticism, *The Novelist at the Crossroads*.
Starting from the work of Robert Scholes and Robert Kellog on
the generic history of the novel, I suggested that there were four
aesthetic options open to the contemporary novelist: traditional
realism, fabulation, the nonfictional novel, and the problematic or
metafictional novel.* Later I wrote a book and several articles
applying Roman Jakobson's distinction between metaphor and
metonymy to the typology of modern fiction.† Later again I used
the Bakhtinian typology of fictional discourse to try and define the
formal characteristics of different period styles in the modern
novel.‡ The general orientation of the conference, in short, has
been a longstanding interest of mine.

None of those books and articles, however, made more than
passing reference to Nabokov. In recent years, too, I have lost
touch with the latest academic theorizing about the novel. Since
retiring from my teaching post at Birmingham in 1987, I have been
a full-time professional author, chiefly occupied with writing
fiction and dramatic work for stage and television. It was a long
time since I prepared a paper for an academic conference. For all
these reasons I approached the task with some trepidation, which
was not eased by an unexpected distraction of a kind typical of the
freelance writer's life. A long-nourished project to adapt a play of
mine for television was suddenly given the green light, and I was
obliged to write the scripts and attend rehearsals during the very
period I had set aside for preparing and writing this paper. There

---

* *The Novelist at the Crossroads*, London, Routledge, 1971, pp. 3–34.
† *The Modes of Modern Writing*, London, E. Arnold, 1977; "Modernism,
Antimodernism and Postmodernism", in *Working with Structuralism*,
London, Routledge, 1981, pp. 3–16.
‡ *After Bakhtin: essays on fiction and criticism*, London and New York,
Routledge, 1990.

were times when I thought I might find myself in the same position as my character Rodney Wainwright in *Small World*, who for different reasons finds himself behind the lectern at Morris Zapp's Jerusalem conference on "The Future of Criticism" with a paper consisting of just two and three-quarter pages of double-spaced A4 typescript, and is only saved from professional disgrace by an outbreak of Legionnaire's Disease in the hotel accommodating the conference – a form of reprieve I could neither expect nor wish for.

Well, I did finish the paper, but its subtitle was always intended to be a kind of defensive gesture, waiving any pretensions to expertise on the subject of Nabokov, and absolving myself from the scholarly obligation to check all secondary sources pertaining to my topic before venturing to make my own contribution. I thought I would consider the question of the generic identity and period-style of Nabokov's novels as a practising novelist rather than as an academic critic. However, this proved almost as difficult a task for me as writing a conventional scholarly paper.

Nabokov is very much a "writer's writer", a novelist who has been a significant influence on several distinguished novelists of a younger generation – Martin Amis and John Banville are just two that immediately come to mind. But I cannot myself claim to have been deeply influenced by Nabokov in my own fictional practice. I came to his work, I think, too late for that. The formative literary influences of my apprenticeship years were Graham Greene, Evelyn Waugh and James Joyce. I could write about them in a spirit of *hommage*, but not about Nabokov. Furthermore, one could say of critics what they say about Catholics: once an academic, always an academic. When I came to write this paper I found myself inevitably reaching for the terminology and concepts of the formalist critical tradition in which I laboured myself for many years, and it could equally well be subtitled, "Nabokov and the Typology of Fictional Form". It is, in other words, something of a hybrid.

Whether what I have to say will be new to any Nabokov scholar I very much doubt, but perhaps the simplicity with which I say it will give it an effect of novelty. Sometimes the most obvious features of a writer's work are overlooked precisely because they are so familiar; or because, with our attention closely focused on the intricacies of individual texts, we fail to perceive the character of the whole *oeuvre*, missing the wood for the trees. I want to stand back at a good distance from Nabokov's *oeuvre*, and consider, from this simplifying perspective, how his practice as a writer might be described and placed on the historical map of fictional form. Fortunately the differences between the Russian and English versions of Nabokov's earlier novels are of little consequence to this exercise, since I am entirely unqualified to comment on them.

Nabokov's novels, needless to say, exhibit great variety of form, as of content, but there are family resemblances between them. If we consider them primarily as *narratives* – that is, simply as representations of events connected in space-time – we will be struck, I think by how many of the events depicted concern crimes, misdemeanours, detection, arraignment and judicial punishment. The popular fiction which deals with these subjects – both the classic whodunnit (in which the emphasis is on the solution of a mystery) and the thriller (in which the emphasis is on suspense, generated by the repetition, or threatened repetition, of evil acts, to thwart which the hero risks his safety) – seems to have provided the narrative model for the majority of Nabokov's novels, though none of them conforms to the formulaic patterns I have just described. That is to say, Nabokov plays with, experiments with, inverts and subverts the novel of crime and detection. These are some of the ways by which he does so:

1. Centring the story on the criminal or miscreant rather than on characters representing social order and justice, making his efforts to conceal his crime, rather than the efforts of the law to unmask him, the major source of suspense (as in *Lolita*).

2. Portraying the criminal character as a bungling incompetent (as in *King Queen Knave*, where the malevolent Martha concocts absurdly impacticable plans to kill her husband and eventually dies herself of a chill contracted in her final murderous attempt – and even more brilliantly in *Despair*, where the protagonist has committed what he thinks is the perfect crime based on a misapprehension

which renders it totally transparent to the investigating police).

3. Making the character who occupies the position of criminal in the story completely innocent (as in *Invitation to a Beheading*, where the condemned man never discovers what his crime was supposed to be, and in *Transparent Things*, where the hero strangles his wife in his sleep).

4. Making the characters occupying the positions of criminal and detective turn out to be one and the same (as in *The Eye*); or signally refusing to apportion punishment justly in the resolution of the story (as in *Laughter in the Dark*, where Albinus is punished for his infidelity not only by being deceived in his turn, but by being accidentally blinded, in which state he is cruelly abused and exploited by his mistress and her lover, and finally killed in the attempt to revenge himself).

5. Making the character who occupies the position of hero in a thriller-plot fail – desolatingly – to escape from or overcome the evil forces conspiring against him (as in *Bend Sinister*).

The whodunnit and the thriller are in their most typical manifestations deeply conventional and ideologically conservative literary forms, in which good triumphs over evil, law over anarchy, truth over lies. Nabokov's novels, needless to say, offer no such reassurance. Nevertheless the paradigm of the crime novel underlies much of his fiction throughout his long career, and one cannot help wondering whether Nabokov's frequent denigration of Dostoevsky was not a symptom of the "anxiety of influence", because *Crime and Punishment* seems such an obvious precursor of Nabokov's thought-provoking and disturbing mutations of the crime story, as does *Notes from Underground* of his disturbingly eloquent, morally repellent narrators: Sumurov, Herman, Humbert, Kinbote.

The crime in Nabokov's crime fiction is usually murder. The favoured weapon is a pistol, an object which crops up again and again in his novels, often with a sexual connotation. The most common motive for murder – committed, premeditated or alleged – is indeed sexual infidelity, e.g. *King Queen Knave, Laughter in the Dark, Transparent Things*. In *Lolita* the primary crime is the seduction and abduction of a minor (though by a characteristic Nabokovian twist the criminal is to some extent seduced by his far from innocent victim), but murder also enters into the story, first virtually in Humbert's unfulfilled plots to murder Charlotte, and then really in his messy execution of Clare Quilty.

Perhaps the frequent appearance of murderers and murder weapons in Nabokov's fiction strikes me all the more forcibly because they are signally absent from my own fiction. There are very few deaths in my novels and they are all from natural or accidental causes. The only firearms occur in *Ginger, You're Barmy*, a novel about military service, and they are only fired on the rifle range. However I think I am a fairly typical English literary novelist in this respect. Excluding crime fiction, and novels about war, there are not many guns or shootings in the canonical authors of the century – Henry James, E.M. Forster, James Joyce, Virginia Woolf, D.H. Lawrence, Evelyn Waugh, Henry Green. The exceptions would be Conrad and Graham Greene, both of whom wrote out of the imperialistic adventure-story tradition – and, in Greene's case, the gangster-film genre. Contemporary, postmodern literary novelists are more apt to find violent crime, or crimes of violence (not quite the same thing), attractive subject-matter for their fiction – and the two novelists I mentioned earlier as being in some sense followers of Nabokov, Martin Amis and John Banville, would be examples in English and Irish writing respectively. Guns are of course ubiquitous in modern American fiction for cultural and histori-cal reasons – the frontier tradition, the constitutional right of citizens to bear arms, the influence of the Western (America's only indigenous literary genre), the routine arming of police, etc. Nabokov's fascination with guns and their murderous power is one reason, perhaps, why his "English" novels sit so comfortably in the context of modern American literature.

The novel of crime and detection, however twisted, displaced and subverted, depends for its coherence as a narrative on *causality*. The corpse in the classic whodunnit is an effect without an immediately obvious cause, or causer. The narrative consists of the process of identifying that causer, reconstructing the chain of events that led up to the effect by interpreting and fitting together various clues which are synecdoches of the total matrix of events.

This kind of novel is therefore a metonymic form in Jakobson's typology, based on relationships of contiguity such as cause and effect, part and whole, rather than similarity. The thriller is a metonymic form in a more straightforward way, since it narrates in chronological order a sequence of contiguous events that keep the hero in continual jeopardy. Despite Nabokov's bold and disconcerting deviations from the stereotypes of these sub-genres, it seems to me that his novels are fundamentally metonymic in Jakobson's terms. This may seem a surprising thing to say of a writer who was almost incomparably gifted and lavish in the coining of metaphors; but I am speaking now of deep structure, not surface structure. The coherence of Nabokov's novels depends crucially on sequence and causality. They are for the most part classically constructed, with a clearly defined beginning, middle and end, and often have an Aristotelian reversal-and-discovery in their conclusion (for instance, Herman's realization in *Despair* that his murder of Felix was bound to be discovered and that he himself is therefore a fool and a failure; or Humbert Humbert's discovery that Lolita is married and pregnant and his belated recognition that he can never make amends for robbing her of her childhood).

There is another group of novels within Nabokov's *oeuvre* that do not significantly involve crime, but also have a metonymic deep structure. These are the pseudo-memoir or pseudo-autobiographical novels: *Glory, The Defence, The Real Life of Sebastian Knight, Ada.* (*The Gift* also belongs in this sub-group, inasmuch as it is made up of several biographical narratives.) Fiction modelled on biography is an essentially metonymic form because it reconstructs the chronological sequence of events that make up a life – with inevitable gaps and ellipses, which may be foregrounded (as in *The Defence*) but seldom with the continual shuttling backwards and forwards in time that is characteristic of the modernist, symbolist novel of consciousness (e.g. *Ulysses, To the Lighthouse*). There is also a lot of overlap between the two sub-groups in Nabokov's *oeuvre*: some of the novels about crime subvert the genre by being cast in the form of autobiographies or confessions by the criminal (e.g. *Despair, Lolita*), and some of the pseudo-biographical novels (e.g. *The Real Life of Sebastian Knight*) are strongly influenced by the novel of detection.

A general characteristic of modernist fiction is the attenuation of its narrative element. As the modernist novel developed, its mimetic impulse was focused more and more upon consciousness, the subconscious and the unconscious, and less and less upon the external world seen objectively, as the arena for action. In consciousness and the unconscious the causal and temporal relationships between events are scrambled and distorted by memory and desire, and truth and meaning are adumbrated through mythical allusion and poetic symbolism. There is a congruence in this respect between the masterpieces of modernist fiction and the masterpieces of modernist verse like *The Waste Land* and the *Cantos*. In Jakobson's terms, modernist aesthetics forced the innately metonymic form of prose fiction towards the metaphoric pole which had always been the appropriate domain of poetry. Joyce's progress from the realistic but enigmatic stories of *Dubliners* to the symbolist *A Portrait of the Artist as a Young Man*, to what T.S. Eliot called the "mythical method" of *Ulysses* (based on a metaphorical substitution of Leopold Bloom for Odysseus, and a drastic reduction of the scale of the epic action), to *Finnegans Wake*, in which the differences between personages and events are swamped by a punning insistence on the resemblances between them – this development was paradigmatic. Virginia Woolf's polemical essays, "Modern Fiction" and "Mr Bennett and Mrs Brown", proclaiming the obsolescence of the traditional realistic novel, are well-known expositions of the modernist poetics of fiction.

Nabokov, needless to say, is not to be bracketed with Arnold Bennett and John Galsworthy. He was far from being an unreconstructed exponent of the classic realist text. He shared some of the aesthetic principles of modernism – a quasi-religious faith in the value of art, for instance, and a corresponding commitment to the pursuit of perfection in his chosen form. He learned several techniques from modernist fiction and deployed them on occasion (e.g. passages of interior monologue in *King Queen Knave*, and synchrony, or "spatial form" as it used to be called, in *Pale Fire*). The lyrical strain in his prose frequently reminds us of the "epiphanies" of Joyce, Woolf, Lawrence and Proust. Nevertheless it is true to say that narrative as a *structural principle* is more important to his work than it was to theirs, and one symptom of this is his fondness for stories of crime and detection, in which narrative interest is heightened by being associated with major crises of life and death and major transgressions of the moral code. But the simple hermeneutic tease of the whodunnit, which merely challenges us to guess the solution to the enigma presented by the crime before the detective does, or the simple narrative lure of the thriller, which keeps us wondering how the hero will survive and triumph, are, as I said earlier, displaced or ignored in Nabokov's fiction. Instead of being the passive recipient of clearly labelled clues and narrative excitements, Nabokov's reader is usually engaged from the start in a strenuous activity of making-sense-of-the-story, and a good deal of mystery and suspense is generated by the narrative method itself. Although this is also true of modernist fiction, there is I think something more playful or ludic about the little puzzles, traps and surprises Nabokov sets for his reader.

The Defence, for instance, begins: "What struck him most was the fact that from Monday on he would be Luzhin."[*] Superficially this resembles the modernist practice of beginning a novel by plunging the reader into a stream of ongoing experience in which he must orient himself by a process of inference and deduction, for example the beginning of Virginia Woolf's *Mrs Dalloway*: "Mrs Dalloway said she would buy the flowers herself."[†] But the effect is actually completely different. In the Virginia Woolf text we do not know who Mrs Dalloway is or why she needs to buy flowers, but we are confident that we shall find out sooner or later and meanwhile there is nothing innately problematic about a woman intending to buy flowers. In contrast, "from Monday on he would be Luzhin" is a much more paradoxical and unsettling mystery. It seems that the male subject of the sentence expects to acquire – involuntarily – a new name on a specific day in the near future. In what circumstances could this happen? The question cannot be put on hold, it nags away at us as we read, until by interpreting and connecting other clues in the discourse we arrive at the solution to the enigma: the subject is a young boy

[*] *The Defence*, London, Panther, 1967, p. 11.
[†] Virginia Woolf, *Mrs Dalloway*, London, Hogarth Press, 1960, p. 5.

who is about to begin attending school, where he will be
addressed by his surname.

In the same book – and in *Look at the Harlequins* – Nabokov
first refers to the most important woman in the hero's life by the
anonymous pronoun "she", and keeps us waiting for some
pages before introducing her properly. In other novels he tricks
us into sharing an illusion or misapprehension of the focalizing
character (for instance the terrified Albinus's conviction in
Laughter in the Dark that his mistress is hiding in his house from
his brother-in-law, when what he thinks is a tell-tale glimpse of
her red dress behind a piece of furniture is in fact the corner of a
cushion placed there by himself); or the hoax perpetrated by
Ivor and Iris Black in *Look at the Harlequins*, pretending very
plausibly that Iris is dumb.

One of the trademarks of Nabokov's fiction from the beginning was the sudden swerve of the discourse in space-time or
from one point of view to another without the usual courtesy of
an explanatory link or punctuating break in the text. In *King
Queen Knave* and *Laughter in the Dark*, for example, he switches
from one point of view to another between paragraphs or even
in mid-paragraph.* In *Bend Sinister* there is an abrupt transition, rather like a cinematic jump-cut, from Krug phoning
Ember, to Ember later composing a letter to someone else
about Krug's call, without any explanation or break in the text
between the two scenes: what would be obvious enough in film,
because of the shift from one setting to another, is by no means
instantly comprehensible in the novel.† Even more striking is
the temporal ellipsis in *The Defence*, which Nabokov himself
fondly compared to an unexpected move in chess, by which
sixteen years in the hero's life are passed over in a single
paragraph.‡ In *Glory* a description of one of Martin's banal
letters written from Cambridge to his mother in Switzerland,

---

* E.g., *King Queen Knave*, pp. 83–84: the paragraph beginning, "She
would switch the radio from song to speech," seems to be continuous with
the preceding paragraph, which is focalized through Franz, and we read it
as such until we encounter the statement, "And all the time she would be
thinking: 'How much longer would he need to get started?'" which locates
the narrative in Martha's consciousness.

† *Bend Sinister*, Harmondsworth, Penguin, 1974, p. 33.

‡ *The Defence*, London, Panther, 1967, p. 55.

and of the envelope in which he sent it, after changing an inkblot into the image of a black cat, is followed directly, within the same paragraph, by the sentence, "Mrs Edelweiss preserved this envelope along with his letters" and then, still in the same paragraph, by a description of how she read the letters "years later . . . with such anguish" – a premonition, for the reader, of Martin's tragic fate.[*]

These are small deviations from the conventions of traditional novelistic discourse, what Barthes calls the *lisible* text – certainly much less radical than, say, Joyce's. But the effect is to keep the reader actively engaged in the task of construing the narrative, and aware that he or she is reading a literary fiction. In a way their effect is what the Russian Formalists called "baring the device", and they are related to much bolder frame-breaking moves in Nabokov's fiction, which distinguish him both from classic realism and from modernism, and have been much imitated by later postmodernist writers. I mean his introduction of himself as a peripheral character in his own fictions, or the showing of his own hand as author of the novel we are reading. In *King Queen Knave* the wretched Franz, trapped in the coils of the mad, malevolent Martha, whom he no longer finds even desirable, is tormented by the repeated sight of a serenely happy couple, a bronzed "elegantly balding" man with a butterfly net and his attractive wife, at the seaside resort where the story reaches its climax – clearly Nabokov and his wife Vera (though not many readers of the novel on its first publication in 1928 would have seen the joke: Nabokov was not then the world's most famous lepidopterist). At the end of *Bend Sinister* the author takes pity on the unbearable sufferings of his hero, mercifully makes him mad and then despatches him with a bullet as he rushes towards a wall where his enemy cringes:

> and the wall vanished, like a rapidly withdrawn slide, and I stretched myself and got up from among the chaos of written and rewritten pages to investigate the sudden twang that something had made in striking the netting of my window.[†]

Perhaps Nabokov's most characteristic device for testing and

[*] *Glory*, Harmondsworth, Penguin, 1974, pp. 74–5.
[†] *Bend Sinister*, p. 200.

challenging his reader is the unreliable narrator. This is also a feature of modernist fiction, but Nabokov's use of it seems to me distinctively different. In James's *The Turn of the Screw*, for instance, or Ford's *The Good Soldier*, the ambiguity generated by the unreliability of the narrator is never finally resolved or dissolved: the use of an unreliable narrator affirms the impossibility of ever establishing the objective truth of a human situation. But in Nabokov the truth *is* established, sooner or later. In *Despair*, for instance, Herman's reluctance to face the fact that he has bungled his crime keeps us for a very long time ignorant that a crime has been committed, and then mystified as to the motive behind it, but eventually all is made clear.

Nabokov's most brilliant and beautiful feat in this line, and an excellent example of his transformation and displacement of the crime fiction model, is *Pale Fire*. It is in a sense a double crime story, or the story of a crime and a misdemeanour: there is the mystery of the murder of Shade, which Kinbote "solves" in a way that answers to his own self-aggrandizing fantasies, and there is the misappropriation of Shade's poem – Kinbote unscrupulously exploiting the circumstances of Shade's death to get possession of the manuscript of the as yet unpublished work. His commentary is in part a self-justifying account of this action. Like *Despair* and *Lolita*, it is a kind of confession or apologia written by a wanted or imprisoned man. What is so fascinating and devilishly clever about *Pale Fire* is the way in which the reader is led to see that Kinbote's notes are not what they purport to be, and to construct the truth from Kinbote's distorted versions of events. The clues are as much stylistic as factual. What alerts us to the unreliability of Kinbote are, in the first place, the sudden breaches of scholarly decorum in his "notes" to Shade's poem. For instance, the apostrophe to the reader, "Canto two, your favourite,"* or the asides about the circumstances in which he is composing his notes, such as: "There is a very loud amusement park right in front of my present lodgings."† His disregard of evidence, and of the protocol of editorial procedure, becomes more and more flagrant, until any old word in Shade's poem will serve as a hook on which to hang some nostalgic fantasy about Zembla; but this development

---

* *Pale Fire*, London, Corgi, 1966, p. 13.
† *Ibid.*, p. 14.

also, rather poignantly, reflects Kinbote's deepening disappointment with the actual content of Shade's poem and the palpable lack of any reference within it to the Zemblan story.

I have to dissent from the interpretation of *Pale Fire* put forward by Brian Boyd in the second volume of his monumental biography of Nabokov, greatly as I respect the scholarship and critical acumen displayed in that work. I mean the idea that the whole text – poem and editorial apparatus – is supposed to have been written by John Shade. The main evidence for this interpretation put forward by Professor Boyd is an unpublished scrap of verse written by Nabokov some years after the composition of *Pale Fire*, which he attached as an *envoi* (playfully attributed to Shade) to a draft of his foreword to a revised edition of *Speak Memory*:

As John Shade says somewhere:

> Nobody will heed my index,
>   I suppose,
> But through it a gentle wind *ex*
>   *Ponto* blows.[*]

The argument is that this reveals Shade to have been the compiler of the index to *Pale Fire*, in which case he must have written the commentary too, and thus invented the character of Kinbote and the story of how he himself is murdered. This interpretation seems to me a classic instance of the intentional fallacy as defined by Wimsatt and Beardsley in their famous essay,[†] namely that it is a mistake to judge or interpret a literary text by seeking evidence of the author's intentions outside the text. The fragment of verse does not in fact unequivocally assert that Shade wrote the index to *Pale Fire* – it could refer to another index. And even if Nabokov did mean to imply when he wrote the verse that Shade compiled the *Pale Fire* index, it does not follow that he intended such a meaning

---

[*] Brian Boyd, *Vladimir Nabokov: the American Years*, Princeton, Princeton U.P., p. 445.

[†] W. K. Wimsatt and Monroe C. Beardsley, "The Intentional Fallacy", reprinted in *Twentieth Century Literary Criticism*, ed. David Lodge, London, Longman, 1971, pp. 334–44.

when he wrote the novel four years earlier; he might have been playing whimsically with the possibility after the event, or thinking of teasing his readers with this possibility in the spirit of a hoax or practical joke, and in any case he suppressed the thought and did not publish the verse. But the main objection to this reading of *Pale Fire* is that it is not required by the text itself, while it drastically impoverishes the meaning and beauty of the text and indeed creates further problems of interpretation which are I believe unresolvable.

I can best express this by saying that, as a practising writer, I cannot conceive of myself doing what Shade, according to this interpretation, is supposed to have done: that is, written a transparently autobiographical poem about coming to terms with one of the most painful and tragic events that can happen to a man, the suicide of his own child, and then attached to it a comic, ironic and satirical fiction, in the form of a commentary on his own poem, about a deranged émigré scholar, which entails a description of Shade himself being murdered just after he has completed the poem. Surely Shade himself would have to be deranged to use his own daughter's suicide in this way, as a means of showing up the vanity and self-deception of a fictitious lunatic? (Kinbote must be a fictional creation of Shade's under this interpretation, because Shade could not, for legal reasons, attribute to a real person the actions and motives he attributes to Kinbote.) Of course, since we know nothing about Shade beyond what we learn from the poem and its editorial apparatus, it is theoretically possible that Shade also invented his daughter's suicide, or invented his daughter, or indeed invented everything within the covers of the book – which is of course precisely what Nabokov has done. A *reductio ad absurdum* of Brian Boyd's interpretation abolishes the distinction between Shade and Nabokov. But the power and beauty of *Pale Fire* surely depend on our accepting that there is within it a distinction between the fictional and the real that corresponds to the distinction between the world of the novel and the world in which Nabokov wrote it and we read it. And the only place where you can draw such a line without the whole text unravelling is between the poem and its commentary. The pathos and poignancy of the daughter's death, the force of the contrast between Shade's bleakly stoical meditation on it, and Kinbote's ripping yarn about Charles, the exiled king of Zembla, depend on our believing that, within the imagined world of the novel, the daughter's death is real, and the story of the exiled King of Zembla is a fiction pretending to be fact, the compensatory fantasy of a gifted but deeply flawed human being.[*]

I think this issue is of more than local significance. Nabokov's art assumes that there is a common perceptual world, in which actions have real and sometimes irreversible consequences, and that people who for their own psychological purposes deny or ignore this are deranged and dangerous. He does not, like the classic realist novelists of the nineteenth century, believe or pretend to believe that this world is unproblematic, or totally knowable, or supervised by a benign Providence, or amenable to human notions of what is just and reasonable. On the contrary, the world he describes is full of violent and random occurrences which are tragic or comic in their lack of rational motivation. But he does not follow the modernists in supposing that reality is wholly subjective. He does not endorse solipsism. Solipsism is a nightmare from which many of his characters awake, usually too late to undo the consequences: Herman in *Despair*, Sumurov in *The Eye*, Kinbote in *Pale Fire*.

---

[*] Brian Boyd, who was present at the conference, defended his interpretation by saying that Nabokov had in fact exploited the painful trauma of the political murder of his father (mistaken by the assassin for someone else) in composing *Pale Fire*, just as Shade exploits the suicide of his daughter, and acknowledged this by making the date of Shade's death the same as that of his father's birthday, 21 July. I completely agree that the assassination of Nabokov's father is one of the imaginative sources for *Pale Fire*; but the analogy is inexact. Nabokov fictionalized, and thus distanced himself and his readers from, his painful personal experience in the *whole* creation of *Pale Fire*; Shade (according to Boyd's interpretation) only in the commentary. To draw a more exact analogy, we should have to imagine that Nabokov wrote a memoir of his father, including a detailed account of his assassination, that was completely factual and also movingly introspective; and then attached to it a much longer parodic scholarly commentary, supposedly written by a deranged academic, who insinuated himself into Nabokov's domestic life, and fed him with some paranoid fantasy about himself which he subsequently reads into Nabokov's text, which he purloined after leading the novelist inadvertently to his death. Quite apart from the logical impossibility of a writer's describing his own death, would we not feel that there was something distinctly odd and misjudged about such a production?

It is a commonplace critical observation that Nabokov wonderfully celebrates the thingness of things. His novels are full of objects, often homely and humble, that are noted and described not necessarily because they are of significance in the plot or because they are signifiers of character and milieu, or vehicles of thematic symbolism, but simply because they are there, because the world is full of forgotten, abandoned, contingent objects, every one of which in fact has its own history and pathos, and a primary duty of the artist is to remind us of this. Martha, in *King Queen Knave*, rummaging through the drawers of her husband's desk for his revolver:

> found several sticks of gold-tinted sealing-wax, a flashlight, three guldens and one shilling, an exercise book with English words written in it, his grinning passport (who grins in official circumstances?), his pipe, broken, that she had given him long ago, an old little album of faded snapshots, a recent snapshot of a girl that might have been Isolda Portz had she not worn a smart ski suit in the photo, a box of thumbtacks, pieces of string, a watch crystal, and other trivial junk the accumulation of which always infuriated Martha. Most of these articles, including the copybook and the winter sports advertisement, she deposited in the wastebasket. She thrust back the drawers violently, and leaving the deafened desk, went up to the bedroom.*

To Martha, intent only on murder, these miscellaneous objects are merely irritants, obstacles in her path which she consigns to oblivion. Only her husband's passport photograph evokes a reflective (though hostile) response from her. If she had been more attentive, she would have found among them clues to the fact that her husband has a mistress (he took Isolda Portz to the ski resort; perhaps he was smiling in anticipation in the passport photograph). Her lack of respect for objects, as for anything other than her own selfish ends, is implied by the dully denotative style in which she registers them. The vivid metaphor of the "deafened drawer" is of course the narrator's, expressing sympathetic solidarity with the things so insensitively treated by Martha.

* *King Queen Knave*, p. 184.

As the narrator of *Transparent Things* explains, such humble objects are microcosms of human effort and ingenuity: to contemplate the full history of their existence opens up dizzying vistas of contingency. Hugh Parsons finds in the drawer of the desk in his hotel room, for instance:

> a very plain, round, technically faceless old pencil of cheap pine, dyed a dingy lilac. It had been mislaid ten years ago by a carpenter who had not finished examining, let alone fixing, the old desk, having gone away for a tool that he never found. Now comes the act of attention.
>
> In his shop, and long before that at the village school, the pencil has been worn down to two-thirds of its original length. The bare wood of its tapered end has darkened to a plumbeous plum, thus merging in tint with the blunt tip of graphite whose blind gloss alone distinguishes it from the wood. A knife and brass sharpener have thoroughly worked upon it and if it were necessary we could trace the complicated fate of the shavings, each mauve on one side and tan on the other when fresh, but now reduced to atoms of dust whose wide, wide dispersal is panic catching its breath but one should get above it, one gets used to it fairly soon (there are worse terrors).[*]

The narrator concludes after quite a few more lines that "the solid pencil itself as briefly fingered by Hugh Person still somehow eludes us", but as readers we are more likely to feel that we have never known a pencil described so completely.

Nabokov's description of objects is very different from the *chosisme* of Alain Robbe-Grillet, in whose fiction consciousness is entirely solipsistic, and the material world is all geometrical planes and surfaces, all surface and no depth, described in language from which every metaphorical trope has been rigorously purged. It is not quite like, either, the whimsical anthropomorphism and moody pathetic fallacies of the nineteenth-century novel, or the lyrical epiphanies of the modernist novel, though it has affinities with them. More often than not, the metaphorical tropes in Nabokov's fiction are purely local in

---

[*] *Transparent Things*, London, Weidenfeld & Nicolson, 1973, pp. 6–7.

effect, and not motivated by the focalizing character's consciousness. The midges in *Laughter in the Dark*, "continually darning the air in one spot"; "the waxed moustache" of a burnished clock at ten minutes to two in *Sebastian Knight*; the "square echo" of a car's slammed door in *Bend Sinister*; the magazine that "escaped to the floor like a flustered fowl" in *Lolita* – such tropes, which swarm over the pages of Nabokov, are, in the Russian formalist sense, primarily defamiliarizing in effect – they allow us to see the phenomenal word afresh, and hence to value it. And even when metaphor *is* charged with the emotion of the perceiving subject, this does not interfere with its fundamental task of doing justice to the phenomenal world. For example, this exquisitely sensuous description of Lolita eating an apple:

> She tossed it up into the sun-dusted air and caught it – it made a cupped, polished plop . . . she grasped it and bit into it, and my heart was like snow under the crimson skin.[*]

The combination of onomatopoeic phonology and double metaphoric reference – to the physical properties of the apple and to Humbert's feelings – is breathtaking. In such passages Nabokov comes closest to the Joycean epiphany, though there is a romantic rapture in the language that Joyce could never invoke without immediately subjecting it to an effect of ironic bathos.

"The detail is all," Ada asserts in a passage lyrically celebrating the discipline of natural history, one branch of which Nabokov himself practised with distinction.[†] It is the most empirical, least abstract, of the natural sciences. One of the reasons for Nabokov's obsessive hostility to Freud and Freudianism was that its interpretations tried to explain everything in terms of something else, the surface in terms of the putatively hidden, whereas Nabokov thought we should stay on the surface and make sense and sensation out of *that*. This doesn't condemn the writer to a drab realism. What Van de Veen says of Hieronymus Bosch would seem to be Nabokov's own aesthetic philosophy:

[*] *Lolita*, London, Corgi, 1961, p. 61.
[†] *Ada*, London, Weidenfeld & Nicolson, 1969, p. 71.

I don't give a hoot for the esoteric meaning, for the myth behind the moth . . . what we have to study is the joy of the eye, the feel and the taste of the woman-sized strawberry that you embrace *with* him.[*]

The profusion of sharply observed and vividly described detail in Nabokov's novels is one reason why, although their stories often deal with sensational actions associated with the crime novel and the thriller, they are not "page-turners", not "good reads", to use the phrases commonly used about successful popular fiction. Roland Barthes in his essay, "Introduction to the Structural Analysis of Narrative", proposed a distinction between what he called, with the structuralist's love of jargon, nuclei and catalysers.[†] Nuclei open or close alternatives that are of direct consequence for subsequent development of the narrative, and cannot be deleted without altering the story. Catalysers expand or fill up the spaces between the nuclei and *can* be deleted without altering the story. In the "good read" the proportion of nuclei is very high. In Nabokov's novels it is very low. The travelogue writing in Part Two of *Lolita*, for example, which must have dismayed many of the readers who bought the book on its scandalous reputation, consists of pages and pages of catalysers without a single nucleus.

There is an interesting passage in *Glory* concerning a book written by the hero's friend Darwin. Purporting to be a book of short stories, it apparently consists of short descriptive dissertations on commonplace things, like corkscrews, parrots, playing cards – "their history, beauty and virtues." Martin is enchanted with the book, and the narrator comments:

If Martin had ever thought of becoming a writer and been tormented by a writer's covetousness (so akin to the fear of death), by that constant state of anxiety compelling one to fix indelibly this or that evanescent trifle, perhaps these dissertations on minutiae that were deeply familiar to him might

[*] *Ada*, p. 437.
[†] Roland Barthes, *Image Music Text*, edited and translated by Stephen Heath, London, Fontana, 1977, pp. 79–124.

have roused in him a pang of envy and desire to write of the same things still better.[*]

The association of the writer's obsessive desire to give permanent form to what he perceives, however trivial, with the fear of death crops up again in slightly different form in a passage in *Pnin*:

> With the help of the janitor he screwed on to the side of the desk a pencil-sharpener – that highly satisfying, highly philosophical implement that goes ticonderoga, ticonderoga, feeding on the yellow finish and sweet wood, and ends up in a kind of soundlessly spinning ethereal void as we all must.[†]

The sudden transition from the lyrical celebration of the commonplace to a chilling reminder of mortality seems to me quintessentially Nabokovian. It is difficult to think of a modern literary novelist whose works end more often with a death, usually a violent one – murder, execution, suicide. *King Queen Knave, The Defence, Laughter in the Dark, Glory, Invitation to a Beheading, The Real Life of Sebastian Knight, Lolita, Pale Fire, Transparent Things*, all end with one or more deaths, and they and the other novels frequently include other deaths in the progress of the story. As we know, violent, untimely and pointless death tragically marred Nabokov's own life when his father was murdered in mistake for somebody else – an experience which left its mark on both the form and the content of his fiction. But unless one has a very naïve fundamentalist religious faith, in a sense death is always irrational, outrageous, unjust, whether it comes violently and early in life or late and from natural causes (as it did for Nabokov himself). The story in Nabokov's novels nearly always carries that bleak message, while the vivacity of the style defies it. The frame-breaking devices in his fiction, and the intertextual allusions which teem beneath its surface, are clear acknowledgements of the limits of art, its artificiality and conventionality. Art cannot overcome or indefinitely postpone death, but it was for Nabokov our best consolation against it, above all in its defamiliarizing celebration of the particularity of the phenomenal world.

[*] *Glory*, p. 64.
[†] *Pnin*, Harmondsworth, Penguin, 1960, p. 58.

Creative Writing: Can it/Should it be Taught?

In April 1995 the Royal Society of Literature held a one-day seminar on the subject, "Creative Writing: can it be taught?" The idea for the event originally came from Hilary Mantel, and it was chaired by P.D. James. The audience consisted of a mixture of writers, aspirant writers and teachers of writing. This was my contribution (slightly expanded here) to the opening panel discussion.

PENNY You told me earlier what I was doing
     wrong. I understand that, I think. Now I
     want to know how to do it right.
LEO (*slowly*) You want me to tell you how to
     produce literary works of enduring value?
PENNY Please.

LEO *shakes his head.*

PENNY I know it's not a simple matter.
LEO You bet your sweet – bet your life it
     isn't.
PENNY But you *are* a teacher of creative
     writing.
LEO I offer criticism. What my students do
     with it is up to them.
                    – *The Writing Game*, Act I Scene 5

How does one become a writer? One thing is certain: nobody
ever wrote a book without having read at least one – and more
probably hundreds – of approximately the same kind. Most
writers, whether they take courses in creative writing or not, are
kick-started – that is, they begin by imitating and emulating the
literature that gives them the biggest kicks. The pleasure and
the enhanced sense of reality that you get from reading gives
you the urge to try and produce that effect on others. And it is
from reading that you acquire basic knowledge of the structural
and rhetorical devices that belong to a particular genre or form
of writing. To a large extent this learning process is intuitive and
unconscious, like learning the mother tongue.

Three writers who I believe had a formative influence on me
when I started to try and write prose fiction were James Joyce,
Graham Greene and Evelyn Waugh. No doubt the fact that all
three were Catholics, and wrote, in very different ways, about
Catholic subjects, was one reason why I was drawn to their
work in late adolescence, for I was brought up in that faith

myself. I also read them as a student of modern English Literature, with exams to pass and degrees to get. But from my immersion in their work I absorbed many lessons about the techniques of fiction, some of which I did not put into practice until many years later. For example: from Greene, how to use a few selected details, heightened by metaphor and simile, to evoke character or the sense of place; from Waugh, how to generate comedy by a combination of logic and surprise, of the familiar and the incongruous; from Joyce, how to make a modern story re-enact, echo or parody a mythical or literary precursor-narrative. I learned many other things from these writers as well – above all, I would like to think, a craftsmanlike approach to the business of writing, a willingness to take pains, a commitment to making the work as good as you can possibly make it.

Can such things be taught, systematically, rather than personally discovered and intuitively assimilated? Henry James thought they couldn't, and said so in a famous essay called "The Art of Fiction". This was written in 1884 as a riposte to a lecture with the same title, delivered in that year to the Royal Institution by Walter Besant. Everybody interested in the subject knows James's essay, but not many have read the text which provoked it, for it is quite difficult to obtain. Besant was a prolific and versatile man of letters, typically Victorian in his energy and industry. He boasted of having written 18 novels in 18 years, and also wrote on and translated French literature, and published books and journalism on many other subjects. He was a tireless philanthropist, and a key figure in the professionalization of authorship in the late nineteenth century.

In the same year that he published his "Art of Fiction", Besant founded the Society of Authors, and it is clear in retrospect that the lecture was part of his mission to raise the professional status of writers. He begins by arguing that novelists are not taken seriously as artists because, unlike painters, sculptors and musicians, they receive no national honours and awards, they "hold no annual exhibitions, dinners or conversazione; they put no letters after their name; they have no President or Academy", and they do not attempt to teach their art to aspirant practioners:

How can that be an Art ... which has no lecturers or teachers, no school or college or Academy, no recognized rules, no text-books, and is not taught in any University? Even German universities, which teach everything else, do not have Professors of fiction, and not one single novelist, so far as I know, has ever pretended to teach his mystery.

All these things have come to pass, for good or ill, and Besant can take some of the credit for that. Certainly, if anyone deserves the title "Father of Creative Writing Courses" it is he. To tyros who lightly assume that "anyone can write a novel," he sternly recommends "that from the very beginning their minds should be fully possessed with the knowledge that Fiction is an Art, and, like all other Arts, that it is governed by certain laws, methods and rules, which it is their first business to learn."

Henry James welcomed Besant's insistence that the novel is a work of art, which might be analysed and discussed, counteracting the "comfortable good-humoured feeling" more common in England, that "a novel is a novel as a pudding is a pudding, and that our only business with it could be to swallow it." On the other hand he was sceptical of Besant's claim that "the laws of fiction may be laid down and taught with as much precision as the laws of harmony, perspective, and proportion":

The painter *is* able to teach the rudiments of his practice and it is possible, from the study of good work (granted the aptitude), both to learn how to paint and how to write. Yet it remains true ... that the literary artist would be obliged to say to his pupil much more than the other, "Ah well, you must do it as you can!" If there are exact sciences, there are also exact arts, and the grammar of painting is so much more definite that it makes the difference.

The essence of James's argument, eloquently developed later in the essay, is that the novel is an organic form:

I cannot imagine composition existing in a series of blocks, nor conceive, in any novel worth discussing at all, a passage of dialogue that is not in its intention descriptive, a touch of truth of any sort that does not partake of the nature of incident, or an incident that derives its interest from any other source than the general and only source of the success of a work of art – that of being illustrative. A novel is a living thing, all one and continuous, like any other organism, and in proportion as it lives will it be found, I think, that in each of the parts there is something of each of the other parts.

Since you cannot isolate and identify the various components of a novel, James seems to be saying, it follows that you cannot teach people how to use them.

Was he right? Well, one hesitates to disagree with Henry James, but I think he overstates his case. Let me invoke another great modern writer, T.S. Eliot. In his essay "The Function of Criticism" Eliot said: "the larger part of the labour of an author in composing his work is critical labour, the labour of sifting, combining, constructing, expunging, correcting, testing: this frightful toil is as much critical as creative." That is precisely what I mean by the willingness to take pains. It can be done intuitively – but it can also be done consciously and analytically. We learn our mother tongue without learning grammar first, but we need the metalanguage of grammar to understand and explain (explain to ourselves as well as to others) how a language works – what are its rules and possibilities, and why some utterances fail in their communicative purpose. I don't say it is *essential* for a writer to have such a metalanguage at his fingertips – just as Molière's M. Jourdain found he had been speaking prose all his life without knowing it, a novelist may use, for example, free indirect style without knowing what it is called or being consciously aware of what its rules and constraints are – but I don't think it does any harm, either, to acquire the metalanguage, and it may help in that essential process of self-criticism which Eliot describes so well. In short, I see no incompatibility between the formalistic critical study of literature and the effort to produce new writing of one's own.

Walter Besant's mistake was to base his proposals not on rhetoric, which can be taught (*that* effect is produced by *this* technique), but on general aesthetic "rules" or "laws" which are either matters of subjective opinion or so vague as to be useless for pedagogic purposes. He sums them up as follows:

The Art of Fiction requires first of all the power of

description, truth and fidelity, observation, selection, clearness of conception and of outline, dramatic grouping, directness of purpose, a profound belief on the part of the story-teller in the reality of his story, and beauty of workmanship.

Well, yes – but whose truth, whose beauty? And what makes one description more powerful than another? On what principles is "selection" based, and what exactly do the terms "outline" and "dramatic" mean in the context of narrative prose? Besant never tells us, and he never illustrates his maxims with quotation – an abstention that becomes almost comically frustrating at times. One would dearly like to know how

> in some well-known scenes which I could quote, there is not a single word to emphasize or explain the attitude, manner and look of the speakers, yet they are as intelligible as if they were written down and described.

In short, Besant's "rules" and "laws" of the art of fiction amount to little more than vague invocations of the conventional literary taste of his time. As Henry James observed, with his usual suave courtesy, "They are suggestive, they are even inspiring, but they are not exact, though they are doubtless as much so as the case admits of."

Creative writing courses can help the aspirant writer to acquire a descriptive vocabulary for and explicit awareness of such technical matters as (in prose fiction, for instance) point of view, narrative voice, frame-breaking, time-shifting, etc., etc., to entertain a wider range of possibilities in these respects than the writer might have discovered independently, and to appreciate how important are the choices made in these categories to the final effect of a narrative text. These things can be "taught" in a variety of ways: by systematic exposition, by practical criticism of model texts, by set writing exercises, and by workshop or tutorial discussion of the student's own spontaneously generated work.

Those words, "own" and "spontaneously", however, bring us to the problematic heart of the matter. I have suggested that the teaching of creative writing is best seen as a special application of formalist criticism. But it is a peculiar feature of criticism, and especially of literary criticism, that the licence to criticize does not carry with it an obligation to explain how the fault complained of might have been avoided or how it might be repaired. The reviewer of a novel may complain that a certain phrase is a cliché without being obliged to produce a fresher one; may protest that a certain character's actions are implausible without having to suggest more credible behaviour. Indeed, for a critic to propose such emendations would be regarded as out of order. The reason is very simple and very obvious: once you start trying to rewrite somebody else's work, you take it away from them and make it your own. To that extent James was right: creative writing cannot be "taught" – as, say, perspective can be taught to an aspiring artist – by correcting the student's work or showing him how it should be done. Indeed a creative writer who tries to make his students clones of himself is doing them the worst possible service.

I believe anyone's expressive and communicative skills can be improved by practice and criticism. If the teacher is competent, anyone who takes a creative writing course ought to be producing or capable of producing better work at the end of it than at the beginning. And certainly the experience of trying to write under systematic guidance will enhance the student's understanding and appreciation of literature as a reader. For that reason I believe there should be a creative writing component of the set-exercise type in all English education up to and including the tertiary level. But no course can teach you how to produce a text other people will willingly give up their time – and perhaps their money – to read, although it has no utilitarian purpose or value.

This raises another kind of problem as regards courses which are offered to students with serious aspirations to become professional writers. Since you cannot guarantee that any of them will succeed in this ambition, is it ethical to take their money to teach them? Responsibly taught courses do their best to mitigate this problem by careful selection of students. But ultimately success cannot be guaranteed and this should be made clear to everybody involved. In one sense, literature is not differently placed from any of the other arts in this respect. You can be taught to draw and paint competently but you cannot be taught to produce paintings of enduring value. But there is a difference too: you can draw and paint for your own pleasure, but, to be satisfying, writing needs an audience and a permanent existence in print. It needs to be published. And as we know, crossing that threshold is very difficult. There is no such thing as an "amateur" novelist, or a "Sunday novelist" – or if there is, it is not a status that anyone would take much pride or satisfaction in, I think. One common argument in favour of creative writing courses, especially long-term ones, is that they provide a supportive yet critical community in which the budding writer can develop and test his or her talent. Certainly many graduates of such courses have testified that this was their experience. Others find the competitiveness and self-exposure of the situation intimidating and inhibiting. But in either case, the community of the course is a small and artificial one. Sooner or later the students must submit their work to the judgement of readers – publishers, agents, editors, scavengers of the slush-pile – who don't know them personally, and this can be a deeply discouraging experience. The more advanced the course, the more heartbreak is likely to be associated with it.*

"The only obligation to which in advance we may hold a novel, without incurring the accusation of being arbitrary," said Henry James in his essay, "is that it be interesting." It goes without saying that not every successful novel can be interesting to every potential reader. But there are novels which are interesting to nobody except the author and perhaps his or her family and friends, and it is inevitable that a great many, perhaps the majority, of works produced in creative writing classes will fall into this category.

What makes a novel "interesting", however, is as difficult to define as any of Walter Besant's categories; though we all recognize the quality when we encounter it and are aware of its absence when it is missing. It is not subject-matter, as James

---

* Walter Besant's advice for dealing with rejection is brutally blunt: "if a novelist fail at first, let him be well assured it is his own fault; and if on his second attempt, he cannot amend, let him for the future be silent." In an appendix to the printed lecture he relented somewhat: "persevere, if you feel that the root of the matter is in you, till your work is accepted; and *never*, NEVER, NEVER pay for publishing a novel."

himself was anxious to affirm: "We must grant the artist his subject, his idea, his *donnée*: our criticism is applied only to what he makes of it." But it is not just a matter of technique either. It is like a chemical, or alchemical, reaction between form and content. So many factors are involved in the production of a literary text: the writer's life-experience, his genetic inheritance, his historical context, his reading, his powers of recall, his capacity for introspection, his fantasy life, his understanding of the springs of narrative, his responsiveness to language – its rhythms, sounds, registers, nuances of meaning, and so on. Even a single sentence in a novel is the complex product of innumerable chains of cause and effect which reach deep into the writer's life and psyche. To distinguish, analyse and retrace them all would be impossible. Even the most sophisticated literary criticism only scratches the surface of the mysterious process of creativity; and so, by the same token, does even the best course in creative writing.

The Novel as Communication

This is the text of a lecture delivered at Cambridge University under the auspices of Darwin College in an interdisciplinary series entitled "Communication". Other contributors included Horace Barlow ("Communication and representation within the brain"), Noam Chomsky ("Language and mind") and Jonathan Miller ("Communication without words"). The eight lectures were collected and published under the title *Ways of Communicating* in 1990.

There are two possible ways of approaching this topic. One is to take for granted that the novel is a mode of communication, and to analyse its formal features as techniques of communication; the other is to question the assumption that the novel is communication – to ask what is implied by that assumption, and what excluded. I shall try to do a little of both. I shall also consider the subject from two points of view: that of the critic and that of the practising novelist. Some of what I have to say applies to literature generally, but much of it is specific to the novel, the literary form in which I am most interested, both as a critic and as a creative writer.

I suspect that it is assumed by most people, including those who planned this series of lectures, that language is a means of communication – that that is what it is *for*; and that since literature is made out of language, it too must be a kind of communication, as defined by, for instance, the Collins English Dictionary: "the imparting or exchange of information, ideas, feelings". A commonsense view of the matter would say that that definition covers the composition and reception of a novel.

The classic novelists certainly seem to have thought of their activity as communication. Henry Fielding, for example, in the eighteenth century, draws his masterpiece, *Tom Jones*, to its conclusion with a metaphor of social intercourse:

> We are now, reader, arrived at the last stage of our journey. As we have, therefore, travelled together through so many pages, let us behave to one another like fellow-travellers in a stage coach, who have passed several days in the company of each other; and who, notwithstanding any bickerings or little animosities which may have occurred on the road, generally make up at last, and mount for the last time into their vehicle with cheerfulness and good humour; since after this one stage, it may possibly happen to us, as it commonly happens to them, never to meet more.

The intrusive authorial voice exemplified in this passage, and generally typical of the classic novel – the voice that confides, comments, explains and sometimes scolds – the voice to which we rather casually give the name that appears on the title-page (Henry Fielding, Charles Dickens, George Eliot, or whoever) is the most obvious sign that these writers saw themselves as engaged in an act of communication with their readers. In this kind of novel the act of narration is modelled on a speech act in which one person tells a story to another. George Eliot begins her novel *Adam Bede* thus:

> With a single drop of ink for a mirror, the Egyptian sorcerer undertook to reveal to any chance comer far-reaching visions of the past. This is what I undertake to do for you, reader. With this drop of ink at the end of my pen, I will show you the roomy workshop of Jonathan Burge, carpenter and builder in the village of Hayslope, as it appeared on the 18th of June, in the year of Our Lord, 1799.

By apostrophizing the reader, the act of writing is transformed here into a kind of speaking. Through the figure of the drop of ink, at once miraculous and homely, the act of telling is transformed into a gesture of showing. This offer to transport us out of our own world, with all its problems, unfinished business, boredom and disappointment, into another world where we may escape these things or negotiate them vicariously, is perhaps the fundamental appeal of all narrative. What is peculiarly novelistic about George Eliot's opening gambit is its pseudo-documentary specificity – the proper names and the date: "the roomy workshop of Jonathan Burge, carpenter and builder in the village of Hayslope, as it appeared on the 18th of June, in the year of Our Lord, 1799".

The novel is a form of narrative. We can hardly begin to discuss a novel without summarizing or assuming a knowledge of its story or plot; which is not to say that the story or plot is the only or even the main reason for our interest in a novel, but that this is the fundamental principle of its structure. (These two terms, incidentally, story and plot, are sometimes used to describe two opposed types or aspects of narrative, but they are also used as interchangeable synonyms and I shall use them as such.) The novel therefore has a family resemblance to other narrative forms, both the purely verbal, such as the classical epic, the books of the Bible, history and biography, folktales and ballads; and those forms which have non-verbal components, such as drama and film. Narrative is concerned with *process*, that is to say, with change in a given state of affairs; or it converts problems and contradictions in human experience into process in order to understand or cope with them. Narrative obtains and holds the interest of its audience by raising questions in their minds about the process it describes and delaying the answers to these questions. When a question is answered in a way that is both unexpected and plausible, we have the effect known since Aristotle as *peripeteia* or reversal. All this applies to the novel as to every other form of narrative, whatever its medium.

Verbal narrative, as distinct from narrative which includes an element of performance or visual images, has two basic modes of representation: the report of characters' actions by a narrator, and the presentation of the characters' own speech in dialogue. These two modes – narrator's voice and character's voices, or summary and scene, telling and showing, as they are sometimes called – are the woof and warp of all verbal narrative, from the story of Little Red Riding Hood to *War and Peace*. The novel, however, exhibits particularly subtle and complex interweavings of these modes of presentation, as I shall indicate more fully later on. Its discursive variety and complexity is one of the reasons why it imitates the social world with a verisimilitude unequalled by other literary forms. Another reason is that pseudo-documentary specificity I mentioned in connection with the opening of George Eliot's *Adam Bede*. In short, the novel is characteristically a *realistic* form of narrative. Early critical discussion of the novel, which acquired a distinctive generic identity in the eighteenth century, focused on this quality: its illusion of reality. Clara Reeve, for instance, writing in 1785, said:

> The Novel gives a familiar relation of such things as pass every day before our eyes, such as may happen to our friends, or to ourselves, and the perfection of it is, to represent every scene in so easy and natural a manner, and to make them appear so probable, as to deceive us into a persuasion (at

least while we are reading) that all is real, until we are affected by the joys or distresses, of the persons in the story, as if they were our own. (*The Progress of Romance*)

A much later, much more sophisticated critic, Ortega y Gasset, said much the same thing:

> . . . the novel is destined to be perceived from within itself – the same as the real world . . . to enjoy a novel we must feel surrounded by it on all sides . . . Precisely because it is a preeminently realistic genre it is incompatible with outer reality. In order to establish its own inner world it must dislodge and abolish the surrounding one. ("Notes on the novel", 1948)

Out of a thousand possible illustrations of this point one might cite the testimony of William Smith, the nineteenth-century publisher, on his first reading of the manuscript of Charlotte Brontë's *Jane Eyre*.

> After breakfast on Sunday morning I took the ms of Jane Eyre to my little study and began to read it. The story quickly took me captive. Before 12 o'clock my horse came to the door, but I couldn't put the book down. I scribbled 2 or 3 lines to my friend saying I was sorry circumstances had arisen to prevent my meeting him, sent the note off by my groom, and went on reading the ms. Presently the servant came to tell me lunch was ready. I asked him to bring me a sandwich and a glass of wine, and still went on reading Jane Eyre. Dinner came; for me the meal was a very hasty one, and before I went to bed that night I had finished reading the manuscript.

The peculiar verisimilitude of the novel's representation of reality, and the peculiarly hypnotic spell the novel casts upon its readers, have always made it an object of some suspicion, both morally and aesthetically. Is there not something fundamentally unnatural and unhealthy about a form of art which suspends the reader's awareness of his own existence in real space and time? Is not the pleasure of the novelistic text akin to day-dreaming, wish-fulfilment fantasy? Freud certainly thought so (see his paper on "Creative Writers and Day-Dreaming"). On such grounds it has been argued that the novel is not authentic communication, notably by the Marxist critic Walter Benjamin.

Benjamin drew a distinction between storytelling, which he saw as, in its purest form, an oral-aural transaction between a narrator and an audience physically present to each other, and the novel, which is produced in one place by a solitary silent author, and consumed in another place by a solitary silent reader. The rise of the novel, he observed, was coincident with the decline of storytelling; and in consequence he says, in a striking phrase, "the communicability of experience is declining".

> The novelist has isolated himself. The birthplace of the novel is the solitary individual, who is no longer able to express himself by giving examples of his most important concerns, is himself uncounselled and cannot counsel others. ("The Storyteller")

In recent years there have been many attacks on what is sometimes called the classic realist novel on similar grounds: that far from being a means of communication it is a means of ideological domination and repression, reproducing on the cultural level the processes of industrial capitalism, making its audience passive consumers, reconciling them to their alienated state instead of liberating them from it, by making it appear normal or natural. (One of the most recent of such polemics is *Resisting Novels: Ideology and Fiction*, by Lennard J. Davis, 1987.)

In fact the classic novelists were well aware of the dangerous power of their art, and took various measures to prevent or warn against its abuse. The intrusive authorial voice itself is often used to point to the formal conventions of the novel, and thus to prevent a naïve confusion of literature with life. When Henry Fielding introduces the word "pages" into his stage coach metaphor ("As we have, therefore, travelled together through so many pages") he reminds his audience that they are reading a book. Jane Austen gives an even sharper jolt at the end of *Northanger Abbey* to "my readers, who will see in the tell-tale compression of the pages before them, that we are all hastening together to perfect felicity." When Trollope says in *Barchester*

Towers, "But let the gentle-hearted reader be under no apprehension whatsoever. It is not destined that Eleanor shall marry Bertie Stanhope," he is teasing rather than indulging his audience.

Henry James did not see it that way. Such authorial admissions that the events of the novel are invented seemed to him "a betrayal of a sacred office". James inaugurated the modern or, as it is sometimes called, the "modernist" novel in England, a kind of fiction which, in pursuit of a more faithful representation of reality, attentuated or eliminated altogether the authorial narrator. Instead the action is narrated as perceived by the consciousness of a character or characters. This can be done in various ways, most of which can be found in eighteenth- and early nineteenth-century fiction, but not used so artfully or extensively. One simple and obvious way of eliminating the authorial voice and giving a realistic effect to the novel is to make a character the narrator, as in *Robinson Crusoe* or *Jane Eyre* or *David Copperfield*. But whereas those first-person narrators are fairly transparent surrogates for the implied authors of those novels, the first-person narrators of modernist texts are more ambiguous, less reliable witnesses to their own experience, and are often framed by or counterpointed with other narrators – as, for example, in Henry James's *The Turn of the Screw* or Conrad's *Heart of Darkness*. A further, characteristically modern variation on the pseudo-autobiographical or confessional novel is the interior monologue, as used in James Joyce's *Ulysses*, where the reader eavesdrops, as it were, on the actual thoughts and sensations of the character as he or she moves through time and space. Here is Joyce's Leopold Bloom, considering his cat:

> They call them stupid. They understand what we say better than we understand them. She understands all she wants to. Vindictive too. Cruel. Her nature. Curious mice never squeal. Seem to like it. Wonder what I look like to her. Height of a tower? No, she can jump me.

This kind of discourse is at the opposite pole from storytelling as defined by Benjamin. Compared to the classic novel, not a great deal happens in the stream-of-consciousness novel – or it happens off-stage, as it were, glanced at in memory and allusion rather than presented directly. The minute registering of "the flickerings of that innermost flame which flashes its messages through the brain", to use Virginia Woolf's words, works best on ordinary experience rather than extraordinary – walking along a street, preparing a meal, knitting a stocking. Interior monologue is particularly ill-suited to narrative purposes – even Joyce uses it only intermittently in *Ulysses*, in combination with other kinds of discourse, including free indirect style.

Free indirect style is a mode of narration which as it were fuses and interweaves the authorial narrator's speech and the speech of the character. By reporting the character's thoughts in the third person, past tense, as in traditional narrative, but keeping to vocabulary appropriate to the character, and omitting some or all of the tags that normally introduce reported speech (like "he thought", "she wondered", etc.), an effect of intimate access to the character's inner self is produced, without relinquishing the task of narrating to the character entirely, as in the pseudo-autobiography or interior monologue. This type of discourse – free indirect speech or free indirect style – is peculiar to the novel; it makes its appearance in the late eighteenth century and Jane Austen was probably the first novelist to realize its full potential. Here for instance is her rendering of Emma Woodhouse's thoughts, having just received a most unwelcome proposal of marriage from Mr Elton, whom she had supposed to be in love with her protégée, Harriet, as a result of her own matchmaking contrivances:

> She had taken up the idea, she supposed, and made everything bend to it. His manners, however, must have been unmarked, wavering, dubious, or she could not have been so misled.

So far there is a discreet element of authorial summary in this representation of the heroine's thoughts as she reviews the supposed courtship of Harriet by Mr Elton. But in the following sentences – unfinished, fragmentary, as spontaneous as speech – we seem to be placed right inside Emma's head.

> The picture! – How eager he had been about the picture! – and the charade! – and an hundred other circumstances; – how clearly they had seemed to point at Harriet. To be sure

the charade, with its "ready wit" – but then, the "soft eyes" – indeed, it suited neither; it was a jumble without taste or truth. Who could have seen through such thick-headed nonsense?

Jane Austen uses this technique sparingly, to represent moments of inner crisis, in combination with the more traditional modes of authorial report and direct speech. But Virginia Woolf's mature novels consist almost entirely of long passages of introspection by the characters in free indirect style, punctuated by banal conversational remarks and parenthetical reports of trivial actions. Here is another fictional matchmaker, Mrs Ramsay, in *To the Lighthouse* (1927):

> Foolishly, she had set them opposite each other. That should be remedied tomorrow. If it were fine, they should go for a picnic. Everything seemed possible. Everything seemed right. Just now (but this cannot last, she thought, dissociating herself from the moment while she talked about boots) just now she had reached security; she hovered like a hawk suspended; like a flag floated in an element of joy which filled every nerve of her body fully and sweetly, not noisily, solemnly rather, for it arose, she thought, looking at them all eating there, from husband and children and friends . . .

Thus Mrs Ramsey at her dinner table, thinking her thoughts, "dissociated from the moment", plotting a match between Lily Briscoe and William Bankes, while Lily Briscoe at the same table is thinking wistfully of quite another man.

The emergence of the stream-of-consciousness novel at the end of the nineteenth and beginning of the twentieth centuries was obviously related to a huge epistemological shift in culture at large, from locating reality in the objective world of actions and things as perceived by common sense, to locating it in the minds of individual thinking subjects, each of whom constructs their own reality, and has difficulty in matching it with the reality constructed by others. If the modern novel is a form of communication, then paradoxically what it often communicates is the difficulty or impossibility of communication. One of the modernist arguments for removing the intrusive authorial voice – wise, omniscient, reliable, reassuring – from the novel was that it was false to our experience that life is in fact fragmented, chaotic, incomprehensible, absurd. The trouble with the classic realist novel, in this view, was that it was not realistic enough: truth to life was sacrificed to the observance of purely narrative conventions. "If a writer could . . . base his work upon his own feeling and not upon convention," said Virginia Woolf, in her celebrated essay, "Modern Fiction", "there would be no plot, no comedy, no tragedy, no love interest or catastrophe in the accepted style . . .". Instead she called for a kind of fiction that would record the atoms of experience "as they fall upon the mind, in the order in which they fall," that would "trace the pattern, however disconnected and incoherent in appearance, which each sight or incident scores upon the consciousness."

The modernist novel thus tends to endorse the philosophical argument known as solipsism – that the only thing I can be sure exists is myself as a thinking subject. This lays it open to Walter Benjamin's critique even more than the classic realist novel, for it is still further removed from his concept of storytelling. Another Marxist critic, the Hungarian Georg Lukács, attacked modernist fiction on similar grounds: "Man, for these writers, is by nature solitary, asocial, unable to enter into relationships with other human beings." Unable therefore to communicate, and unable to act upon history. And of course a familiar populist complaint about modernist fiction is that it does not communicate its meaning to the reader in a clear and comprehensible way. It is obscure, difficult, esoteric, élitist.

The standard defence of the modernist novel is based precisely upon these qualities, on its formal complexity and difficulty: the "revolution of the word" is seen as either essential to, or more important than, any political revolution. The paradigmatic case is James Joyce. After the psychological hyper-realism of the early chapters of *Ulysses*, the text is taken over by a bewildering variety of voices and discourses – parodic, travestying, colloquial, literary: newspaper headlines, oratory, women's magazines, pub talk, operatic songs, encyclopaedia articles, and so on; while the narrative level of the text is full of gaps, non sequiturs, anticlimaxes and unsolvable enigmas, and the chronological order of events is broken down and re-arranged by the operations of memory and the association of ideas in the consciousness of characters. Reading such a text we are reminded that the world we inhabit is constructed, not given; constructed in language. As Gabriel Josipovici has said, "To imagine, like the traditional novelist, that one's work is an image of the real world, to imagine that one can communicate directly to the reader what it is that one uniquely feels, that is to fall into the real solipsism, which is, to paraphrase Kierkegaard on despair, not to know that one is in a state of solipsism" (*The World and the Book*).

That is, I think, a somewhat tendentious description of the classic realist novel, and, in fact, writers like E. M. Forster, D. H. Lawrence, Ernest Hemingway, Evelyn Waugh and Graham Greene have written fiction that answers to the twentieth century's sense of moral and philosophical crisis without deviating violently from the conventions of classic realism. In the experimental fiction of our day that is sometimes called "post-modernist" these conventions – such as the omniscient and intrusive authorial narrator – are retained in exaggerated and parodic forms that remind one of the metafictional jokes of Fielding, Sterne, Thackeray and Trollope (one thinks for instance of Muriel Spark and John Fowles in this respect). In short, I am suggesting that there is more continuity than discontinuity in the development of the novel as a literary form.

The emergence of the modernist novel of consciousness is often described in terms of a shift of emphasis from "telling" to "showing" – but showing in this context is a metaphor. Written language cannot literally show us anything except writing. Speech cannot show us anything except speech. Language is not an iconic sign system, in which the signifier has a visual resemblance to the signified (as in the traffic signals for "falling rocks" or "hump-backed bridge"), but a symbolic one in which the connection between signifier and signified is arbitrary. The stream-of-consciousness novel only "shows" us the operations of the mind by another kind of telling than straightforward authorial report. And even those modern fictional texts, such as the novels of Samuel Beckett, that seem dedicated to demonstrating the impossibility of communicating anything to anybody about anything, do so by alluding to a paradigmatic act of storytelling, a paradise lost of communication:

Where now? Who now? When now? Unquestioning. I, say I. Unbelieving. Questions, hypotheses, call them that. Keep going, going on, call that going, call that on. Can it be that one day, off it goes on, that one day I simply stayed in, in where, instead of going out, in the old way, out to spend day and night as far away as possible, it wasn't far. Perhaps that is how it began. (*The Unnamable*)

To recapitulate: the novel tells a story, which has some kind of generalizable thematic significance, by means of a tissue of interwoven discourses. There is the discourse of the narrator, who may be a character or an authorial persona, who, if the latter, may be covert or overt; and there are the discourses of the represented characters, as manifested in their direct speech, or what we usually call "dialogue", and as manifested in the representation of their thoughts through soliloquy, reported speech, free indirect style, interior monologue and so on. But all these discourses will also contain echoes of, allusions to, anticipations of, other discourses both spoken and written – the discourses of popular wisdom, literary tradition, cultural institutions, social classes, and so on. It is this multivocal quality that distinguishes prose fiction from poetry, as Mikhail Bakhtin, the great Russian theorist whose work has only recently become well-known in the West, observed:

> The possibility of employing on the plane of a single work discourses of various types, with all their expressive capacities intact, without reducing them to a single common denominator – this is one of the fundamental characteristics of prose. Herein lies the profound distinction between prose style and poetic style . . . For the prose artist the world is full of other people's words, among which he must orient himself, and whose speech characteristics he must be able to perceive with a very keen ear. He must introduce them into the plane of his own discourse, but in such a way that this plane is not destroyed. He works with a very rich palette.

But this richness and complexity of discursive texture in the novel, what Bakhtin called the novel's "polyphony", offers a certain resistance to the idea of the novel as communication.

The basic model of communication is a linear sequence:

addresser→message→addressee

The addresser encodes a message in language and sends it to the addressee via speech or writing and the addressee decodes it. But who is the addresser in prose fiction? The French critic Roland Barthes quotes a passage from Balzac's story "Sarrasine", in which a young sculptor falls in love with a castrato disguised as a woman. The words of the text are as follows: *"This was woman herself, with her sudden fears, her irrational whims, her instinctive worries, her impetuous boldness, her fussings and her delicious sensibility."* Barthes asks:

> Who is speaking thus? Is it the hero of the story bent on remaining ignorant of the castrato hidden beneath the woman? Is it Balzac the individual, furnished by his personal experience with a philosophy of Woman? Is it Balzac the author professing "literary" ideas on femininity? Is it universal wisdom? Romantic psychology? We shall never know, for the good reason that writing is the destruction of every voice, of every point of origin. Writing is that neutral, composite, oblique space where our subject slips away, the negative where all identity is lost, starting with the very identity of the body writing. ("The Death of the Author")

It is time to consider, very briefly, the assault mounted by post-structuralist literary theory on the idea of literature as communication – indeed on the idea of communication itself.

The trouble with the model of communication in which the addresser encodes a message and sends it to the addressee, who decodes it, is, as another post-structuralist theorist has pointed out, that "every decoding is another encoding". Perhaps I may be permitted to quote from Morris Zapp's lecture on "Textuality as Striptease" in my novel, *Small World*:

> If you say something to me I check that I have understood your message by saying it back to you in my own words, for if I repeat your own words exactly you will doubt whether I have really understood you. But if I use *my* words it follows that I have changed *your* meaning, however slightly . . . Conversation is like playing tennis with a ball made of Krazy Putty, that keeps coming back over the net in a different shape. Reading of course is different from conversation. It is

more passive in the sense that we can't interact with a text, we can't affect the development of the text by our own words, since the text's words are already given. That is what perhaps encourages the quest for interpretation. If the words are fixed once and for all, on the page, may not their meaning be fixed also? Not so, because the same axiom, every decoding is another encoding, applies to literary criticism even more stringently than it does to ordinary spoken discourse. In ordinary spoken discourse the endless cycle of encoding – decoding – encoding may be terminated by an action, as when for instance I say, "The door is open" and you say, "Do you mean you would like me to shut it?" and I say, "If you don't mind", and you shut the door, we may be satisfied that at a certain level my meaning has been understood. But if the literary text says, "The door was open" I cannot ask the text what it means by saying that the door was open, I can only speculate about the significance of that door – opened by what agency, leading to what discovery, mystery, goal?

In other words, the fact that the author is absent when his message is received, unavailable for interrogation, lays the message, or text, open to multiple, indeed infinite interpretation. And this in turn undermines the concept of literary texts as communications. If Jane Austen's *Emma*, for instance, is a communication, what is its message? Hundreds of articles and chapters of books have been published, purporting to explain what that novel "means", what it is "about", and we can be sure that hundreds more will be published in the future. They all differ to a greater or lesser extent from each other in their conclusions and emphases; indeed if they did not differ there would be no need for more than one to be published. Does this mean that the message hasn't got across, that Jane Austen has somehow failed to communicate? This is the perennial paradox in which literary criticism finds itself implicated: that, as Michel Foucault observed:

> the commentary must say for the first time what had, nonetheless, already been said [by the original text] and must tirelessly repeat what had never been said [by other com-

mentators]. Commentary . . . allows us to say something other than the text itself, but on condition that it is the text itself which is said, and in a sense completed. ("The Order of Discourse")

The fact that we cannot identify the author of a text simply and straightforwardly with any of the discourses which make it up, especially in the polyphonic novel-text, and the fact that literary texts resist interpretive closure, has led some modern critics to deny that literature is communication. Rather they see it as *production* – the production of meaning by the text itself when activated by the reader. Roland Barthes again:

> The text is a productivity. This does not mean that it is the product of labour (such as could be required by a technique of narration and the mastery of style) but the very theatre of a production where the producer and reader of the text meet: the text "works", at each moment and from whatever side one takes it. Even when written (fixed) it does not stop working, maintaining a process of production. The text works what? Language. It deconstructs the language of communication, representation, or expression (when the individual or collective subject may have the illusion that he is imitating something or expressing himself) and reconstructs another language, voluminous, having neither bottom nor surface . . .

This is a forceful attack on not only the idea of literature as communication but also on the idea of communication itself. Note that communication is described as an "illusion" which literary language "deconstructs". Barthes is here influenced, no doubt, by the founder of deconstruction, Jacques Derrida, who argued that contrary to the traditional view that speech is the exemplary case of language in use, and writing an artificial substitute for speech, writing ought to be privileged because it exposes the fallacious metaphysics of presence, of the autonomy of the subject, which speech encourages.

Deconstruction marginalizes the author, or seeks to do away with the author altogether, replacing him or her with what Foucault called the "author-function", that is, a culturally and historically determined role over which the individual writer has no control. As we see from the passage quoted from Barthes, the work or labour that the writer puts into composing his text is brushed aside as of no importance. Rather it is the text that "works", and the text is not something that the author creates and hands over to the reader, but that the reader produces in the act of reading it – and by writing his own text about it. For the production-model of the literary text is a very academic one. It has its origin in the academic institution's need to justify the endless multiplication of commentaries, from undergraduate essays to doctoral dissertations and scholarly articles. It offers an escape from the double bind of commentary pithily summarized by Foucault in the passage I quoted just now. In this perspective there is no essential distinction between primary and secondary texts, between so-called creative and critical writing.

Most writers and readers of fiction outside the academy, it must be said, still subscribe to the communication model of the literary text. That is, they regard a novel as the creation of a particular human being, who has a particular vision of the world, which he or she tries to communicate to his or her readers by employing the codes of narrative and language in a particular way, and is responsible for the novel's success or failure in this regard, and deserves praise or blame accordingly. That is the basis on which most novels, including my own, are actually written, published and received in our culture.

As a practising novelist, my instinctive reaction is to repudiate the deconstructionist position. Barthes says the text is not "the product of a labour (such as could be required by a technique of narrative or a mastery of style)." I know empirically that a novel *is* the product of such labour. (So, I believe, were Barthes's own books, if we substitute "argument" for "narrative" in his formulation.) But is it a labour of communication? A major difficulty, here, is that the idea of communication is tied up with the idea of intention, and intention is a very tricky concept in literary criticism. It is fairly easy to demonstrate that the meaning of a text cannot be constrained by reference to a writer's intentions. Let me give a trivial but I hope interesting example from my own experience. In *Small World* the middle-aged English academic Philip Swallow has a wife called Hilary and has a passionate affair with a younger woman called Joy, who reminds him of his wife when she was younger and prettier – when he first meets her, Joy is even wearing a dressing gown like one Hilary used to wear. Reviewing the novel in the London *Times*, A. S. Byatt noted approvingly that this theme of identity and difference was neatly encapsulated in the names of the two women, Hilary being derived from the Latin *hilaritas*, or joy. Now I can be quite sure I had not intended this pleasing symmetry. I called Philip's wife Hilary in a previous novel, *Changing Places*, because it is an androgynous name and at that stage of their marriage she was the dominant partner in the marriage, or, as the saying is, wore the trousers. I called Joy Joy because when Philip falls in love with her he is in pursuit of what he calls "intensity of experience", an essentially Romantic quest with a capital R, and joy is a key word in Romanticism. At the moment of consummation, Philip shouts aloud the word "Joy", which is both exclamation and apostrophe. I had no conscious awareness of the Latin root of the name Hilary until Antonia Byatt pointed it out to me. Nonetheless the play on words is there in the text, and is appropriate. It seems a good case of what Barthes calls the text working.

Another difficulty with the idea of the novel as an intentional act of communication is that until the writer has completed it he doesn't know what it is that he is communicating, and perhaps doesn't know even then. You discover what it is you have to say in the process of saying it. However carefully and thoroughly you prepare the ground, you cannot possibly hold the whole complex totality of a novel in your head in all its detail at any one moment. You work your way through it word by word, sentence by sentence, paragraph by paragraph, trying to hold in your head some idea of the totality to which these bits are contributing. What you have written already and what you plan to write in the future are always open to revision, though such possible revisions will be constrained by their mutual effect on each other. The future of a novel in the process of composition is always vague, provisional, unpredictable – if it were not so, the labour of writing it would be too tedious to bear. When you have finished the novel it is not that you have really finished it, but that you have decided to do no more work on it. If you sat down and made another fair copy of the manuscript, you would infallibly find yourself making new adjustments and emendations to it. And when the novel is published and goes out of your control to modify it, it also goes out of your control to intend the meaning of it. It is read by different readers in a bewildering variety of ways, as reviews and readers' letters attest. Can this be described as a process of communication?

I think it can, as long as we realize the inadequacy of the simple linguistic model of communication (addresser–message –addressee) not only to literary discourse, but to any discourse. The model only works at the level of the textbook example, the single isolated sentence. But there are no isolated sentences in reality. Here we must reintroduce Bahktin. Language, according to Bakhtin, is essentially dialogic. Everything we say or write is connected both with things which have been said or written in the past, and with things which may be said or written in response to it in the future. The words we use come to us already imprinted with the meanings, intentions and accents of others, our speech is a tissue of citations and echoes and allusions; and every utterance we make is directed towards some real or hypothetical Other who will receive it. "The word in living conversation," says Bakhtin, "is directly, blatantly directed towards a future answer word. It provokes an answer, anticipates it and structures itself in the answer's direction."

The same is true of literary discourse, in a more complicated way. To write a novel is to manipulate several different codes at once – not simply the linguistic codes of grammar and lexis, denotation and connotation, but the narrative codes of suspense, enigma, irony, comedy and causality, to name but a few. To write a novel is to conduct imaginary personages through imaginary space and time in a way that will be simultaneously interesting, perhaps amusing, surprising yet convincing, representative or significant in a more than merely personal, private sense. You cannot do this without projecting the effect of what you write upon an imagined reader. In other words, although you cannot absolutely know or control the meanings that your novel communicates to its readers, you cannot *not* know that you are involved in an activity of communication, otherwise you will have no criteria of relevance, logic, cohesion, success and failure, in the composition of your fictional discourse. The generation of meaning unintended by the author, in the reading process, is dependent on a structure of intended meaning: the Hilary–Joy equivalence in *Small World*, for instance, is brought into play partly by the percipience of A. S. Byatt and partly by the fact that the novel is by intention full of doubles and pairs and symmetries and heavily connotative names. Perhaps I may conclude by repeating what I have written elsewhere:

> As I write, I make the same demands upon my own text as I do, in my critical capacity, on the texts of other writers. Every part of a novel, every incident, character, word even, must make an identifiable contribution to the whole . . . On the other hand (there is always another hand in these matters) I would not claim that, because I could explicate my own novel line by line, that is all it could mean, and I am well aware of the danger of inhibiting the interpretive freedom and of the reader by a premature display of my own, as it were, "authorized" interpretation. A novel is in one sense a game, a game that requires at least two players, a reader as well as a writer. The writer who seeks to control or dictate the responses of his reader outside the boundaries of the text itself, is comparable to a card-player who gets up periodically from his place, goes round the table to look at his opponent's hand, and advises him what cards to play. ("Small World: an Introduction"; in *Write On*, 1985.)

It might be profitable to pursue this idea further: the novel not as communication, not as production, but as play. But that would be another lecture.

PART TWO

Mixed Media

Novel, Screenplay, Stage Play: Three Ways of Telling a Story

This is the revised text of a lecture I have given on several occasions, in different versions. It serves as a general introduction to some of the essays which follow.

The dominant forms of fictional narrative in our culture are the novel, the stage play, and the motion picture (including television drama). What narrative properties are peculiar to each medium, and what are common? What makes a writer gravitate towards one rather than another? What prompts him or her to switch to another medium, and what do they discover in that process about the nature of narrative? In addressing these questions, I shall be drawing for illustration largely on my own experience, because it is the most convenient database for the purpose. I have been writing prose fiction for more than 30 years, and I think of myself primarily as a novelist. But some years ago I wrote a stage play, *The Writing Game*, which has had three professional productions, and over the same period I have adapted my novel *Nice Work*, and Dickens' *Martin Chuzzlewit*, and *The Writing Game*, for television. I have also had a long-standing interest in narrative as an academic literary critic, and in what follows I shall be making some use of literary theory as well. And I shall hazard some generalizations which are purely intuitive and speculative.

What makes a writer tend towards one narrative medium rather than another? Ultimately this is probably an unanswerable question, but we can surmise that the choice will be determined by a combination of factors: innate or genetic talent; personal temperament as formed by personal circumstances; and the wider cultural/historical/institutional context in which the writer operates.

To consider the last of these first: it is fairly obvious that if Shakespeare had been born in the nineteenth century instead of the sixteenth, he would have been a novelist rather than a dramatist, because the Victorian theatre was simply not capable of accommodating a creative genius of that order and allowing him to realize his expressive potential. A confirmation of that judgement is the case of Charles Dickens – a creative genius of comparable stature to Shakespeare, who became a great novelist, though his natural bent was towards the theatre. As is well known, Dickens was addicted to the theatre, loved to act in and produce amateur theatricals and charades, and finally killed himself by enormously successful, intensely theatrical public readings of his own work. In the Elizabethan age, he would certainly have been a dramatist rather than a novelist, and as it is his novels – especially the early ones – have a strongly theatrical quality.

Another example: the fact that so many British literary novelists have in the last two decades written original screenplays or screen adaptations of their own or other novelists' work – something very rare in the Fifties and Sixties – has a great deal to do with the expansion of the television networks and their hours of broadcasting, the opening up of British television to independent producers, the shift in taste from studio-based drama (essentially theatrical in its conventions) to the more novelistic, location-based filmed drama, and the success of Channel 4 as a prime commissioner of low-budget movies of artistic quality, provoking the other channels to compete in the same area. These developments created a market for screenplays that could not be satisfied by a relatively small cadre of professional TV playwrights like those who dominated the medium in the era of Play for Today.

Such external, material factors, beyond the individual writer's control, and sometimes below the threshold of his or her conscious awareness, obviously have an effect on individual careers. Equally obviously, their influence is not absolute or exclusive. Personal temperament and personal biography come into play. Most writers, I suspect, discover their vocation by imitation and emulation, by wanting to produce something like the effect they have experienced themselves as a result of reading or watching work that stirred and excited them. Most novelists were, in their formative years, great readers of novels; most playwrights had access to the theatre in childhood or youth. As to the determining effect of personal circumstances and temperament, this is much more difficult to gauge. From reading literary biographies it is my impression that novelists are very often people who were somewhat lonely and isolated in early life – either through being only children or through a confining illness – and were thus thrown back on the resources of fantasy and imagination that private reading affords. They tend to be introspective and depressive; they like to observe rather than participate; in the Freudian sense they are anal-retentive types, hoarders of information, jealously possessive about their work, often perversely reluctant to finish it and let it go. Playwrights, in contrast, are likely to be more extrovert, exhibitionist, gregarious, manic and oral.

It would be hard to draw the profile of the typical screenplay writer in the same way, partly because of the overlap of this role with that of director. People who have a natural bent towards making movies usually want to be directors, writing their own screenplays. Screenplay writers who are not directors rarely begin their careers as such, but move into it from some other kind of writing – novels or stage plays. In fact, these three forms – novel, stage play, screenplay – may be distinguished according to the diminishing degree of artistic control that the writer has over the work as it is received by the audience, and this is in turn related to the formal means they use to communicate.

The novelist's medium is almost exclusively language. I say "almost" because novels are sometimes illustrated, and commonly were in the nineteenth century, and today they usually have illustrative covers or dust jackets which presumably have some influence on the way the text is received. And I say "presumably" because I am not aware that any research has been done in this area, though a great deal of time and money and attention is expended on the design of book jackets in the publishing industry. It is certainly crucially important in the *marketing* of fiction. The buyers for big bookselling chains apparently place their orders for a new novel mainly on the look of the cover and the author's sales record, since they do not have time to read the books presented to them. Publishers may spend up to 20 per cent of the unit cost of a hardback novel on the jacket. The hope that a striking cover will attract the attention of the browsing punter in a crowded bookshop is probably well-founded. But whether the cover illustration actually affects the reader's *reading* of the text – whether *Nice Work*, for instance, is differently received when wrapped in Paul Cox's fluent watercolour of the hero and heroine's cars passing each other in a Rummidge street (Secker & Warburg hardback), when imprinted with Ian Boyd's decorative lettering, illuminated with industrial and academic motifs (first Penguin edition), or when bound with a photographic still of Warren Clarke and Haydn Gwynne in hard hats on the front (Penguin TV tie-in edition) is an unplumbed mystery.

In any case, this aspect of the novel's reception hardly affects its composition. Novelists may take a keen interest in the design of jackets for their novels (I certainly do) but normally only *after* the book has been written. The novelist's medium is the written word. One might almost say the printed word, since the novel as we know it was born with the invention of printing. Typically, the novel is consumed by a silent, solitary reader, who may be anywhere at the time – in bed, on the beach, in the bath, on a train or aeroplane. I even knew a man (British, of course) who in the 1950s used to read while he was driving across the great empty prairies of America. Nowadays he would have novels on audio-cassettes to listen to – a new form of storytelling that has become hugely popular in the age of the traffic jam. Whether these artefacts should be categorized as prose fiction or drama is a nice question that I haven't time to pursue here. The paperback novel is, however, still the cheapest, most portable and adaptable form of narrative entertainment. It is limited to a single channel of information – writing. But within that restriction it is the most versatile of narrative forms. It can go –

effortlessly – anywhere: into space, into people's heads, into their bodies, into palaces or prisons or pyramids, without any consideration of cost or practical feasibility such as the dramatist or screenplay writer has to take into consideration. It can be, if we include the short story under the general category of novel, virtually any length. In determining the shape and content of his narrative, the writer of prose fiction is constrained by nothing except purely artistic criteria.

This doesn't necessarily make his task any easier than that of the writer of plays and screenplays, who must always be conscious of practical constraints such as budgets, performance-time, casting requirements and so on. The very multiplicity and indeed infinity of choice enjoyed by the novelist is a source of anxiety and difficulty. But the novelist does retain absolute control over his text until it is published and received by the audience. He may of course be advised by his editor or others to make some revision of his text before it is published; a publisher may even make such revision a condition of publication. But if the writer refused to meet this condition, no one would be surprised. And it is not unknown for a well-established novelist to deliver his or her manuscript and expect the publisher to print it exactly as written, entertaining no editorial suggestions for revision, deletion or emendation. Not even the most well-established playwright or screenplay writer would submit a new script and expect it to be performed without any rewriting. This is because plays and motion pictures are collaborative forms of narrative, employing more than one channel of communication.

The production of a stage play involves, as well as the words of the author, the physical presence of the actors, their voices and gestures as orchestrated by the director, spectacle in the form of lighting and "the set", and possibly music. In film, the element of spectacle is more prominent, of course, in the sequence of visual images, heightened by various devices of perspective and focus (close-up, wide shot, telephoto, zoom, etc.), all controlled by the directing and editing process which imposes a uniform point of view on all the spectators. In film, too, music tends to be more pervasive and potent than in straight drama. So, although the script is the essential basis of both stage play and film, it is a basis for subsequent revision negotiated between the writer and the other creative people involved; and in the case of the screenplay the writer may have little or no control over the final form of his work. Contracts for the production of plays protect the rights of the author in this respect. He is given "approval" of the choice of director, and actors. He has the right to attend rehearsals and is usually paid his expenses for doing so. Often a good deal of rewriting takes place in the rehearsal period, and sometimes there is an opportunity for more rewriting during previews before the official opening night. The playtext is not usually printed and published until the acting script has been agreed by all concerned.

In film or TV work the screenplay writer usually has no contractual right to this degree of consultation or approval. Practice in this respect varies very much from one production company to another, and according to the nature of the project and the individuals involved. As a rule television, at least in Britain, is more friendly towards writers, and more apt to involve them in the production and post-production process, than feature films. A friend of mine who adapted his own novel for a feature film made in Hollywood was actually banned from the set on the ground that he was interfering too much.

In the case of *Nice Work* the director, Chris Menaul, made it clear that he didn't want me present throughout rehearsals. (This was probably because, inexperienced in these matters, I intervened over-enthusiastically at the first rehearsal I attended.) Instead he invited me in at the end of each day to watch a run-through of the scenes the actors had been working on and listened to my comments. I was welcome to observe as much of the shooting as I liked, but at this stage there is very limited opportunity for modifying the script or performances. Although I was also free to observe the fine-cut editing, the director and his editor had already worked out the basic selection and sequence of shots. And in the finished product there were many shots and sequences that were in effect new content, not in my screenplay, added by the director on his own initiative. (For example, Vic Wilcox, driving away from his "goodbye" scene with Robyn Penrose in somewhat melancholy mood, with Randy Crawford singing plangently of broken hearts on the car's hi-fi, suddenly becomes aware that he is entirely surrounded on the road by Riviera Sunbed vans belonging to the covert business venture of his moonlighting colleague Brian Everthorpe, and is so tickled by the absurdity of the situation that he bursts out laughing. This, the final image of Vic, gives a welcome lift of spirits to his character and the audience. Not only was this entirely Chris Menaul's idea, but I didn't even know he had planned it until I saw the rough cut of the final episode.)

In short, while the script is going through its various drafts the writer is in the driver's seat, albeit receiving advice and criticism from the producer and the director. But once the production is under way, artistic control over the project tends to pass to the director. This is a fact mysteriously overlooked by most journalistic critics of television drama, who tend (unlike film critics) to give all the credit or blame for success or failure of a production to the writer and actors, ignoring the crucial contribution, for good or ill, of the director. In the case of *Nice Work* I did feel occasional frustration and resentment at having artistic control taken out of my hands; however, I have to admit that in almost every respect the results justified the director's judgement.

In this area much depends on the authority and experience of the writer, and his relationship with the producer and the director, and the personalities of all of them. My own feeling is that if there isn't a certain amount of friction between them then the result will be uninspired; some conflict and debate and mutual criticism is healthy. On the other hand, unresolved disagreements can have an unhappy effect on the final product (see the discussion of the ending of *Martin Chuzzlewit* later in this volume). As writer, you may win an argument with your director about a particular scene in the script, but you can't make him shoot it with flair and conviction if he doesn't believe in it, so it's best to at least reach a compromise. No wonder that writers who work mainly in this medium usually end up wanting to direct their own work (e.g. Peter Barnes and the late Dennis Potter). On the other hand, there are obvious dangers in doing so – losing the creative tension of collaboration.

I want to turn now to a more abstract and theoretical consideration of the similarities and differences between these three narrative forms: novel, stage play, screenplay. My basic tool is the distinction made by the Russian Formalists between the *what* and the *how* of narrative, which they called the *fabula* and the *sjuzet*. The *fabula* is the raw material of the narrative –

the story as it would have been enacted by real people in real time and space; and the *sjuzet* is the representation of that action in a discourse – which may be a novel-discourse, a play-discourse or a film-discourse, or indeed some other kind of discourse. The *sjuzet* is always a motivated deformation of the *fabula*. That is to say, its selections, exclusions, rearrangements, and repetitions of the raw material of the *fabula* are what determine its meaning or import.

Take, for example, a story of adultery – any adultery. This will affect us differently according to whether it is presented from the point of view of the injured party or the guilty party or the third party; though in the *fabula*, as in real life, it would involve all three parties equally. The novelist might try to achieve this effect by presenting the adultery from all three points of view in succession, but in the *fabula* it would be happening simultaneously to all of them. The novelist might attempt to present the affair impartially from some omniscient fourth position, but in the *fabula*, as in reality, there is no such position – it is a literary convention, or an article of religious faith. And the story will affect us differently according to whether it unfolds chronologically (as in *Anna Karenina*) or in reverse order (as in Pinter's *Betrayal*) or in an order jumbled in the minds and memories of the participants, jumping between past, present and future (as in Graham Greene's *The End of the Affair*). And all these differences between *fabula* and *sjuzet* will be conditioned by the possibilities of the narrative medium – some of the choices I have described as open to the novelist are scarcely practicable in drama or film, and the reverse is also true.

The novel, for instance, is of all three the best equipped to represent thought, and therefore the subjectivity of experience. The devices of soliloquy and aside in drama, or of voice-over in film, are comparatively clumsy compared to the novelist's use of free indirect style* and interior monologue. Of course, resourceful dramatists and film-makers can find a way round the inherent constraints of their medium. Peter Nichols in his *Passion Play*, which is a story of adultery, has two actors and two actresses performing the two principal parts – one speaking the

---

* For an explanation of this term, see above, pp. 186–7.

character's actual utterances, the other, assumed to be invisible to the rest of the cast, speaking the character's private thoughts. In the film *Alfie* the philandering hero, played by Michael Caine, periodically turns to the camera and confides his thoughts and feelings directly to the audience in the form of an aside. But such devices are exceptional in drama and film – they are what Irving Goffman calls "frame-breaking" moves – whereas in the novel the reverse is true. In the novel we *expect* to have access to a character's thoughts and feelings, and if a novel remains resolutely on the surface, representing only speech and behaviour, with no interiority, as in Malcolm Bradbury's *The History Man*, and some of Muriel Spark's novellas like *The Driver's Seat* and *Not to Disturb*, a disturbing and alienating effect is created. It is in fact difficult *not* to present experience subjectively in the novel, and difficult therefore not to privilege the character from whose subjective point of view the action is dominantly presented. The dramatic form is much more impartial, and there is no authorial voice in the drama text which may betray a sympathy for one character over another. In two of my novels, *Changing Places* and *How Far Can You Go?*, I adopted a scenario form at the end to avoid declaring an authorial preference for one position out of several being presented in the text.

The plot of *Changing Places* is a highly stylized and symmetrical one, in which two professors of English, Philip Swallow of Rummidge University and Morris Zapp of Euphoric State, exchange jobs and to some extent their attitudes, habits and values. They also have affairs with each others' wives. In the final chapter, called "Ending", all four meet in a hotel in New York, halfway between the two fictitious campuses, to sort out their futures. When I began the novel I had no idea how I would end it, and as I approached the end I became reluctant to settle the story in favour of England or America, marriage or divorce, divorce with remarriage or divorce without it, or to discriminate between the different desires and needs of the four main characters. So I wrote the final chapter in the form of a film scenario in which every possible resolution of the story is discussed by the four characters, and none of them is privileged by any insight into their thoughts and feelings, or by the narrator's tone of voice – for there is no narrator. The scenario form also gave me a way of escape from choosing any one resolution of the plot, by exploiting the fact that an open or inconclusive ending is easier to accommodate in a film because the audience doesn't know when it's coming. The last words of the scenario are given to Philip:

> I mean, mentally, you brace yourself for the ending of a novel. As you're reading, you're aware of the fact that there's only a page or two left in the book, and you get ready to close it. But with a film there's no way of telling, especially nowadays, when films are much more loosely structured, much more ambivalent, than they used to be. There's no way of telling which frame is going to be the last. The film is going along, just as life goes along, people are behaving, doing things, drinking, talking, and we're watching them, and at any point the director chooses, without warning, without anything being resolved, or explained, or wound up, it can just . . . end.
>
> PHILIP *shrugs. The camera stops, freezing him in mid-gesture.*
> THE END

After point of view, time is probably the category in which there is most difference between *fabula* and *sjuzet* in the three media. Gérard Genette, in his *Discours du Récit*, breaks down the category of time in narrative discourse into three sub-categories: order, duration and frequency. I have already touched on chronological order and deviations from it in discussing possible treatments of an adultery story. By frequency, Genette means the relation between the number of times something happens in the *fabula* and the number of times it happens in the *sjuzet*. A good example is the fateful leap of Jim in Conrad's novel *Lord Jim* from the ship full of sleeping pilgrims which he thinks is just about to sink, an action which reveals a fatal flaw in his character and destroys his career as a merchant navy officer. This action is described again and again in the course of the book, as Jim tells his story in court, compulsively tells it to other people, and other narrators also discuss it. So although the jump only happens once in the *fabula*, it happens many times, as it were, in the *sjuzet*. The cinema can produce this effect very easily and powerfully by means of the flashback and the replay; the stage play perhaps less easily.

Duration concerns the relation between the putative length of time occupied by an action in the *fabula* and the time it occupies in the *sjuzet*, which may seem longer or shorter or roughly the same. Considered objectively, most narrative discourses are shorter in duration than the sequence of actions they represent, because of the deletion of large slabs of non-significant event, but in our experience of them there is considerable variation.

In the work of Henry James or Virginia Woolf, for instance, a simple conversational exchange will seem to be stretched out beyond normal duration because of the amount of introspection and analysis that is represented in the minds of the characters between their quoted speech. In Proust or Robbe-Grillet descriptions of simple actions read like slow-motion replays in films because of the meticulous detail with which they are rendered. In an adventure story, by contrast, the duration of events tends to be compressed to provide a constantly renewed state of jeopardy for the protagonist. In a film, though, moments of crisis (a man clinging by his fingertips to a ledge, for instance) may be drawn out in the editing to increase suspense. A lengthening of real time can be most easily achieved in film by using slow-motion, but this has a distancing effect for the viewer because it is "unrealistic" – it is a way of aestheticizing violence in the adventure film, for instance. Film can certainly produce the effect of an accelerated tempo in events – perhaps it can do this even better than the novel: by the simple device of the cut it can jump instantly from one critical point in time to another without the need to explain how the character got there, since all such explanation has a retarding effect. In fact it is doubtful whether any medium can match the movies for this kind of narrative excitement. Stage drama can of course cover a given *fabula* more or less quickly by varying the length of individual scenes, and by what it chooses to leave out. But while the characters are speaking a normative duration is imposed on the *sjuzet*. Speech spoken on the stage takes roughly the same time as speech spoken in reality, though it is usually much more "well-formed" grammatically and carries much more information, and a play inevitably consists mostly of speech.

There is another aspect to duration in the play and screenplay which Genette doesn't touch on, because he is exclusively concerned with prose fiction, and that is the total duration of the work in performance. This is a formal constraint on both stage play and screenplay which has enormous implications. A work of prose fiction can be more or less any length the writer chooses: as long as Vikram Seth's *A Suitable Boy* or as short as Ernest Hemingway's "A Very Short Story", which will fit on a single sheet of A4 typing paper. It can take minutes or days, even weeks, to read. A stage play, however, is hardly viable if it is more than four hours or less than an hour in performance, a feature film if it is more than two hours and a quarter or less than an hour and a half. A TV serial or "mini-series" can be anything from three to twelve hours long, and soaps can in theory go on for ever, but each episode must fit into a precisely measured time slot, prescribed by the broadcasting company that commissions it. Nineteenth-century novelists who wrote for initial publication in serial form were rather similarly placed to today's TV screenplay writers, for their instalments often had to fit exactly into pre-determined spaces in the magazines for which they wrote; but modern novelists don't have to worry about such matters. When they sit down to begin their novel they may have it in mind to write a short novel, but if the idea develops into a longer, more complex work than they envisaged they can carry on without any other consideration than the artistic possibilities of the subject. The playwright and the screenplay writer, however, are *always* acutely conscious of the time-frame within which they must fit their story, constantly having to weigh what they want to say (i.e. want their characters to say) against the time available to say it; and much revision of TV screenplay writing in particular is carried out not for reasons of dramatic effectiveness but to achieve a temporal target.

Again, however, the crucial role in fitting the filmic artefact into a precisely measured time-slot is that of the director and editor, rather than the writer. How long a given script will occupy in screen time is something the writer can only roughly estimate; it all depends on how the director shoots and edits it. Frequently the format of a serial is changed during or after actual production. In the case of both *Nice Work* and *Martin Chuzzlewit*, the serial as broadcast was much longer than stipulated in the contract for the script, and my carefully planned episode breaks were replaced by new ones engineered in the editing suite.

Prose fiction consists formally of scene and summary (or dialogue and description). Drama and film consist entirely of scene. Drama can incorporate summary in the form of report – like the long descriptions of events that happen offstage given by messengers in classical drama – but this seems to go against the grain of the film medium. A character's deposition in a court of law, for instance, if it is of any length, will usually fade into a flashback sequence in which the events are enacted, not verbally reported. In a film, everything that needs to be told ought to be shown, as a rule. In *Nice Work*, for instance, Robyn Penrose's attendance at the meeting of Asian shop stewards, at which she reluctantly retracts the assertion that caused the walkout from the foundry, is reported in a summary form by her to her boyfriend Charles, in the novel and also in my first draft screenplay. But the producer and director quite rightly asked me to present this scene dramatically.

This meant actually adding new material to the novel. But in general, because of the different status of duration in each medium, adapting novels for film or TV almost always involves a process of reduction, condensation and deletion, rather than expansion. This can be very frustrating for the writer, but it can also be illuminating. Working on the script of *Nice Work*, I was struck by how much of the dialogue and narrative description in a given scene in the novel I could dispense with, while still getting across the same point. This was even more striking in the case of *Martin Chuzzlewit*. This does not necessarily mean that the dialogue and description of the original were superfluous. It is a matter of the type of attention demanded of the audience by narrative in each medium, and a matter of the type of redundancy each employs.

I do not use the word "redundancy" here in the usual colloquial sense of material which is unnecessary, and which should be eliminated, but in a technical sense. In information theory, redundancy is the surplus of signal over message. Redundancy is essential to human communication because a message with zero redundancy would overload the receiver's capacity to assimilate the information. The repetitions, hesitations, interjections, self-glossing, etc., which characterize casual speech are *functional*. A prepared speech has less redundancy; a literary text still less; and they correspondingly demand more concentrated attention on the receiver's part. But they still contain a good deal of redundancy, and must do so. In a novel such redundancy would include, for instance, the repeated allusion to certain traits by which characters are identified and distinguished from each other, and speech tags like "he said" and "she said". Strictly speaking a character trait needs to be described only once, but it assists comprehension if we are constantly reminded of it. And usually we can infer who is speaking in a scene of dialogue from the content and the layout on the page, but speech tags make reading easier.

Stage drama, which consists mostly of speech, imitates and reproduces the redundancy of real speech with various degrees of stylization. In some modern dramatists, e.g., Beckett and Pinter, this is taken to an extreme, so that the dialogue seems to consist almost entirely of redundant language, whose function is purely phatic (merely establishing contact between the two speakers), leaving us in the dark as to what is being communicated (see the essay on Pinter below).

In film, it seems to me, redundancy is mainly on the level of the image. We are shown much more of the landscape of the Western, for example, than we strictly need for the articulation of the narrative. In a film of modern urban life, we see more of people moving through time and space – driving a car, walking down a street – than we strictly need to follow the story. Such sequences are like the repetition of character traits or the speech tags of prose fiction. The pictures tell us what we already know – that this girl is young and vital, that this man is middle-aged and affluent – they fill up the gaps between moments of significant action, they provide intermittent relief from the bombardment of narrative information. And just because this redundancy is built into the cinematic image, cinematic *dialogue* can afford less redundancy. The more repetition, expansion, checking back by the interlocutors, self-glossing, etc., there is in filmic dialogue, the more artificial and tedious it is likely to seem, because we will be getting redundancy on two channels at once.

In adapting a novel for the screen there is a natural

temptation to dramatize the information supplied by narrative description in the original text by turning it into dialogue, but this is generally to be resisted. Where possible it should be translated into action, gesture, imagery. Much of it can be dispensed with altogether. The novel, at least in the realist tradition, is bound by a code of plausibility based on cause and effect; and since the reader is in control of his reception of the text – can stop and ponder and re-read and check back – this code requires a great deal of explanation, covering of contingencies, anticipation of the reader's objections, etc. Much of this apparatus is unnecessary in film: first, because films don't give their viewers time to think through the logical implications of what is shown, and partly because the presentation of events in them sweeps away the audience's scepticism by its vividness and immediacy. (The videorecorder does of course give the viewer the same control over film as the reader has over a book, but using the pause and reverse buttons is much less natural, much more disruptive of the aesthetic experience of film, than stopping and referring back in reading a book.)

What makes a writer who has specialized in one narrative form experiment with another? What, for example, makes a novelist turn his hand to adapting novels for television, or try writing a stage play? There may be all kinds of reasons, some aesthetic, some materialistic. Writing screenplays is a useful source of supplementary income for a novelist (though writing for television is not particularly well-paid), and undoubtedly a successful TV serial will boost the sales of the novel on which it is based and sometimes the author's other work. Speaking for myself, these were welcome effects of my involvement in television adaptation, but not the essential motivation for it.

In 1985 I sold the TV rights in *Small World* to Granada, and observed the long and complex process of "development", production and post-production which eventually brought it to the screen as a six-part serial in 1988. I didn't feel that I had the time available, or indeed the appropriate experience, to propose adapting the novel myself, and that task was ably undertaken by Howard Schuman. But I was shown the scripts in various drafts, and invited to comment on them, and welcomed to attend rehearsals and make suggestions to Howard and the director, Bob Chetwyn. I got to know the actors, and enjoyed talking to them about the project and in due course I observed some of the actual filming. In short, I became fascinated by the whole business of movie-making and determined to get creatively involved myself at the next opportunity. After abortive attempts to adapt *Out of the Shelter* and *How Far Can You Go?* I finally had the satisfaction of seeing *Nice Work* through to a successful production. This experience coincided with my decision to retire from academic life and become a full-time writer. In many ways the collaborative activity of making television drama has replaced the collegiate activity of university teaching in my life. Both yield satisfactions, and frustrations, that are absent from the solitary and individualistic activity of novel-writing. This is even more true of writing and producing a stage play, for reasons already suggested.

All my ventures into television drama to date have been adaptations of stories – my own or other writers' – that already exist in another form. The challenge is to find ways of translating the story from one medium to another, balancing the claims of the original to be "faithfully" rendered against the aesthetic requirements and possibilities of the new medium. It is essentially work of a technical, problem-solving kind – creative up to a point, but not as taxing and anxiety-making as writing something from scratch. My stage play, *The Writing Game*, was an original work, like my novels (though later I had the interesting experience of adapting it for television). It concerns the relationships of three writers who are tutors on a short residential course for creative writing students – relationships of sexual and professional power, possession and rivalry. The play originated in the experience of teaching such a course myself – not because its plot bears any resemblance to what happened on that course, but because it struck me that the bare situation possessed the classic dramatic unities of time, place and action. Indeed it would be true to say that I invented the plot of my play to fulfil the dramatic possibilities inherent in the situation.

Another source of the play was my experience over the last decade or so of reading my work in public, at literary festivals, bookshop signings and similar meet-the-author events which have become such a ubiquitous feature of the marketing of fiction in the last fifteen years or so. There is an element of performance in these occasions which I thought would lend itself to incorporation in a play, and provide a way of dramatizing what seems inherently undramatic: the normally silent and private business of writing and reading prose fiction. In the course of *The Writing Game*, each of the three writers reads from their work to the audience – who stand in, as it were, for the circle of students who are supposed to be listening. I couldn't of course have any of my characters read a whole short story or a substantial chapter, as they would have done in real life, since three such readings would take up most of the time available for the whole play; so devices had to be found to limit the duration of the three readings by interruptions or unexpected curtailments of various kinds, which themselves motivated further developments in the plot. This is a good example of how the practical constraints of dramatic form fundamentally affect the narrative content of the drama.

A more detailed account of the pleasures and pains of writing for the theatre will be found below. I conclude by mentioning two aspects of writing drama (whether for the stage or screen) which are absent from the novel, and may tempt the novelist out of the workshop inside his head where he has complete control. One is the extra dimension of feeling and suggestion that can come from performance – the thrilling discovery that your words had more potential expressivity than you were aware of yourself. The second is the possibility of simultaneous communication on several different channels. For all its versatility and flexibility, writing only works on one channel – one word, or word-group, at a time. Even in registering a pun we cannot receive both meanings exactly at the same time. When reading a novel, we cannot take in a line of dialogue and simultaneously observe the reaction of the person it is addressed to. We cannot fuse the description of the hero *and* of the sunset into which he rides into a single instanteous image, let alone hear the strains of appropriate music at the same time. But a play or a film, when it works well, can achieve that rich synaesthesia, and for the writer that seems worth a certain sacrifice of artistic autonomy and control.

Adapting *Nice Work*
for Television

I finished writing my novel *Nice Work* early in 1988. Not long
before, I had made the acquaintance of Chris Parr, a TV drama
producer based at the BBC's Birmingham Centre, Pebble Mill,
working under Michael Wearing, an executive producer with a
distinguished track record especially in the field of realistic,
socially relevant drama series like *The Boys From The Black Stuff*
and *Blind Justice*. They expressed an interest in my writing
something "regional and topical" for production at Pebble Mill.
I told them I had the very thing, and gave them the typescript of
Nice Work. They liked it, and after one meeting, in April 1988,
commissioned me to write the screenplay. Unusually, the
contract was for the complete script, and did not stipulate
approval of a treatment or first episode. This was an encouraging act of faith in a writer with no proven ability to write a
screenplay (none of my few previous attempts had made it into
production), and a warrant of their serious commitment to the
project. But there was a pragmatic reason for proceeding as
quickly as possible: we all recognized that it was important to
broadcast the TV version of the novel while its picture of
Thatcher's Britain was still recognizable, and the winter-spring
calendar of the story meant that the serial would have to go into
production by the following February, or be postponed for
another year. I had, therefore, to produce the complete script by
the end of 1988, But I did not begin work immediately. I waited

until I had corrected the proofs of the novel and seen the revises, so that the text was irrevocably fixed, before beginning the screenplay. It was as if the story was having two different "lives", and I wanted the first to be over, as far as I was concerned, before the second one began.

The most important single component of a TV writer's brief is the temporal format of the drama, especially if it is a serial. No narrative form is as precisely timed as an episode of a TV series. When transmitted, it must fit a preordained slot measured in minutes and even seconds. Such precision can only be achieved in the editing, rather than in the writing process; but the writer must turn in a script that will fit the programming slot at least approximately. This is an exceedingly difficult matter to judge, especially for a beginner; and the rule-of-thumb that a page of script equals a minute of screen-time is a very rough guide indeed.

With a serial there is the additional problem of dividing up the whole narrative into a number of blocks of equal duration, each of which will have a satisfying dramatic structure and end with some kind of "lure" (to borrow Roland Barthes' term) to encourage the audience to watch the next episode. The production of *Nice Work* was hampered, and perhaps ultimately impaired, by exasperating changes of mind concerning its format by the powers in the BBC who determine these matters.

At my initial meeting with Chris Parr and Mike Wearing, Mike suggested a format of two parts of 75 minutes each. By the time the contract was drawn up, this duration had been redistributed as three episodes of 50 minutes. Later it was expanded to three episodes of 60 minutes; and, after much cutting and rewriting, that was the form in which I delivered the "final" script in December 1988, and the form in which it was subsequently typed up as a rehearsal script. In the course of filming* the director, Christopher Menaul, became increas-

---

* Strictly speaking, I should say "recording", since *Nice Work* was made on videotape, not celluloid. There are differences between these two media and the techniques that go with them which are of great interest to professionals, but they have little bearing on the concerns of this essay. The director used a single video camera, connected to an Outside Broadcasting van on location, much as a movie director uses a film

ingly concerned that he would end up with too much material to fit into three hours. This was partly the consequence of his own highly creative visual imagination, which was continually adding effects not envisaged or required by the script.

During production he pressed Chris Parr to ask the higher echelons of the BBC for permission to divide the series into four episodes of fifty minutes each, giving us an additional twenty minutes in all, but the word always came back: no, 3 x 60 minutes is what it has to be. In consequence, already pushed for time, the two Chrisses decided to cut or abbreviate several scenes in the screenplay – scenes which everybody concerned liked very much – because they were quite certain that they would not be able to include them. Some small adjustments to other scenes were required by these cuts.

A few days after shooting had finished, and the actors and crew had irretrievably dispersed, the word came from London that, after all, a series of four episodes of 50 minutes was required – shortly afterwards expanded to 4 x 55 minutes (in which form it was eventually transmitted). In Birmingham we had mixed feelings about this *volte-face*. On the one hand we were delighted to have the additional thirty minutes of screen time, because it was already evident, from the early editing, that much of what had been recorded would have had to be drastically cut to fit a 3 x 60 format. On the other hand what we had in the can only just filled the newly available time, and it was bitterly frustrating to think of the scenes we had needlessly sacrificed. In particular I mourn the loss of (1) a scene (not in the novel) in which Charles refuses to accompany Robyn to Sunday lunch at the Wilcoxes – his first rebellion against the force of her will in their relationship, a relationship which could have done with a bit more detail in the TV version; (2) a sequence in the swimming pool and gym of the German hotel where Vic and Robyn have their brief affair, which would have made this development seem a little less abrupt; (3) a scene in which Vic, changing out of his business suit on returning home in the late afternoon, absent-mindedly puts on his pyjamas and gets into bed – a scene both amusingly expressive of his

camera, and although the editing processes for each method are technically different, they use the same "grammar".

emotionally traumatized state and one that would have provided a smooth transition to the nightmare sequence that immediately follows in the TV serial.

One consequence of the last-minute change of format, of course, was that my carefully worked-out climaxes for episodes One and Two had to be scrapped, and three new episode-endings created in the editing room. There is a scene in the second episode as transmitted where Robyn is in bed with Charles, who challenges her about returning to the factory; if the acting and direction seem a little over-emphatic here it is because this was originally going to be the final scene of episode One. My episode Two had ended with Robyn in bed with Vic in Germany, saying "I prefer to be on top." Now it ended rather inconclusively with Vic and Robyn returning from their walk after Sunday lunch, followed by a wordless sequence in which Vic drives to work listening dreamily to Jennifer Rush singing "The Power of Love". At Chris Menaul's request, I wrote some additional dialogue in which Robyn urges Vic to address the workforce at the factory about his rationalization plans, thus providing a link to the first scene of the next episode, and the principal actors were recalled to record these lines, which were dubbed over a rear-view shot of them re-entering the Wilcox house. There were, it has to be said, some dramatic gains from the reformatting of the series. The superbly acted morning-after scene in Germany, for instance, is all the more effective for coming immediately after the scene in bed the night before, rather than separated by an episode-break.

The German part of the story provided perhaps the most striking example of how external circumstances can affect the form and content of a television drama. In the novel, Vic Wilcox goes to a trade exhibition in Frankfurt to buy an expensive machine tool for his foundry, taking with him his Industry Year "shadow", Robyn Penrose. Through her knowledge of German, she protects him from some rather sharp practice by the German businessmen with whom he is dealing, and this action precipitates their brief affair. Very early in the process of turning *Nice Work* into a TV serial – before, indeed, the contract with the BBC was even signed – Chris Parr and I had what we thought was an amazing piece of luck in this connection: we discovered that the principal foundry trade show in Europe, which is only mounted once every four years, was to be held in Düsseldorf in May 1989, exactly the time when we would want to shoot the German scenes in *Nice Work*. The organizing body, GIFA, readily agreed to let us film inside the exhibition. A participating company agreed to let us use their stand. I accordingly wrote the screenplay showing Vic and Robyn, as in the novel, making their way through a crowded hall in which massive machines are in simulated operation. It promised to be a spectacular scene of a kind which couldn't possibly be faked. It seemed too good to be true, and it was.

In February 1989, when *Nice Work* was already in production, alarm bells rang. Someone had sent to Germany the script, not only of the scenes in the Exhibition hall, but also of a subsequent scene in a restaurant, in which the German businessmen are shown trying to pull the wool over Vic's eyes about the specification of the machine he is seeking to buy from them. GIFA had immediately withdrawn their permission to film, not only inside, but anywhere near the show, on the grounds that we were portraying German businessmen in a dishonourable light.

We pleaded that our film also showed British businessmen indulging in deception – but to no avail. We appealed to GIFA's sense of humour: it didn't apparently exist. Desperately we offered to make the offending characters German-speaking Swiss. No dice. In the end I had to rewrite the episode so that Vic visits a German *factory* to appraise and purchase his automatic core-moulder. There was no time to find a suitable factory in Germany. The location we used was a factory in Stourbridge that made core-moulders under licence (another irony here, since I thus discovered that in reality Vic wouldn't have had to travel to Germany to buy his machines). German-language notices were put up on the walls, and German actors imported to take part in the scene. Strenuous efforts were made to tidy up the factory floor, though it still, I'm afraid, fell well short of normal German standards in this respect. Visually, the scene was much less spectacular than the one I had originally envisaged in my screenplay. But dramatically, I believe it was an improvement. Deprived of spectacle, the scene had to be more carefully researched and imaginatively written. The technical discussions were more convincing in the new scene and the comedy of Robyn's pretending to be Vic's dumb Rummidge bimbo was much enhanced. It also helped that by the time I wrote the new scene I had observed the actors, Warren Clarke and Haydn Gwynne, working together in rehearsals, and had a good idea of how brilliantly they would perform it.

Turning a novel into a film, even a serial film several hours long, is inevitably mostly a matter of condensation rather than expansion. This is because, very simply, it usually takes longer to perform an action, including a speech act, than it does to read a written report of the same action. But there is another reason, which I explained in the preceding essay: novels contain a great deal of information that is superfluous in film, because the presentation of events in the latter hardly allows the spectator time to analyse their plausibility, and sweeps aside scepticism by its vividness and immediacy. The fundamental narrative device of film (one which modern novelists have of course borrowed and exploited) is the cut, which moves the story instantly from one spatio-temporal context to another without explanation.

I can perhaps illustrate these points, and the essentially collaborative nature of making television drama, by describing the evolution of the first part of the first episode of the televised *Nice Work*. Readers of the novel may recall that the first chapter consists of a leisurely description of Vic Wilcox waking on Monday 13 January 1986, getting up, getting dressed, having breakfast, and driving to work, combined with a fairly detailed account of his biography and family background. Chapter Two does the same for Robyn Penrose, as she gets up and goes to the University on the same morning; and reference is made in it to a one-day strike of University staff, planned for the following Wednesday, in which Robyn intends to take part. Chapter Three describes the activities of these two characters at their respective workplaces later the same day, alternating between the University and the factory, and also introduces, via the character of Philip Swallow, the Shadow Scheme which will bring them together. At the end of the day, both are pressured into participating in the scheme, which is due to start the following Wednesday. Vic is mistakenly informed that his shadow is a male "Robin".

These three chapters make up Part One of the novel, covering Day One of Week One of the action, which is also the first week of the University term. Chapter 1 of Part Two picks up the story ten days later, on the Wednesday of Week Two, when Robyn makes her first visit to the factory. The reader learns that she postponed her visit for a week because she would have been "strike-breaking" if she had gone on the Wednesday of Week One. On this second Wednesday, she is delayed by a heavy snowfall. When she finally arrives, Vic recognizes her as a participant in a demonstration outside the University gates that delayed him on his way to work the previous Wednesday. This provokes a discussion about the strike which sets them at odds at the outset of their acquaintance.

At the first moment of thinking about adapting *Nice Work* for the screen I decided to use the essentially cinematic cross-cutting device of my third chapter at the very beginning of the screenplay. Episode One therefore begins with a sequence of short scenes alternately set in Vic's house and Robyn's house, showing them getting up and preparing for the day's work at roughly the same time. In the novel, the processes of washing and dressing afforded opportunities for detailed descriptions of the physical appearance of each character, but in the TV version this information is of course continuously transmitted by every shot in which the actors appear. Conversely, the detailed biographical data provided about the characters in the novel had to be reduced to a few vital pieces of information that could be spoken or shown. This led me to have Robyn's boyfriend, Charles, present in the first scenes of the screenplay (in the novel he has returned the previous evening to his own University of Suffolk) to show rather than report their relationship, and to provide an interlocutor for Robyn.

My first draft screenplay followed the sequence of events of Day One in the novel; but it then showed in chronological order what was reported retrospectively (via the interiorized rendering of Robyn's consciousness and Vic's consciousness) in Part Two of the novel: her participation in the AUT demonstration outside the University on the Wednesday of Week One, which delayed him on his way to work. And in the screenplay I sent her to the factory later that same day. I simply dropped her scruple about strike-breaking, and made her picket duty the reason for her being late for her appointment with Vic. This moved the story on more quickly. It also provided a convenient explanation for her lateness to replace the snowstorm in the original novel (since it would have been prohibitively expensive to cover all the relevant locations with artificial snow).

The change had important consequences for the effect of the narrative when Robyn finally arrives at the factory. What is an enigma in the novel (Vic feels he has seen Robyn somewhere before, but cannot immediately remember where or when) becomes an irony in the screenplay (the viewer will have already seen Robyn on the picket line that delays him). There is an additional irony in the picket-line scene itself, since the viewer knows, as neither character does, that their fates are already entwined through the Shadow Scheme.

Chris Parr's reaction to the first draft screenplay of Episode One was generally encouraging, but he said it was too long, and too leisurely in following the main characters as they got up and went to work on the first morning of the action. He suggested using a split screen to present some of these scenes simultaneously. This seemed like a good idea, which I implemented in a second draft. (Later it was dropped, and split screen was used instead for some of the many telephone conversations in the story.) I also made some cuts, but essentially the second draft of the episode was structurally the same as the first.

While I was working on Episodes Two and Three, Chris Menaul was appointed as director, and at another conference about the script of Episode One he suggested that the AUT demonstration should happen on Day One of the action, so that Robyn gets up and goes straight to the picket line, which delays Vic on his way to work. In this way the ideological opposition between the two main characters is established dramatically in the first five or six minutes of the film. Instead of just ironically juxtaposing them, the screenplay now showed them in conflict or potential conflict. This was neatly underlined by Chris Menaul's direction of the scene when it was finally shot: Robyn approaches Vic's car with a leaflet, and almost speaks to him, before she is distracted by a cheer from her fellow-pickets.

These changes, however, entailed others. If the University

Staff were on strike on Day One, then the Shadow Scheme could not be discussed and settled on that day. So Robyn's interviews with Swallow about her job and about the Shadow Scheme, and other University scenes, were postponed to Day Two, along with several scenes in the factory. In the novel Robyn and her colleague Bob Busby have an argument with Swallow about the efficacy of the strike on Day One, before it happens. This was incorporated in the film by having Swallow challenged by Busby and Robyn as he drives through the picket line – again, a more dramatic handling of the topic.

These changes were a huge gain in cinematic terms, but they entailed some improbabilities which would have been unacceptable to me in a novel. First of all, they violate the facts of history. The novel makes reference to many current events, taken from the newspapers of the day, and the realism I was aiming at in it is partly created by the documentary accuracy of this dimension of the story. There actually was an AUT one-day strike on Wednesday 15 January 1986. It is highly unlikely in any case that the AUT would ever hold a demonstration on the first day of term – it would be too difficult to organize. The one-day strike was a national event, raising the question of why Charles is lingering in Rummidge instead of taking part in the strike at his own University. I solved that one by making the Rummidge strike a local day-of-action. Some of my university colleagues may have been bothered by these implausibilities and inconsistencies, but I am quite sure that the vast majority of the audience will not have been bothered by them, or even noticed them.

Condensation – cutting out superfluous material, accelerating the tempo of events – and dramatization – translating narration and represented thought into speech, action and image: these are the fundamental tasks of the adapter. But it is not always easy, especially for the author of the original novel, to see what is essential and what is not. It seemed to me, for instance, that the episode in which Robyn goes to Sunday lunch at the Wilcoxes, and afterwards for a walk through the university halls of residence with Vic, was not essential to the development of the plot, and so I cut it out of my first draft screenplay, in order to save time. The two Chrisses persuaded me to put it back –

and of course they were absolutely right: it is one of the most effective scenes in the whole serial, expressing, through beautifully played comedy of manners, all the conflicts and contrasts between the various generations and classes portrayed in the story. One of Vic's children, his daughter, did however disappear in the course of the various rewrites. Her part became so abbreviated by the exigencies of overall timing that we thought it was better to cut her out of the story altogether. Robyn's friend, Penny, also disappeared. Her function as confidante, useful in the novel, seemed unnecessary in the screenplay and made for rather static scenes. One such scene in the first draft screenplay had Robyn reading out to Penny extracts from Charles's letter announcing his intention of becoming a merchant banker. This was my attempt to "dramatize" the letter in the original novel. Letters, so at home in prose fiction (some of the earliest classic novels were written in the form of letters), are apt to seem clumsy devices in films about modern life. At the prompting of the two Chrisses, I wrote a new scene in which Charles waylays Robyn at the University to announce his change of career and make a proposal of marriage (the subjects of two separate letters in the novel). This is much more effective visually and dramatically. We see Charles in his sleek yuppie suit, already transformed from the rumpled don of the earlier scenes. His special pleading and Robyn's response are acted out in terms of her getting into her car and driving away, resisting his attempts to detain her or follow her.

Adapting *Nice Work* consisted mostly of reducing and reworking material in the original novel. A few new scenes were added, however, not just to solve problems created by the processes of condensation, but to convey additional meaning. These were the dream sequences, in which Vic sees Robyn transformed into the figure of the goddess Diana. The origin of these scenes in the novel was a passage describing Vic's thoughts, as he sits in his office one evening after an excursion with his "shadow". She has just revealed to him that she has a lover (Charles) and he finds himself surprisingly disturbed by this information.

She was the most independent woman he had ever met, and

this had made him think of her as somehow unattached and – it was a funny word to float into his mind, but, well, *chaste*.

He recalled a painting he had seen once at the Rummidge Art Gallery on a school outing – it must have been more than thirty years ago, but it had stuck in his memory, and arguing with Shirley the other day about nudes had revived it. A large oil painting of a Greek goddess and a lot of nymphs washing themselves in a pond in the middle of a wood, and some young chap in the foreground peeping at them from behind a bush. The goddess had just noticed the Peeping Tom, and was giving him a really filthy look, a look that seemed to come right out of the picture and subdue even the schoolboys who stared at it, usually all too ready to snigger and nudge each other at the sight of a female nude. For some reason the painting was associated in his mind with the word "chaste", and now with Robyn Penrose. He pictured her to himself in the pose of the goddess – tall, white-limbed, indignant, setting her dogs on the intruder.

This is very characteristic "novel-discourse", the interiorized rendering of a character's thoughts, using free indirect style, and a very literary kind of irony at Vic's expense, appealing over his head to the educated reader to supply the missing information that explains why Vic associates Robyn with chastity and with the painting: the subject of the painting was Diana, the goddess of chastity, something he was told by his teacher but has forgotten. The technique of the passage is antithetical to film and has no essential narrative function in the book. It did not occur to me to try and incorporate it into my screenplay. But Chris Menaul, at a fairly late stage in the evolution of the screenplay, was still looking for some way of expressing the turmoil of Vic's inner emotional life as he becomes romantically infatuated with Robyn, and he saw this passage as a possible key: in dream and reverie Vic could picture Robyn as Diana, the chaste, forbidden, angry, unobtainable object of his desire. His actual acts of voyeurism – spying on her through the peephole when she first arrives at the factory, and involuntarily glimpsing her naked breast when he first calls at her house – provoke visions in which he re-enacts watching Diana bathing with her nymphs and is pursued by the huntress and her hounds. As the

BBC at Pebble Mill had considerable resources for studio-based set-design and special effects, which were not otherwise bespoken at the time, Chris Menaul was able to stage these scenes on a lavish scale. A large warm-water pond, complete with waterfall, was constructed in order to produce a *tableau vivant* of Titian's famous picture of Diana surprised by Acteon. Lasers were used to cast an eerie light over Haydn Gwynne's impersonation of Diana as huntress, in the other Titian painting of this mythical story.

The main problem for me as screenplay writer was how to convey to the audience the reason for the associations between Robyn and Diana in Vic's mind. These associations could be mysterious up to a point, but eventually they would have to be explained. The solution I arrived at, in discussion with Chris Menaul, was to have a flashback scene in which Vic recalls himself as a boy looking at the painting in the Rummidge Art Gallery, then another scene set in the present in which he revisits the gallery to track down the picture and overhears an art historian lecturing some students about it, relating the myth of Diana. A large painting in the style of Titian, in which Diana bears a faint resemblance to Haydn Gwynne, was produced by the Pebble Mill design team, and the gallery of the Royal Birmingham Society of Artists was hired for the two scenes.

When the series was well into production, Chris Menaul asked me to write some additional lines for the art lecturer to cover the camera movements he had planned for the second of these scenes. I promised to do so, but there was some confusion about the deadline. One morning, just as I was leaving my house to go to London, I received a phone call from Chris Menaul at the Art Gallery, saying he was about to start shooting the scene and hadn't got the extra material. I raced down to the Art Gallery where, standing in the lobby in my raincoat, I wrote several lines of art-historical jargon about the nude and voyeurism and the male gaze, using a ball-point pen and the back of a discarded page of script, before rushing off to catch my train to London. Whatever the quality of the lines (actually, I thought they came across rather well in performance), writing a novel was never so exciting.

Adapting *Martin Chuzzlewit*

In the late summer of 1992, I had a phone call from Chris Parr, who had produced the TV serial of *Nice Work* for the BBC in Birmingham four years earlier. That had been a happy experience, and we both hoped to work together again one day. A couple of ideas had been floated, but sank for one reason or another. One was *Dombey and Son*, which the BBC drama department thought had been done too recently to justify a new version. Now Chris was calling to propose a serial adaptation of Dickens' *Martin Chuzzlewit*. He had taken the novel with him to America, where he was working on another project that summer, and was enthusiastic about its potential as a TV serial. It had some of Dickens' greatest characters in it, notably Pecksniff and Mrs Gamp. Furthermore, he told me, it had never been adapted before. I told Chris that I would read the novel immediately, and give him an answer.

Although I am a great admirer of Dickens, and taught a "special option" on his novels at Birmingham University, and wrote scholarly articles about them, it so happened that *Martin Chuzzlewit* was, at that date, the only one that I had never read – partly because it is not very highly rated by modern critics of Dickens and seldom studied in English Literature courses. Though this omission is somewhat embarrassing to confess, I think it was an advantage to me as a potential adapter to approach the book with no preconceptions. It helped me see more clearly what elements in it would and would not work in dramatic terms, and to identify what would be most interesting and appealing to a modern television audience, most of whom would also be encountering the story for the first time. My overall assessment of the novel was that despite its prolixity and structural flaws (it perfectly illustrates Henry James's characterization of the typical Victorian novel as "a large, loose, baggy monster") it was full of wonderful things, and that these were precisely the things which would lend themselves most readily to adaptation. I was particularly attracted by the comic element in the novel, which is generated by the speech and interaction of the characters rather than by the style of the narrator. Dickens' authorial voice – sardonic, prophetic, and inventively metaphorical – is the dominant one in novels like *Dombey & Son, Hard Times, Bleak House* and *Little Dorrit,* giving the adapter a hard choice between sacrificing this level of meaning altogether or retaining it through the use of a "voice-over" narrator, which can so easily seem clumsy and intrusive. (The same problem is presented by most classic nineteenth-century novels.) In *Martin Chuzzlewit,* however, it seemed to me, apart from a few set-pieces like the description of Todgers' and its environs, or Tom Pinch's coach-ride to London, the authorial voice was not as prominent and important as it usually is in Dickens. The narrator uses his omniscience sparingly. Instead of making explicit judgements of the characters, or telling us what they are thinking and feeling, he allows them to reveal themselves by their actions, and above all by their words: the good characters (e.g. Tom Pinch, Mary Graham, Mark Tapley) by the transparent sincerity of their speech, and the morally flawed characters (e.g. Pecksniff, Tigg Montague, Mrs Gamp) by their reliance on specious rhetoric. Nowhere in Dickens' *oeuvre* is the essentially theatrical nature of his genius so clearly evident. There were many scenes in the novel, it seemed to me, that could be performed almost as written; and at least a dozen juicy roles of the kind that British actors excel in playing.

I also perceived that, as classic novels go, it contained little action that would be difficult and very expensive to film, apart from the American episodes, most of which would have to be cut anyway on grounds of dramatic and narrative irrelevance. Nearly all the essential action of *Chuzzlewit* takes place in an English country village (of which there are many comparatively unspoiled examples available for location filming) or on the open road, or in London, and many of the most important London scenes take place indoors. Television is not suited to epic drama with big spectacular scenes such as battles and crowds: the screen is too small to do them justice, and the budgets are too small to do them convincingly. (There was a legendary BBC production of *A Tale of Two Cities* in which the storming of the Bastille was done with twelve extras.) The most characteristic forms of TV drama – those peculiar to the medium, like soaps and sitcoms – consist largely of people talking to each other in small spaces; and so, it seemed to me, did most scenes in *Martin Chuzzlewit*. I noted only one big spectacular scene that was indispensable – when Jonas Chuzzlewit embarks with Mercy on a cross-channel steamer at the Thames embankment – and I thought we could probably manage that (rightly, as it turned out: it was convincingly designed and shot at Gloucester docks). These were important considerations. They meant that one could make a TV version of Dickens' novel that would not seem, even to Dickensians, a travesty or pale shadow of the original. I called Chris Parr to say yes.

It was not an easy or lightly taken decision. I was getting ready to start a new novel (*Therapy*) and I knew that undertaking *Chuzzlewit* would delay the completion of that book, one way or another, by six months. But I couldn't resist the opportunity and the challenge. One of the attractions was certainly the thought of being the first adapter to bring this rich and vital work by one of the great geniuses of English literature to a mass audience. This however turned out to be a misapprehension, based on wrong information given to Chris Parr: there had in fact been a BBC "Sunday afternoon serial" version of *Martin Chuzzlewit* made in 1964. We made this somewhat embarrassing discovery after my adaptation had been commissioned by BBC2 on the assumption that it would be a "first". It slightly diminished the glory of the project, but we hardly felt we were going over familiar ground. Like so much TV drama of that era (some of it of the highest quality), the earlier version was not preserved, and survives only in the fading memories of those who watched it, in black and white of course, thirty years ago.

I told Chris that I wanted to make substantial progress with my novel before tackling *Chuzzlewit*, and wouldn't be available till the spring of 1993. I intended then to work on both projects in tandem, but as soon as I started on *Chuzzlewit*, in April 1993, it became an all-absorbing occupation, and I resigned myself to putting *Therapy* aside until I had finished the first draft scripts (in fact they went through two or three drafts before I was able to get back to the novel). I was fooling myself in proposing to do otherwise. I have never been able to work on more than one imaginative project at a time. Creative writing doesn't just go on at your desk. It goes on inside your head continuously, as you turn over the problems and possibilities of the work in progress, and some of your best ideas may come in this way. You can't maintain this ruminative, receptive state in respect of two quite different stories – at least, I can't.

As always, the most important element in my brief was the temporal format of the serial, and, as always, the primary task was one of condensation. In my contract I was asked to write five episodes, of fifty minutes' duration, making a total of four hours ten minutes. Eventually this was extended by eighty minutes, making a total of five and a half hours. Dickens' novel runs to nine hundred-odd pages in most editions. A page of a novel consisting mostly of dialogue, if performed as written (without the narrator's words), will occupy three to four minutes. That is a long time in television. For example, the little scene in Chapter 2 of the novel, in which Pecksniff, recovering from his fall on the doorstep, tells his daughters that he has found a new student to replace John Westlock, would take about seven minutes to perform if every line of Dickens's dialogue were spoken – one-seventh of a fifty-minute episode. In the television version it lasts one minute twenty seconds – and a quarter of that time is occupied by the silent spectacle of Pecksniff downing the hot brandy and water under the anxious scrutiny of his daughters, an action described in a single short sentence in the novel. This bit of theatrical "business" creates a little moment of dramatic suspense, comically relieved by Pecksniff's complacent announcement, "That'll do. I'm better," and the girls' exaggerated show of relief. In other words, adaptation is not just a matter of cutting out material: you must allow for the fact that *in performance* what is retained may take up more time than it did in the original text.

How does one set about reducing an enormous, complex novel like *Martin Chuzzlewit*, which would take about forty-eight hours to read aloud without interruption, to a script that will, when filmed, occupy just a few hours of television? I don't know how other adapters work, but I do it intuitively rather than methodically. I mark in my text situations and actions and lines of dialogue that I think must be incorporated in the script because they are essential to the articulation of the plot, and/or because they would be dramatically effective or exciting or funny. I identify a point in the story which seems a good one to aim at for the final scene of the first episode – one that is dramatically strong, that will raise questions about the future development of the plot in the audience's minds, and that will allow me to cover an appropriate amount of the novel (roughly a fifth for a five-part serial). Then I begin, writing the script straight on to the computer. With original work I like to write the first draft in longhand, a few pages at a time, but in adaptation it helps to see at once how many pages your scenes are taking up in a standard printed format. With practice you develop an intuitive sense of how well you are keeping to your temporal target (which isn't to say that you won't have to make lots of adjustments later).

A general rule of thumb is to include only what is essential to the articulation of the plot, or the motivation of character, for reasons I have already touched on in another essay (pp.213–15): the medium is very intolerant of verbal redundancy, and the television audience (unlike a movie audience) is free to switch to another programme, or to switch off entirely, if its interest is not continuously engaged. Dickens, however, presents a special problem, especially in his earlier novels: what might be called his comic lyricism. Some of his most delightful writing simply revels in the heightened representation of the absurdity and affectation, the vanity and self-delusion of human speech and behaviour, with little regard for the dynamics of narrative. The great dinner at Todgers' in honour of the Pecksniff sisters in Chapter 9 epitomizes the problem. It is one of the most memorable and cherishable parts of the novel, yet it contributes nothing to the story except to initiate Moddle's infatuation with Mercy (such a minor theme at this point that he is not even identified by name) and to underline Charity's jealousy of her sister. The fun is all in the rendering, which is affectionate as well as satirical, of the way Mrs Todgers and her young men strive to imitate a stylish social occasion, complete with speeches and toasts, in a down-market boarding house. Pecksniff gets amusingly drunk, falls into the fireplace in the drawing-room after dinner, and is put to bed with difficulty. In his cups he reveals a licentiousness usually concealed beneath his hypocritical mask, but this is almost endearingly rendered, and he seems to lose no credit by his behaviour. The action is like an interlude, a feast of misrule. It has no consequences for the main story, and could be deleted without any effect on narrative coherence. I knew, of course, that it couldn't be presented in its entirety in the serial – that, for instance, the drawing-room scene would have to go, and (in breach of Victorian protocol) the ladies would have to stay at the dinner table for the speeches. But to pass it over entirely was unthinkable. The solution, it seemed to me, was to make it have consequences.

In the novel Pecksniff has brought his daughters to London to await a promised message from old Martin Chuzzlewit (without telling them the reason). Some days after the great dinner party, old Martin sends a letter (via the General Post Office) proposing to call on the Pecksniffs, and does so. In the screenplay the letter arrives at Todgers', by special delivery, on the morning after the great dinner, announcing old Martin's imminent arrival that very day. I wrote a new scene (not in the novel) in which Charity and Mercy wake their father to present this letter. He has a terrible hangover, which threatens to disable him in his crucial interview with the old man. Thus Pecksniff's greatest desire – to ingratiate himself with old Martin – is jeopardized by his self-indulgence at the dinner party. By cross-cutting that dinner with the dinner given at Salisbury by John Westlock to Tom and young Martin (moved from its temporal position in the novel for the purpose) I tried to give further justification for its inclusion. Even so, the director decided at the editing stage (rightly, I believe) to cut two speeches, by Jinkins and the Man of a Literary Turn, because wonderful as they are, and splendidly performed as they were (pity poor actors whose best lines end up on the cutting-room floor), they just didn't earn their place dramatically.

From the outset, Chris Parr encouraged me to adapt *Martin Chuzzlewit* freely rather than faithfully, and indeed this was the only way to do it in the screen-time available – especially in the original specification. Although I always aimed to be faithful to the spirit of the original, I frequently modified the letter. I felt less hesitant about doing this to *Martin Chuzzlewit* than I would have felt about doing the same to greater and better-known novels by Dickens. Although it was the first of his novels to have a single unifying theme – the effects of selfishness on private and public life – it is a structurally flawed novel, and many of its flaws would be cruelly exposed by a faithful adaptation. The plot is over-complicated, excessively reliant on coincidences (many of them highly improbable), some actions are inadequately motivated, and it is full of digressions and set-pieces of doubtful relevance to the narrative.

Dickens himself set great store by this novel when he was writing it, and was disappointed by the early sales of the monthly numbers in which it was originally published (just over twenty thousand, compared to fifty thousand for *Nicholas Nickleby*). As is well known, he decided to send young Martin Chuzzlewit to America, making use of the copious notes he had taken on his own trip there the previous year, in the hope that a satirical account of the New World would attract new readers to his serial. In fact it made little difference. The introduction of Mrs Gamp was much more effective in this respect, and realizing how popular she was, Dickens gave her more and more scope in the story. But the American episodes occupy a substantial chunk of the text, and present a problem to an adapter, as they always have done to literary critics of the novel.

Dickens's American experience contributed imaginatively to the writing of *Martin Chuzzlewit* before Dickens ever thought of sending his young hero there. At first overwhelmed by the warmth of the welcome extended to him, and the evidence of his fame in the New World, Dickens became increasingly alienated from and disillusioned with American culture and society – its brashness, materialism, chauvinism and racism, its physical and moral squalor (the universal habit of spitting and the flagrant pirating of his books particularly disgusted him). He became more and more depressed as his tour went on, and his riverboat trip down the Ohio river to its junction with the

Mississippi is rendered in his *American Notes* as something like a journey into the heart of darkness:

> The trees were stunted in their growth; the banks were low and flat; the settlements and log cabins fewer in number: their inhabitants more wan and wretched than any we had encountered yet . . . Hour after hour, the changeless glare of the hot, unwinking sky, shone upon the same monotonous objects. Hour after hour, the river rolled along, as wearily and slowly as time itself.
>
> At length, upon the morning of the third day, we arrived at a spot . . . much more desolate than any we had yet beheld . . . At the junction of the two rivers, on ground so flat and low and marshy, that at certain seasons of the year it is inundated to the housetops, lies a breeding place of fever, ague, and death: vaunted in England as a mine of Golden Hope, and speculated in, on the faith of monstrous representations, to many people's ruin.

This is Cairo, the model for "Eden" in the novel; and it was not a mere whim on Dickens part to send his self-deceived hero there to experience a crushing disillusionment, and near-death, from which he is rescued by Mark Tapley's selflessness. The dark vein of misanthropy that runs through the novel, especially in the character of old Martin, would seem to derive in part from Dickens's experience of America, and Eden makes a symbolically appropriate setting for the turning-point in young Martin's moral history. But most of the American episodes in *Martin Chuzzlewit* are written in a quite different style of broad caricature and knockabout farce, and require young Martin to play the part (inconsistent with his portrayal elsewhere) of an urbane, intelligent young English gentleman against whom the absurdities and extravagances of American life are measured. Opinion varies about how amusing these satirical episodes are (personally I find them rather tedious). Some relate to the theme of "selfishness". But for the most part they contribute nothing to the development of the story, and would be the first candidates for deletion in any adaptation of the novel.

From our point of view this was a fortunate flaw, since our budget would not have allowed us to recreate extensive scenes of New York and the American West as they looked in 1840.

The producer and director even wondered wistfully whether we could do without any American scenes at all. I set myself against this. Two components of the American chapters were essential to the story: young Martin's foolish purchase of the property in Eden (squandering Mark's capital as well as his own) and his disillusionment and revaluation of his own character when he gets there. These had to be shown, in context. It would have been unacceptable to have young Martin, absent from the story for two episodes, suddenly turning up on Tom Pinch's doorstep to report that he was a changed man. But how to do it?

These parts of the script went through many drafts, but the solution eventually adopted was to have Martin send two letters to Mary which would give (in his voice, over pictures of her reading the letters) an account of his American adventures, each such sequence framing an acted scene: the first depicting the purchase of the Eden property, and the second the arrival in Eden (this was filmed in a flooded quarry in Gloucestershire). To give some visual variety to the scenes of Mary reading the letters, I suggested that, since Martin is supposed to be a gifted draughtsman, his letters should be illustrated with little drawings and sketches, which the camera could focus on at appropriate moments, but after some experiments at the post-production stage (which I did not see) the director decided against the idea. (This abandoned device explains why the envelopes in which Martin's letters arrive are rather bulky.)

By beginning to publish *Martin Chuzzlewit* in monthly numbers before he had finished it, Dickens deprived himself of the freedom (taken for granted by modern novelists) to revise the earlier part of the text to make it consistent with things he wanted to put in later. Although he had a plan for *Chuzzlewit*, he could not predict, when he drew it up, what ideas would occur to him in the process of composition. As he wrote to his friend Forster, when he was halfway through the book:

> As to the way these characters have opened out, that is to me one of the most surprising processes of the mind in this sort of invention. Given what one knows, what one does not know springs up.

An example might be Mrs Todgers, who seems to be a rather unlikeable character when first introduced, hard and calculating, fawning on the Pecksniffs, and sharing in their snobbish conde-scension towards Ruth Pinch when they visit the copper-merchant's house where she is governess. But in the course of the novel she is revealed as a woman of genuine feeling and integrity, definitely allied to the "good" characters. I thought it prudent to leave Mrs Todgers out of the scene when the Pecksniffs visit Ruth, so as not to send misleading signals to the audience.

There were other opportunities to tighten up links in the plot in the adaptation. For example, if the confession of Lewsome, late in the novel, that he supplied Jonas with drugs with which to poison his father's medicine, seems a somewhat ponderous piece of plot machinery, it is partly because we have never seen Lewsome with Jonas, or heard about Anthony's medicine, before. On the director's shrewd suggestion I wrote Lewsome into the early scene where Jonas arrives with Charity and Mercy at his father's house (Lewsome, evidently desperate to do some shady business with Jonas, accosts him and is brusquely dismissed); and I made him turn up again as Anthony's funeral cortège leaves the house (he faints from the shock of discovering the identity of the corpse). I found a way to focus on the medicine in the scene of Anthony Chuzzlewit's death – but this scene was perhaps the one in which I took most liberties with Dickens' text in the interests of consistency, and is worth discussing in some detail.

In Chapter 18, Pecksniff arrives at the house of Anthony and Jonas Chuzzlewit, having been summoned by Anthony unknown to Jonas. While Jonas is out of the room the ailing Anthony urges Pecksniff to press on with the match between Jonas and Charity Pecksniff which Anthony himself had pro-posed some months earlier. His motivation seems to be that he thinks he is dying and cannot bear the thought of his fortune being wasted by some improvident wife of his son:

> "When I am dead . . . it will be worse for me to know of such doings than if I was alive: for to be tormented for getting that together, which even while I suffer for its acquisition is flung

into the very kennels of the streets, would be insupportable torture."

He favours the match with Charity because he relies on her to be as grasping as her father – "she comes of good griping stock". In short, Anthony's miserliness is shown as persisting to the end of his life – for he dies of a stroke later that same day. He cannot repent of his sin of avarice, and seems to accept that he will be damned for it.

In Chapter 51, however, in the scene where Jonas is accused by old Martin of having poisoned his father, and confronted with Lewsome, who testifies that he supplied him with the poison, we get a very different account from Old Chuffey of Anthony's state of mind immediately before his death. Chuffey reports that Anthony had discovered Jonas's plot to poison his medicine, and refilled the bottle with harmless medicine. But he was devastated by the discovery, and interpreted it as a judgement on himself.

> "Oh, Chuff," he said, ". . . this crime began with me. It began when I taught him to be too covetous of what I have to leave . . . He shall not weary for my death . . . he shall have it [i.e. the fortune] now; he shall marry where he has a fancy, Chuff, although it don't please me . . . I have sown and I must reap. He shall believe I am taking this [the poisoned medicine] and when I see that he is sorry, and has all he wants, I'll tell him that I found it out, and I'll forgive him. He'll make a better man of his own son."

Chuffey's intervention in this scene is a brilliant *coup de théâtre*. Jonas, who believes he *has* poisoned his father, seems to have been unmasked as a parricide, but is exonerated by the testimony of Old Chuffey, whom he has always treated badly. Then just as Jonas is exulting in his escape, Nadgett bursts in with the police to arrest Jonas for the murder of Montague Tigg, a murder he need never have committed because he was being blackmailed by Tigg on the presumption that he had murdered his father.

Chuffey's intervention is therefore crucial to this scene, but it seemed to me that it wasn't entirely consistent with Anthony's behaviour in Chapter 18. There Anthony is an unregenerate miser up to the moment of his death; according to Chuffey he was by this time a chastened and reformed character. I feared that the inconsistency would be more obvious in the adaptation than it is in the book. Consequently I made some bold changes in the earlier scene. I gave Anthony some lines suggesting that he has summoned Pecksniff not to urge on the marriage between Jonas and Charity, but because he is having qualms of conscience about proposing a match based on avarice and involving a man as callous and cold-hearted as Jonas. I also made him have a coughing fit, which requires Pecksniff to give him some of the cough medicine on which suspicion later focuses. Jonas comes in at this point and checks at the sight of the medicine bottle. These additions make Chuffey's revelations later more convincing, I hope. And I made Jonas's demeanour throughout this sequence much more brooding and uneasy than in the novel.

The problem of Anthony's motivation is tied up with the larger problem of the novel's time scheme. Anthony first proposes the match between Jonas and Charity as the Pecksniffs are leaving Todgers', and he does so on avaricious grounds and by appealing to Pecksniff's greed: such a match would be to the material advantage of both their families. A few days earlier, when Jonas entertained Charity and Mercy to dinner, Anthony was portrayed as delighting in his son's "sly, cunning and covetous" character. We must infer, therefore, that Anthony's discovery of Jonas's plot to kill him, and his consequent change of heart, occur at some time between Pecksniff's departure from Todgers', which is in late autumn or early winter, and the day of Anthony's death, which is some time the following spring – Anthony refers to its being "a cold spring" as he pokes the fire. But there is no other reference in the novel to this interval, or what happens in it.

Dickens, unlike most Victorian novelists, is never very specific about the chronology of his stories or their relation to historical time, and this is particularly true of *Martin Chuzzlewit*. There are no dates, or references to datable public events, though there are topical references like the Anglo-Bengalee Disinterested Loan and Life Assurance Company (inspired by a notorious insurance scam of the day). There is a railway in

America, which implies that the action is roughly contemporary with the time of publication (1843–4), but no sign of a train in England, which is presented as still becalmed in the age of the stage coach. There is also a good deal of vagueness and some inconsistency in the internal chronology of the story, which are hardly perceived in the reading of it, but which had to be sorted out in the process of adaptation. For example, in order to ensure that the external locations in the shooting schedule would have an appropriate seasonal look, it was necessary for me to work out a rough calendar for the story. This revealed that there are two incompatible time-schemes in the novel.

We know that the story begins "pretty late in the autumn of the year" – say, late October – when old Martin and Mary Graham arrive in the village (it is never given a name, another "timeless", universalizing touch, and I was obliged to invent one, Little Hadding). Old Martin must be laid up sick for some days, perhaps more than a week, to allow the relatives, including Chevvy Slyme and his associate Montague Tigg, to descend on the village (though it is never explained how they discovered his whereabouts). Then Pecksniff holds the family council, and old Martin and Mary leave the village on the same day. It cannot be more than a few days later that young Martin arrives, because some days after his arrival Tigg and Chevvy Slyme are still staying at the Blue Dragon, unable to leave because they cannot pay their bill of three pounds. The morning after young Martin's arrival at his house, Pecksniff receives the letter summoning him to London (the breakfast at which he reads the letter is shown as being young Martin's first in the house – he shocks Tom by helping himself to Pecksniff's bacon) and Pecksniff goes off that night with his two daughters. It follows that young Martin receives no tuition in architecture from Pecksniff at all, before setting off to America to make his fortune as an architect, which seems a little implausible, even given his vanity and naïvety. It also means that from the adapter's point of view there is very little time in which to show Pecksniff's plan to marry off one of his daughters to young Martin (on the assumption that he will be reconciled with his grandfather) actually in operation, for they are all together for less than two days.

The Pecksniffs settle into Todgers', and for "four or five

days", during which time the dinner takes place, Mr Pecksniff goes to the General Post Office hoping to find a message from old Martin. On the fifth day the message is received and old Martin makes his visit. Pecksniff says he will return home "at the end of the week". He and his daughters have been away perhaps two weeks, so it is presumably November by now. Pecksniff orders young Martin out of his house on his return, and young Martin goes to London and spends some weeks making ineffectual attempts to arrange his passage to America. He meets up with Mark Tapley, the hostler at the Blue Dragon, who has preceded him to London, and has been looking unsuccessfully for new employment, though in fact there is hardly any time in which he could have done this, since he is involved in the scene about the settlement of Tigg's and Slyme's bill at the Blue Dragon. (In the screenplay young Martin and Mark leave the village on the same day and meet up on the road.) It seems that young Martin and Mark sail to America in late December. They have a five-week voyage, stay in New York for a while, and then travel slowly westwards to Eden. It is evidently late spring or early summer when they get there because it is hot and humid and people are dying from fever. They stay there for some months before returning to England, which they reach, the narrator says, about a year after their departure. That would be in December. But in fact it is clear that they return in the summer, about six or seven months after setting off. They are in England when the story of Jonas reaches its climax, beginning with his attempt to flee to the Continent and ending with his suicide five days later, and this is clearly happening in the summer, since Ruth Finch eats cherries when she and Tom dine with John Westlock on the day Jonas boards the boat for Antwerp.

In short, if you try to construct a detailed calendar of events for *Martin Chuzzlewit*, its implausibilities and inconsistencies become glaringly obvious. Dickens' vagueness about time is therefore functional, lulling the reader's scepticism, and inviting a response rather different from that appropriate to a realist novel like *Middlemarch*. A certain "willing suspension of disbelief" is necessary, for instance, to accept that old Martin could carry off his deception, or that Tom Pinch could be deceived by Pecksniff, for so long. The story owes a good deal to the "timeless" romance and fairy-tale tradition on which Shakespeare drew for his comedies and tragi-comedies, and it is fascinating to learn that on his trip to America the year before he started work on *Martin Chuzzlewit*, Dickens took with him a pocket edition of Shakespeare's plays, a parting gift from John Forster, and carried it everywhere with him on his travels. The book was, he wrote back to Forster, "an unspeakable source of delight". No wonder that, as Steven Marcus points out (in *Dickens from Pickwick to Dombey*), *Chuzzlewit* is more densely saturated with Shakespearian quotations and allusions than any other novel by Dickens. What it most resembles, perhaps, are the so-called "problem plays" or "dark comedies" of Shakespeare, *All's Well that Ends Well* and *Measure for Measure*, in which there is an exciting but sometimes disconcerting mixture of comic, satiric and tragic elements, and the most interesting and memorable characters are those who are morally flawed. It was this Shakespearian spirit that I hoped to get into the adaptation, and it was a wonderful bonus to have the part of old Martin (which so strikingly resembles that of the Duke in *Measure for Measure*) played by one of our greatest Shakespearian actors, Paul Scofield. I remember rehearsing the scene in which Jonas is finally exposed and arrested, after which Old Chuffey (touchingly portrayed by Sir John Mills) enquires about the whereabouts of Mercy, and old Martin offers to take him to her. That was the line in the script, "I'll take you to her." But Paul used the more Shakespearean phrase, "I'll bring you to her," and it sounded so right that we persuaded him to keep it in.

All through the late spring and summer of 1993, I worked on the screenplay of *Chuzzlewit* in the 5 × 50-minute format, submitting my drafts to Chris Parr and Nell Denton, who had been appointed script editor to the project. When adapting classic novels with many-stranded plots the first episode is always particularly difficult, and usually goes through most drafts, because you have to introduce a large number of characters *and* advance the story sufficiently to interest the audience in their subsequent fortunes. It is also the episode on which most reviews will be based. The deeper I got into the serial, the more confident I became in the strength of the story and the characters. By August I had produced a complete script that satisfied us all. We all agreed that if our audience stayed with us as far as Episode Two they would be hooked.

By this time, Chris Parr had been appointed Head of Television Drama at Pebble Mill, the BBC's regional headquarters in Birmingham. This undoubtedly helped forward the production of *Chuzzlewit* (many a script is accepted and paid for without being put into production, because of lack of support at the higher executive levels where funds are allocated and programming decisions made). The next stage was to appoint a director. This is always an anxious moment for the screenplay-writer because, once the director is appointed, he has primary artistic responsibility for the production, and naturally he will have comments to make about the script, especially if it is an adaptation of another text with which it can be compared. Ideally, the director should collaborate with the writer from the earliest stages of the evolution of the script, but production companies are generally unwilling to retain the services of a director for a project they may never make. Therefore, however many drafts your script has been through, you always expect to have to do some rewriting when the director comes on board. In the case of *Chuzzlewit*, this turned out to be very considerable.

Chris Parr, in consultation with Mike Wearing (the BBC's Head of Series and Serials in London), offered the job of director to Pedr James. Pedr is a very experienced director who, like many others, had started off in theatre and then moved into television. He made his name many years ago with a delightful film written by Willy Russell called *Our Day Out*. More recently he had had some success with a serial about contemporary sexual mores called *Nice Town* and Mark Lawson's political satire, *The Vision Thing*. He had never made a classic period drama, but this was a positive recommendation in the eyes of Chris Parr and Mike Wearing. They thought he would bring a fresh approach to the project, and make it work for a modern audience.

After a week or so, Pedr accepted the job. We had a mutually wary telephone conversation in which he expressed admiration for some (unspecified) parts of the script, but said, "Chris tells me you're very professional about doing re-writes," which I didn't find altogether reassuring. He then took the novel and the script off to his country cottage in Wales and read them extremely carefully. He came back a month later with twenty closely typed pages of notes on the first two episodes alone.

As I said earlier, I had been encouraged by Chris Parr to adapt *Chuzzlewit* pretty freely, and in doing so so I had favoured the comic and villainous characters. Essentially Pedr wanted me to give more weight to the "good" characters, especially Tom Pinch, and to follow Dickens' plotting much more faithfully. Though I disagreed strongly with some of his notes, I accepted that at least half of them were well-founded. The reason, however, why I had left out so many things that he wanted to restore was that there was not room for them – and there never would be in a 5 × 50 minute serial.

The deadlock was broken when Chris and Pedr persuaded Michael Jackson, the controller of BBC2, to let us have some additional screen time. But there was a catch – it had to be accomplished within the original budget. By dint of ingenious juggling with the shooting schedule, and keeping changes of location down to a minimum, we were able to add thirty minutes to the first episode, and an extra five minutes to the others (later the serial became even longer). The extension of the first episode was particularly valuable: it allowed me to develop the characters more fully, especially Tom Pinch and Mark Tapley, and to end the episode where Pedr quite rightly saw it should end – with the Pecksniffs apparently triumphant after old Martin's visit at Todgers' (originally it had ended with the delivery of old Martin's letter at the climax of the dinner party). But there was still a long way to go, and a lot of hard argument between Pedr and myself.

In these discussions it often struck me that a strange and unpredictable exchange of professional roles had taken place: I, the novelist and literary academic, was chiefly exercised by what would "work" in television terms, while Pedr, the seasoned director, was fiercely defending the integrity of Dickens' text. Interestingly, something very similar happened between Andrew Davies, the adapter of *Middlemarch* for the BBC, and his director, Anthony Page – except that *their* relations were so strained that they didn't actually meet until the serial was being filmed, all the rewrites being negotiated through the producer. Pedr and I had frequent meetings.

I remember a particularly tense one to discuss the scene where Mary Graham reveals Pecksniff's perfidy to an incredulous Tom Pinch in the village church. Pedr wanted me to preserve the rhetoric of Mary's speeches in the text, which I thought would sound intolerably strained to a modern audience, especially on the small screen. To resolve our dispute we read it aloud, with Chris Parr and Nell Denton participating and arbitrating, first in Dickens's full-blown melodramatic style ('But what is he: oh Mr Pinch, what *is* he: who, thinking he could compass these designs the better if I were his wife, assails me with the coward's argument that if I marry him, Martin, on whom I have brought so much misfortune, shall be restored to something of his former hopes; and if I do not, shall be plunged in deeper ruin?") and then in my simpler, more colloquial version ("And he says that if I marry him he will use his influence with Mr Chuzzlewit to restore Martin's hopes, but if I refuse him he will make sure they are never reconciled. Do you believe me?"). I carried the day on that occasion, but on others Pedr prevailed. For example, one of the things I was most pleased with in my script for the first episode was a "cut" from the breakfast table in Pecksniff's house, when Charity asks, "Where shall we stay in London, Pa?" to the exterior of the boarding house, with Pecksniff's reply in voice-over: "I hope at Mrs Todgers', a most respectable lady . . .", which saved a lot of time rather neatly, omitting the night journey of the Pecksniffs by coach, coincidentally shared by Anthony and Jonas Chuzzlewit. Pedr was very keen to include this journey, and especially the scene in the coach during which Jonas flirts with the girls (a bit of action I had moved into the family conclave scene a little earlier). He nagged away at me about this matter, and eventually I gave in and wrote the night coach scene. I think in retrospect he was right to insist on its inclusion: it establishes the character of Anthony, who is only fleetingly introduced in the family conclave scene, firmly in the audience's mind; and also his bad cough, thus setting up the later scene with the medicine bottle. And Jonas's byplay with the girls is more effective in the intimate confines of the dark coach.

Though I was not well pleased at having to undo so much of the work I had done that summer, I have no doubt that, in the end, a much better script emerged as a result of my arguments with Pedr. As I said in an earlier essay, where there is no disagreement and debate within a television production the result is likely to be bland and self-indulgent. There was no danger of that happening to *Martin Chuzzlewit*. Pedr and I had very different views of the novel and the task of adaptation, but our disagreement was creative, even if the personal tension between us sometimes became acute. Pedr is in many ways a somewhat Dickensian character himself, even in appearance: short and stocky, with granny glasses and a cherubic face wreathed in a curly white beard and hair; emotionally volatile and stubborn in defending his views. He is not a literary scholar. I was unable to persuade him that "todger" did not have its modern slang meaning of penis in Dickens's day, and that the novelist would have been as innocent as Tom Pinch of any *double entendre* in the line, "I was touching the organ for my own amusement", but that didn't matter. He had a real empathy with Dickens' emotional and moral fervour, and was not afraid of taking it on board, as perhaps I had been. Sometimes I thought he was obsessed with the character of Tom Pinch, but undoubtedly I had skimped that character's part in my first script. Revised and expanded, and beautifully performed by Philip Franks, it added a necessary dimension of innocence and pathos to the story.

All through October and November I did rewrites, wondering how scriptwriters ever managed before the invention of the word-processor and the fax machine. Eventually I delivered a script that, give or take a point or two, satisfied Pedr, Chris Parr and myself. But then, just before Christmas, there was a new crisis: it had been calculated that this script couldn't be filmed in the seventy working days allowed by our budget. The assistant director, John Greening, produced a schedule estimating how many hours every scene in the six-hundred-page script would take to shoot, and Pedr and I went through it looking for cuts that would save seven days' filming. This was not an easy or enjoyable exercise, but it was not, I think, seriously damaging to the production. What we lost were the scene-setting or mood-establishing sequences, links between the dramatically essential scenes. But the *mise-en-scène* was never going to be the strong point of our production, partly because we didn't have the budget for it, partly because everyone concerned – director, producer, designer and costume designer – was agreed from the outset that this story required a focus on character, not setting. As Pedr remarked to me, if you spend a lot of money on sets and locations, there is always a danger that the camera will spend too much time admiring them. He intended to stay "tight" with the characters, and I thoroughly approved. I had only one reservation about the final look of the serial: we failed to evoke Dickensian London, and especially the environs of Todgers', convincingly. The architecture of King's Lynn, where we filmed most of the London sequences, is the right period, and hasn't been excessively tarted up by the heritage industry; but it is too low-profile to provide the narrow, crooked alleys and tall, light-excluding tenements Dickens describes. This was no fault of the designer, Gavin Davies, who did wonders within the constraints of his budget. I had hoped that we might use the Inns of Court for the several scenes set there, since they are little changed from Dickens' day; but it was explained to me that filming period drama in London is next to impossible because you can never escape the sound of modern traffic for long.

The making of a television serial like *Chuzzlewit* is an enormously complex operation, involving the planning and co-ordination of many distinct tasks and requiring many different skills: writing, casting, designing, costume design, location-finding, studio set construction, make-up, acting, directing, cinematography, stunt arranging, lighting, sound recording, editing and musical composition, not to mention the provision of horses and horse-drawn vehicles of various kinds, and practical matters like arranging catering, transportation and accommodation for the unit on location. Some of these elements are more important than others, but for a really successful show they all need to work, and serious failure in one of the artistic departments can jeopardize the whole production.

Casting is one of the most crucial of these operations, and what makes it particularly nerve-racking is that it is seldom finally settled until the last moment (and sometimes even later than that). There are several reasons for this. One is that actors are generally unwilling to commit themselves long in advance, in case they are offered something more lucrative for the same dates. Another is that producers and directors hesitate to commit themselves too soon in case they end up with incompatible actors or miss the chance of getting a major star. But we were lucky enough to secure the services of Paul Scofield to play old Martin quite early on, and Pedr had the bright idea of persuading him to play the part of Martin's brother Anthony as well. There is a moment in the last episode when old Martin enters Jonas's house to confront him with Lewsome's testimony about the poison:

> JONAS *looks towards the door with a look of terror on his face.*
> OLD MARTIN *is on the threshold. He comes forward into the room and is recognized with relief by* JONAS. MRS GAMP *takes the opportunity to scuttle out of the room.*

> JONAS What the devil d'you mean by creeping into my house like this, uncle?

Dickens describes "a ghastly change in Jonas" as he sees his uncle. It seemed to me that this might well be caused by a family resemblance between the two brothers, leading the guilty Jonas to think he is seeing his father's ghost, so I added a line to that effect, and an appropriate rejoinder by old Martin.

> JONAS By God, I thought I'd seen my father's ghost.
> OLD MARTIN (*grimly*) As well you might.

Reflecting that this would mean casting an Anthony who looked reasonably like Paul Scofield, it struck Pedr that, since the two brothers never appeared in the same scene, Paul could play both.

Although I was not involved in interviewing actors, I was consulted about casting and invited to give my suggestions and comments on the suggestions of others. I was particularly concerned about the casting of Pecksniff. His part was easily the longest in the script, and his hypocritical scheming completely dominated the action of the crucial first episode. If the audience didn't believe in his malevolence *and* find him amusing, we would be lost. Several names, some of which seemed to me quite wrong, were mooted before the part was offered to Tom Wilkinson. I didn't know his work well, having seen him only once that I could recall, in a very different part (the lead in Christopher Hampton's memory play at the National, *White*

Chameleons). But at the very first read-through, in the BBC's bleak tower-block of rehearsal rooms in North Acton, I knew we had found a superlative Pecksniff. It was as if Tom Wilkinson had been waiting all his life to play this part. He eased himself into it like a man pulling on a snug and familiar garment, and I was astounded to read in interviews after the serial was broadcast, and his performance had been acclaimed, that he had never read Dickens' novel, so complete was his grasp of the character. (I couldn't help reflecting that this said something for the script, too.)

The acting in *Chuzzlewit* was almost uniformly excellent, right down to the smallest cameos, and this was absolutely crucial to its success. Dickens offers great opportunities to actors, but also great pitfalls, especially on the small screen. His characters are wonderfully vital and individual, but they are slightly larger than life. If the actors don't "go for it", they miss the unique Dickensian quality, but it is so easy to over-act and lose credibility. Our cast passed the test triumphantly. Unprecedentedly, three out of the four nominations for Best Actor in that year's BAFTA awards were taken from the same cast: Tom Wilkinson, Paul Scofield and Peter Postlethwaite (as Tigg Montague); and though Robbie Coltrane predictably scooped the members' vote (for *Cracker*), Tom Wilkinson at least got his rightful due with the Royal Television Society's award a few months later. Several other actors in *Chuzzlewit* were unlucky not to get among the award nominations – but really there were so many superlative performances that it would be invidious to mention any more names. Working with them was a pleasure and a privilege, and the two-week rehearsal period in particular was one of the most fascinating and rewarding experiences of my professional life. Because of the limited amount of time available, Pedr did not attempt to do any blocking or real acting. Instead the cast sat around a long table and read the script scene by scene, discussed it and analysed it and read it again. It was like a literary seminar at which every participant was committed one hundred per cent – something I never experienced as a university teacher.

There is no real finality in any script – which is to say that its final realization is out of the writer's hands and largely out of his control. I made a few additions and modifications to the script of *Chuzzlewit* while it was being filmed, at Pedr's request, but my significant contribution to the production ended with the rehearsals, when it was still possible to fine-tune the dialogue. I was always welcome to observe the filming, and did so on several occasions, but it is not advisable to try to change a script on the set, and it was hardly feasible with such a tight schedule as ours. You just have to stand quietly and unobtrusively in the background while your lines are spoken again and again in take after take – tested to destruction, I sometimes think. The director is in the driver's seat. And then it is the film editor's turn, working in collaboration with the director. Much of what you wrote can be shifted about, rearranged, given a different spin, or cut altogether, at this stage. It turned out that, in spite of the Christmas cutting exercise, we had much more film in the can than could comfortably fit into five episodes, even with an extra-long first one, and the rushes were perceived to be of such high quality that we were allowed to extend the serial yet again, to six episodes. The final format as transmitted was a first episode of eighty minutes and five more of fifty minutes each, making a total of five and a half hours.* The new six-episode format meant, of course, that my carefully planned and much discussed breaks between episodes all went out of the window, and new climaxes had to be found. Exactly the same thing had happened to *Nice Work*, and I wondered if television drama was *ever* transmitted in the form in which it had originally been commissioned.

Observing the evolution of a television serial in the post-production process is a fascinating and – if it is successful – thrilling experience. First you see the rushes – little snippets of action filmed over and over again, sometimes from different points of view and distances. There is no background sound,

* At a total cost of approximately four and a quarter million pounds, it was a bargain for the BBC. Both *Middlemarch* and *Pride and Prejudice*, for example, cost six million pounds for six hours. These figures seem huge to the layman, but they are very modest compared to the budget for a feature film. Nobody involved makes very large sums of money out of television drama. It is perhaps for that reason a rather friendly, democratic and genuinely co-operative field of artistic endeavour.

and the picture quality is lousy. It is always disappointing and sometimes deeply depressing. Then the editor assembles a rough cut, making choices from the available takes and knitting them together to create a narrative with some coherence and rhythm. Then editor and director produce a "fine cut", something very near to the finished product, tinkering and adjusting the images for maximum dramatic effect, but also struggling to meet the arbitrary requirements of the stipulated episode length. (Some excellent sequences in *Chuzzlewit* had to be dumped at this stage for that simple reason.) Then the background sound is added, and the background music. It is surprising what a difference the former makes to the reality of filmed drama, while the effect of music, for good or ill, is hard to exaggerate. I was enchanted with Geoffrey Burgon's haunting theme music, and had the audio cassette playing constantly at home. It was predominantly lyrical and elegiac in mood, which was perhaps surprising considering the predominantly comic and melodramatic nature of the story, but it gave us an emotional power and sense of reality just where we needed it, in the relationships of love and friendship, and at wordless moments of pathos and longing. And then finally you see the finished product in all its glory, in perfect focus and colour.

Pedr sent me the rough and fine cuts on VHS tapes and I made comments on which he acted as he thought fit. There was only one issue on which we seriously disagreed, and that concerned the very ending of the last episode.

Dickens's novel has a very long-drawn out and complicated final act. It begins with old Martin revealing his true nature to Tom Pinch, and then taking command of the confrontation with Jonas, who subsequently commits suicide. Young Martin, who is excluded from this action, and unaware of his grandfather's transformation, suddenly accuses Tom of being disloyal to him without specifying the grounds. Tom, rather improbably, does not ask him to be explicit, but denies any disloyalty. This seems to be connected with Tom's secret, hopeless, but completely honourable love for Mary Graham, which his sister Ruth now discovers. Old Martin summons a meeting at his London rooms (formerly Tom's workplace) of his nearest and dearest, before whom he denounces Pecksniff and beats him.

He tells the long story of his troubled relationship with his grandson, and of Pecksniff's perfidy. He gives his blessing to the union of young Martin and Mary. Tom and Martin are reconciled: it appears that Martin saw him going into the rooms one day and suspected he was in secret contact with his grandfather when he himself was still estranged from him. Bailey turns up with Mrs Gamp (and Poll Sweedlepipe the barber – the only named character apart from the Americans that I excluded from the serial). Mrs Gamp is dismissed. Old Martin approves Mark Tapley's intention of marrying Mrs Lupin, and encourages the ripening attachment between John Westlock and Tom's sister Ruth. John proposes and Ruth accepts him on condition her brother can share their home. John and Ruth announce their engagement to Tom, who is overjoyed. The penultimate chapter ends with a great celebration supper for the "good" characters, including the three betrothed couples. In the last chapter the scene shifts to Todgers', on the day appointed for Charity's marriage to Moddle. She has invited some of the sponging relatives who attended the family conclave summoned by Pecksniff at the beginning of the story – the Spottletoes, and George Chuzzlewit and the hairy grandnephew are mentioned. A letter arrives from Moddle announcing that he has run away to Tasmania. Charity faints. The final passage in the book is a kind of rapturous vision of Tom grown old, seated at the organ, thinking back over his life. We gather that he gives occasional assistance to the indigent Pecksniff without expecting or receiving any thanks, that he is a beloved member of Ruth and John's household, but also the special favourite of a daughter of Mary's, that his life is "tranquil, calm and happy", and that the memory of his old love "is a pleasant, softened, whispering memory, like that in which we sometimes hold the dead, and does not pain or grieve thee, God be thanked."

There was no way I could get all this into the last episode of the television serial. Some things had to go, and others had to be telescoped (i.e., fitted together into a single scene). I didn't hesitate to cut the misunderstanding between Tom and young Martin. (I have not met many readers of the novel who grasped what it is all about, or understood the cryptic line of dialogue in which it is explained: "Oh Tom! Dear Tom! I saw you,

accidentally, coming here. Forgive me!") It seemed to me that
the final vision of Tom's future, as well as being intolerably
sentimental, was not really dramatizable; and that the immediately preceding scene of the jilting of Charity Pecksniff would be
a very sour note on which to end the entire story. One function
of Charity's wedding-day in the novel is to bring back into the
narrative the grasping minor relatives not seen since the family
council in Chapter 4, and it seemed desirable to preserve this
symmetry in the television serial. Accordingly, I greatly enlarged
the meeting summoned by old Martin, to include the minor
relatives, and Charity. I made it a kind of Shakespearian set
piece, in which justice is dispensed by old Martin, the good
rewarded and the evil humbled and punished. Old Martin
announces that he has made a new will which will put an end to
any further solicitation by members of his family. He gives his
blessing to Mary and young Martin, and Ruth guesses her
brother's secret from his reaction. Pecksniff is denounced and
chastised, giving Charity a spiteful satisfaction. Then she in turn
is humbled, when Moddle's letter announcing that he has
absconded is delivered by Mrs Gamp.

Pedr didn't much like this big ensemble scene, but Chris Parr
persuaded him that it was an elegant solution to the dramaturgical problems. In practice it worked very well, thanks particularly to a magisterial performance by Paul Scofield. The real
disagreement between Pedr and myself concerned the last few
minutes of the serial. The family gathering disperses and, in the
garden of Furnival's Inn, old and young Martin are reconciled.
Ruth weeps sympathetically for her brother's disappointment in
love, and he gently chides her. This is how the serial ended in
the agreed shooting script:

TOM Come, come. This is no crying matter. By her own
　　choice, she is betrothed to Martin, and was, long
　　before either of them knew of my existence. And do
　　you think, even if she had never seen him, that she
　　would have fallen in love with me?

RUTH Yes, of course she would have! It's so unfair.

TOM (*smiles and shakes his head*) You think of me, Ruth,
　　and it is very natural that you should, as if I was a
　　character in a book; and you make it a sort of poetical

justice that I should, by some impossible means or other, come at last to marry the person I love. But there is a higher justice than the poetical kind, my dear. I don't grieve for the impossible. But how did you guess my secret?

RUTH (*bashfully*) Perhaps because I have one of my own.

RUTH *glances at* JOHN WESTLOCK. TOM *follows the direction of her glance.* JOHN *smiles and approaches them.*

TOM You mean – ? (RUTH *nods*) Goodness gracious! I was never so surprised – or delighted – in my life. John, my dear fellow!

JOHN We are brothers, Tom. Give me your hand.

TOM (*overcome*) John! John!

JOHN (*smiling*) But as you are Ruth's guardian, I must ask you formally for her hand in marriage.

TOM Granted, my dear John! And I'll play the organ at your wedding!

5/41 INT. DAY. LONDON CHURCH

TOM, *dressed in a new morning suit, with a flower in his button-hole, is sitting at a really enormous organ. He is looking over his shoulder as if expecting a cue. He seems to get it, nods, and starts playing the Wedding March,* con brio.

5/42. EXT. DAY. LONDON CHURCH.

FINAL CREDITS *over steps and porch of a London church. Sound of the wedding march played inside. The church bells begin to ring. A little group of bystanders have gathered to watch the exit of bride and groom.* JOHN *and* RUTH, *appropriately dressed, come out arm in arm, followed (to the spectators' growing astonishment) by* YOUNG MARTIN *and* MARY, *also dressed as groom and bride, and* MARK TAPLEY *and* MRS LUPIN, *also dressed as groom and bride. All smile and laugh and exchange kisses and handshakes. The organ music fades and is replaced by theme music. A procession of wedding guests emerges from the church:* CHUFFEY, *frail but smiling, escorted by* MERCY (*who is*

visibly pregnant) and BAILEY (*who has just a small plaster on his
forehead*), *a chastened-looking* CHARITY, *and all the*
GENTLEMEN LODGERS *at Todgers'. Last to appear is* OLD
MARTIN, *smiling benignly, his arm round* TOM*'s shoulder.*

THE END

If I remember rightly, it was the script editor, Nell Denton, who
first casually threw out the suggestion of a double wedding –
between young Martin Chuzzlewit and Mary Graham, and
between John Westlock and Ruth Pinch – as the final scene of
the serial. The idea appealed to me as a background to the final
credits, and I developed it into a multiple wedding – incorporating the union of Mark Tapley and Mrs Lupin, and taking the
liberty of marrying Mrs Todgers off to Mr Jinkins at the same
time. Pedr's comment was: "I really hate this," and my
readiness to surrender the Jinkins – Mrs Todgers match did not
placate him. He felt it was a chocolate-boxy, feel-good ending
which undermined the seriousness and pathos of the novel's
conclusion, especially as it concerned the character of Tom
Pinch. "This book is not about marriage," he said to me more
than once.

Well, no, it is not – in the sense that *Middlemarch*, for
instance, is "about" marriage. Indeed, ordinary married life is
conspicuous by its absence from the pages of *Martin Chuzzlewit*.
As I worked on my adaptation it dawned on me what an
extraordinary number of orphans, widows, widowers, bachelors
and spinsters there are in this novel. If you exclude the
American episodes, there is only one "normal" nuclear family
(i.e. two parents with children) in the entire book, and that is
the family of Mr Mould the undertaker, a relatively minor
character. Dickens makes a great point of the serene content-
ment of Mr Mould's domestic life, which is thrown into relief
by the somewhat melancholy nature of his profession, and by
the emotional deprivations of the other characters.

Young Martin, his sweetheart Mary Graham, Tom Pinch and
his sister Ruth, and Bailey, the boy at Todgers' boarding-house,
are all orphans from childhood, and Tom's friend John Westlock is parentless when the story begins. Pecksniff, old Martin
and Anthony Chuzzlewit are all widowers (and the deceased
wives of the Chuzzlewit brothers are never even mentioned).

Mrs Gamp and Mrs Lupin are widows, and Mrs Todgers is either a widow or a deserted wife. It would seem that Tigg Montague has never been married, since there is no information to the contrary, and the same is true of at least a dozen other named characters in the novel, and all of Mrs Todgers' "gentlemen". The only marriage that takes place in the course of the novel is a very unhappy one, between Jonas Chuzzlewit and Mercy Pecksniff, involving physical abuse of the wife, and the novel ends with a jilted bride.

There are facts of social history – like the lower life-expectancy of people in early Victorian England – which partly explain the plethora of orphans, widows and widowers, but the almost complete absence of "normal" family life from the novel must have a more literary motivation. Dickens described the theme of his novel as selfishness, and he deployed incomplete, deviant, or surrogate family groupings to communicate his vision of a society worm-eaten by this vice. The selfish characters create domestic misery for themselves, and try to deny domestic happiness to others. Even old Martin is not blameless in this respect. A widower without living children, he buys himself a surrogate daughter (and perhaps unconsciously a surrogate wife – there is an impropriety about his relationship with Mary that is not entirely in Pecksniff's imagination) by taking Mary from her orphanage, and binding her to a degrading contract, while using his fortune to command the subservience of his grandson, young Martin.

But these warped and exploitative relationships, and the rarity of normal family life in the novel, make marriage all the more potent an image of desired happiness. As in Shakespeare's comedies and tragi-comedies, the removal of obstacles to the union of the young lovers in *Martin Chuzzlewit* confirms the triumph of good over evil, hope over despair, love over selfishness. The story ends with three couples looking forward eagerly to marriage; it didn't seem outrageous licence to end the serial by actually showing, and combining, their weddings.

This argument did not persuade Pedr, but as he went ahead and shot the wedding scene, I assumed that he had conceded defeat on this point. I was wrong. In editing the last episode he concluded it with Tom Pinch's very moving speech to his sister Ruth about her unrealistic hope of "poetic justice". I had shifted this speech from its earlier position in Dickens' text very deliberately, to avoid a formulaic "happy ending". But to end the whole serial with a close-up of Tom saying, "I don't grieve for the impossible," seemed to me intolerably abrupt. I protested to Chris Parr. Pedr was adamant. Chris suggested half-seriously that we might have two endings, Pedr's for the first transmission and mine for the repeat six days later. News of this leaked out, and caused a stir in the press, to the glee of the BBC's publicity department. Rather to my surprise, Pedr seemed to countenance the idea and invited me into Pebble Mill to see an assembly of "my" ending. In the script Tom welcomes the news of his sister's engagement to John, promises to play the organ at their wedding, and is shown doing so, just before the happy couples emerge from the church. Although Pedr had shot these scenes, the number of wedding guests in the procession from the church (and therefore the time it took for them to exit) was drastically reduced – so much so that, in the edited version which I saw, Tom appeared at the door throwing confetti just a few bars into the wedding march he is supposed to be playing, and there was no time to let the theme music take over sooner. Faced with this surrealistic effect, I had no option but to accept Pedr's ending.

The moral of the story is, I suppose, that you can lead a director to the water but you cannot make him drink. I think that both Pedr's ending and my ending were valid efforts to find an equivalent in the condensed, dramatic language of television, for Dickens' final vision of Tom Pinch – mine an upbeat version, his a downbeat one. The loss of the weddings bothered me less than cutting Tom's belated recognition that his sister is in love with his best friend, but it was impossible for technical reasons to detach one from the other effectively at the editing stage. I rather regret, now, that we didn't reach a compromise solution which I tentatively suggested while filming was still in progress – that we should end after the embrace between Tom and John Westlock, with a long-held shot of the two men and Ruth walking away, arm in arm, out of the courtyard and out of the story. Pedr said the location chosen for the scene didn't allow such a shot. From such practical constraints do large consequences often follow in the making of television drama.

Through the No Entry Sign:
Deconstruction and Architecture

In the spring of 1988 Waldemar Januszczak, then Arts Editor of the *Guardian,* invited me to attend and report on a Symposium on "Deconstruction in Art and Architecture" to be held at the Tate Gallery. I presume he thought that what I knew about deconstruction from the literary point of view would make up for my lack of qualifications as a critic of art and architecture. Intrigued by what seemed a highly paradoxical title, and being then something of a professional conference-watcher, I accepted the commission.

The only way you could get into the auditorium for the Tate Gallery's recent one-day symposium on Deconstruction in Art and Architecture was through a swing door clearly marked with the international "No Entry" symbol. Whether this was planned or accidental, it seemed appropriate that we should be trangressing the conventional meaning of this familiar sign all day long (and it was a long day) as we shuffled backwards and forwards between the auditorium and the lobbies; for one of the axioms of Deconstruction is that the bond between the signifier and the signified is not as stable as is generally supposed, but on the contrary "always already" subject to slippage and the play of *différance*. Some who pushed their way through the No Entry sign were hoping to find out what Deconstruction was. Others of us were curious to discover what it could possibly have to do with Art and Architecture.

Deconstruction is the brainchild of the French philospher Jacques Derrida. Over the last twenty years it has been an important – some would say the dominant – element in that general movement in the human sciences known as post-structuralism. It's not so much a method, more a frame of mind – one that has tirelessly questioned the nature and possibility of meaning through analysis of and commentary upon texts – originally philosophical texts, then literary texts. Taking their cue from Derrida's assertion that "language bears within itself the necessity of its own critique," deconstructionist literary critics, especially at Yale, have demonstrated, to their own satisfaction and in the teeth of traditional scholarship, that any text inevitably undermines its own claim to have a determinate meaning. Since this procedure opens up the text to endless multiple interpretations, its appeal to literary critics is perhaps obvious. But how could a movement so deeply invested in the analysis of verbal language be relevant to art and architecture? My first reaction to the announcement of the Tate Symposium was incredulity.

Well, we live and learn. I soon discovered that Derrida himself had published a whole book about the aesthetics of the visual arts, recently translated into English as *The Truth in Painting*, and that he has taken a keen interest in architecture, to the point of collaborating with Bernard Tschumi and Peter Eisenman on projects for the Parc de la Villette, a kind of post-structuralist theme park now under construction (or should one say, under deconstruction?) on a cleared industrial site in the northern suburbs of Paris.

Tschumi and Eisenman are among seven architects whose work is to be exhibited at the Museum of Modern Art in New York this summer under the heading of Deconstruction, or Deconstructivism (there is some mystery and controversy about the exact title), an event awaited with keen interest and the audible sharpening of knives in the architectural fraternity. The Tate symposium was in some sense a preliminary skirmish in the controversy this show is bound to provoke. Peter Eisenman indeed complained that it would be the first time in history that an exhibition was being commented on before it had happened. What he was registering was the crucial place of the international conference as an institution in modern intellectual life. New trends now start not from exhibitions or publications but from conferences. It was, after all, the 1966 conference at Johns Hopkins University, Baltimore, "The Languages of Criticism and the Sciences of Man", attended by Derrida and other Parisian *savants*, that first put the ideas of poststructuralism into circulation in America, where they were developed, institutionalized, and ultimately re-exported to Europe and the rest of the academic world.

It was not surprising, therefore, that the Tate Symposium (jointly sponsored by the Academy publishing group, who are publishing two useful special editions of their handsomely illustrated journals *Art & Design* and *Architectural Design* in conjunction with the event)* was oversubscribed long before the day, especially as Derrida himself was advertised as a

---

* "The New Modernism: Deconstructionist Tendencies in Art", *Art & Design*, Vol. 4, 3–4 (1988). "Deconstruction in Architecture", *Architectural Design*, Vol.58, 3–4 (1988).

participant. Cynical veterans of the international conference circuit were equally unsurprised when Derrida didn't show up. Instead we were shown an edited videotape of an interview with him recorded a few days earlier by Christopher Norris, Professor of English at Cardiff and the leading British expert on deconstruction. Perhaps after all it was fitting that the relentless critic of the idea of "presence" in Western metaphysics should be a palpable absence at the gathering he had indirectly provoked.

On this fuzzy, jerky bit of video (deconstruction, as I discovered last year in the process of making a film for Channel 4 about a similar conference,* seems to have a bad effect on the focal properties of TV cameras) Derrida, seated in a glazed study surrounded by lush greenery, admitted that he had himself once been doubtful about the application of deconstruction to architecture, but the persistence of architectural metaphors in philosophical and theoretical discourse ("foundation", "superstructure", "architectonics", etc.) had encouraged him to investigate further. Architects, he suggested, used deconstruction to challenge the hegemony of architectural principles such as "function" and "beauty", reinscribing this challenge in their work.

What does this mean in practice? Well, it means warped planes, skewed lines, exploded corners, flying beams and what Dr Johnson, describing metaphysical verse, called "heterogeneous ideas yoked by violence together." Take, for instance, Frank Ghery's house in Los Angeles. This is an ordinary suburban shingle house, painted pink by the previous owners, to which Ghery added a visually disorienting extension made of corrugated steel, glass, chain-link, black asphalt and cheap timber posts, full of skewed angles and unexpected gaps, and generally suggestive of a school playground or the back of a film set. It is unpopular with Ghery's neighbours, one of whom has

---

* *Big Words, Small Worlds*, transmitted in November 1987, was a documentary about an international conference on "The Linguistics of Writing" held at Strathclyde University, Glasgow in the summer of the previous year. One of our two cameras had a fault which was only discovered after the event, and in consequence a good deal of the film footage was useless. Most annoyingly, a dialogue between Derrida and Raymond Williams became a monologue by the former.

described it as "a dirty thing to do in someone else's front yard", but a source of intense interest among architects and designers – indeed it is possibly the most written-about house to have been built in the last decade. Ghery himself is cheerfully untheoretical about his work – his answer to the question, what is the difference between art and architecture, being that "the architect is willing to put a toilet in his structure" – but his exploitation of discord, discontinuity and distortion, to break down accepted architectural distinctions between form and function, beauty and ugliness, inside and outside, has made him willy-nilly a sort of figurehead in the deconstructionist movement, and his work will feature in the MOMA exhibition.

Peter Eisenman is a more self-consciously theoretical architect, who has based his work (especially a series of houses known austerely as House I, House II, House III, etc.) on linguistic models. His early work was inspired by Chomskian generative grammar, entailing a series of "transformations" of a geometrical deep structure with total indifference to the comfort and convenience of his clients. His House VI, for instance, has non-functional columns which separate people sitting at the dining table, and a slit in the floor of the master bedroom that makes twin beds mandatory. When climbing the stairs you must take care not to bang your head on a second inverted staircase stuck on the ceiling. The architect's conversion to deconstruction was marked by House X, which has a cantilevered transparent glass floor and no identifiable centre.

Eisenman was the first of a panel of speakers on architecture in the morning session of the Symposium, introduced by Charles Jencks, an American art critic resident in England, with a special, some would say proprietorial, interest in postmodernism. This he defines not merely as an architectural reaction against the severely functional cubic shapes of Corbusier and Gropius, but as a wider cultural phenomenon of "double coding" to be found across the board of innovative contemporary art. Whether deconstruction is part of or the same as postmodernism was one of the recurrent issues of the day's debates. Jencks' view seemed to be that insofar as deconstructionist architecture was distinguishable from postmodernism it was probably not architecture, but a kind of aesthetic joke. His introductory discourse was entitled: "Deconstruction: the sound of one mind laughing."

Eisenman was not amused. "I'm quite fond of Charles," this feisty New Yorker drawled into the microphone, "but enough's enough. Next time could we have an introducer who knows what he's talking about?" To have blood on the carpet so early in the proceedings was a good sign. The audience clapped and sat up expectantly. Jencks, who is used to being the man other people in the art world love to hate, didn't seem unduly disturbed.

Though Eisenman's buildings sound fairly loony in description, his ideas are interesting. His version of deconstruction has a psychoanalytical slant: it breaks down dialectical oppositions to reveal what they have repressed. In the past, visual artists told us truths about architecture that architects preferred to conceal. Munch's paintings reveal the fear and loathing entombed within the bourgeois house. Piranesi deconstructed perspective and point of view by the insoluble riddles of his vaulted staircases. The medieval cathedrals acknowledged what they repressed in the form of decorative gargoyles. "We want to make the repressed structural," said Eisenman, to "cut into the areas of greatest resistance."

Then Bernard Tschumi (Swiss in origin, American-based), sombrely dressed in shades of black and dark grey, showed slides of his prize-winning plan for the Parc de la Villette. Its chief feature is a series of eccentric-looking red buildings, vaguely reminiscent of Russian Constructivism in shape, scattered over the flat site at 120-metre intervals according to a point grid, and called *folies* – a Derridean pun on the English architectural folly and the French word for "madnesses". Derrida himself has given the enterprise an approving commentary: "The *folies* put into operation a general dislocation . . . they deconstruct first of all, but not only, the semantics of architecture." The functions of the *folies* are flexible and ambiguous. One, Tschumi told us, originally earmarked as a children's centre, is now a video studio. Another has been designated at different stages a restaurant, a garden centre and most recently an art gallery. Another was designed with no specific function in mind.

Tschumi's approach to architecture is fiercely historicist in the Popperian sense. The speed of modern communications, he assured us, has made traditional measure redundant. It is no use trying to disguise the abolition of permanence. We live in a period of deregulation – of airlines, of the Stock Exchange and the laws of classical physics. The Parc de la Villette uses permutation and substitution to attack the obsolete logic of cause and effect. This, Tschumi claimed, was a truly postmodernist architecture – the eclectic revivalism which claims that name being merely regressive, a desperate attempt to recuperate a discredited notion of meaning.

There is a bleak, fanatical consistency about Tschumi's vision which seems all too likely to be realized in the Parc de la Villette. Looking at the slides I kept imagining little groups of disconsolate people wandering through the Parc on a wet Sunday, staring numbly at the meaningless red buildings as the rain dripped from the functionless flying beams onto their umbrellas, wondering what was expected of them.

According to Zahar Hazid, a London-based architect of Persian extraction, who spoke next, the new architecture affirms that "much about the twentieth century is very enjoyable", and for me her stunning architectural paintings, drawn as if viewed from the cockpit of a low-flying jet fighter, expressed this hedonistic principle more successfully than Tschumi's *folies*. Hazid's architecture has been described as "anti-gravitational". Her prizewinning design for a club on top of a mountain overlooking Hong Kong is, in her own words, "a horizontal skyscraper," but the cunning arrangement of its slabs and ramps makes it look as if it is about to slide down the side of the mountain. It's a pity the client has suspended the project because of some unspecified trouble with the Hong Kong authorities: it would be interesting to see if it could be built.*

Mark Wigley, the young co-organizer of the impending MOMA show, stressed that the exhibits (they include Hazid's) were not utopian fantasies. Walls might be "tormented", structure and materials brought to the very limits of tolerable stress, but they could all be built. Contrary to Tschumi, Wigley

---

* Since this article was written, Zahar Hazid has become much better known, though still mainly for unbuilt buildings. In 1995 her controversial prize-winning design for an opera house in Cardiff was cold-shouldered by the Lottery Board on whose funding the project depended.

claimed that architectural deconstruction was not a new -ism or *avant garde*, but an effort to uncover the problematics of all architecture. It administered "the shock of the old". On that note we adjourned to a buffet lunch.

The afternoon session, devoted to art and sculpture, was rather more subdued, perhaps because the speakers were all scholars and critics rather than practitioners, perhaps because the quiche lorraine and chocolate gateaux they were digesting slowed them down, but mainly, I think, because the relationship of deconstruction to the visual arts is less specific than in the case of architecture. There are a few artists, such as Francis Bacon, who claim to have been influenced by Derrida, and some, like Valerio Adami and Gerard Titus-Carmel, on whom he has commented sympathetically and at length. But so much modern art is concerned with the interrogation of its own processes and the questioning of *a priori* assumptions about perception and the world, that the term deconstruction can be applied loosely to almost anything, and precisely to almost nothing, from Post-Impressionism onwards. Geoff Bennington of Sussex University, the co-translator of Derrida's *The Truth in Painting* (a task comparable in difficulty to serving spaghetti with a knitting needle), asked rhetorically whether the time had come to name a movement in art "deconstructionist", and gave the impression that only politeness restrained him from giving a negative answer.

The fact is that the term deconstruction is in danger of being appropriated indiscriminately by artists and art critics searching for impressive-sounding theoretical concepts with which to explain and justify the varied assaults of modern art upon common sense. Derrida is on record as saying that "Deconstruction is a word whose fortunes have disagreeably surprised me," and one suspects that he would get some unpleasant shocks browsing through the special issue of *Art & Design* on "Deconstructive Tendencies in Art".

Arguably the application of the term to architecture is just as specious, but the existence of a number of practising architects with some understanding of the theory behind it makes a focused debate possible. This was perhaps one reason why the audience at the symposium rebelled against the organizers' provision for two discussion panels, one on painting, one on architecture, to close the day, and insisted on a single panel of all the speakers. (Another reason was that because the programme was running late, they would have had to miss their tea to attend both panels. Of course, the audience *always* objects to the way things have been arranged towards the end of such events: enforced silence for hours on end while being lectured at generates a kind of collective resentment which has to be discharged somehow.)

It became clear in the last session that the key to the whole symposium was another event that, as Eisenman pointed out, had not yet happened: the MOMA exhibition. What makes this show potentially so important is that it has been "instigated" and co-organized by Philip Johnson, the doyen of American architects. When he was a young man, in 1932 to be precise, Johnson co-organized another exhibition at the MOMA called "The International Style", which launched the work of Corbusier and the Bauhaus in America, and thus in due course changed the face of the modern world. In the late 1970s Johnson was spectacularly converted to postmodernism (he is the architect of the notorious "Chippendale" skyscraper for AT & T in New York), and now it seems he is putting his enormous authority behind a group of architects previously thought of as marginal and eccentric. Is it conceivable that deconstruction could become the new International Style?

A lady of mature years in the audience obviously expressed the misgivings of many when she observed that the architecture displayed in the course of the day had seemed to her both "élitist and sprawling" – what relevance did it have to today's overcrowded world? In reply, Tschumi said his architecture was expressing a revolution that had already happened (he meant an information revolution). Eisenman said his architecture was a critique of architecture. Hazid said architects could inject new ideas into society by re-writing the architectural brief. In short, they retreated behind a shield of professionalism.

It was interesting, and perhaps predictable, that the attack on deconstructionist architecture should have had a political slant, because the same thing has been happening in the field of literary studies. Deconstructionist criticism is in retreat, especially in America, from something called the New Historicism, a quasi-Marxist, quasi-Foucauldian situating of literature in its socio-economic context – so much so that J. Hillis Miller, one of the luminaries of the Yale school of deconstructionists, felt impelled to rally the troops in a remarkable presidential address to the Modern Language Association of America in December 1986, "The Triumph of Theory, the Resistance to Reading, and the Question of the Material Base," in which he affirmed that "the future of literary studies depends on maintaining and developing that rhetorical reading which today is called 'deconstruction'." In the scholarly journals, however, there is an increasing sense that deconstruction is played out. Derrida's own late work has become increasingly whimsical, fictive and difficult to methodize (he himself always denied that it was a method). More recently, the prestige of deconstruction has sustained a blow from which it may never recover in American academic circles: the discovery that Paul de Man, the most revered and authoritative member of the Yale School of criticism, who died, much mourned, in 1983, had, as a young man in occupied Belgium, published a great many newspaper articles sympathetic to the Nazi cause. Imagine that F. R. Leavis was discovered, shortly after his death, to have once been a member of Mosley's Blackshirts and you will have some idea of the impact of this revelation on American academics in literature departments. It has been a gift to those on the intellectual left who have always suspected that deconstruction is dangerous to moral health, that its critique of reason is a pretext for evading social and political responsibilities.

Architects, in short, appear to be scrambling onto the deconstructionist bandwagon just at the moment when literary intellectuals are jumping off. It remains to be seen whether this will save the cause of deconstruction, or consign the architecture to limbo.

Pinter's *Last to Go*:
A Structuralist Reading

This essay was written for and first published in *Harold Pinter: a casebook*, edited by Lois Gordon (New York, 1990), a book aimed primarily at scholars and students. In reprinting the essay I have lightly revised it to make it more general-reader-friendly, but a certain amount of academic jargon is inseparable from the approach.

I was introduced to Harold Pinter at Angus Wilson's 70th birthday party in July 1983, a memorable affair which took place at the London Zoo in a thunderstorm. The next occasion on which we spoke to each other was a much more melancholy one: a reception after the memorial service for Angus in St James's Church, Piccadilly, in the autumn of 1991. Pinter came up to me and said, "Did you write something about a sketch of mine, in a book published in America?" I confessed that I had, and asked him what he thought of it. He was non-committal. "I don't know. I've never read anything like it," he said, staring at me in a searching sort of way. In retrospect it is clear that he was trying to infer from my demeanour if the piece was entirely serious. (It was, of course.) When the American critic Mel Gussow asked him if he'd seen it, the playwright replied, "I couldn't believe it . . . It's only a sketch." (Mel Gussow, *Conversations with Pinter*, Hern Books, 1994.) I know the feeling, of being a nut under some critic's ponderous hammer, but I think that this little sketch illustrates truths about Harold Pinter's work, and about dramatic dialogue and dramatic structure in general, which are worth spelling out. In the circumstances, it is particularly generous of him to allow me to reproduce the complete text as an introduction to this essay.

LAST TO GO

A coffee stall. A BARMAN *and an old* NEWSPAPER SELLER. *The* BARMAN *leans on his counter, the* OLD MAN *stands with tea. Silence.*

MAN You was a bit busier earlier.	1
BARMAN Ah.	2
MAN Round about ten.	3
BARMAN Ten, was it?	4
MAN About then.	5
(*Pause*)	
I passed by here about then.	5a
BARMAN Oh yes?	6
MAN I noticed you were doing a bit of trade.	7
(*Pause*)	
BARMAN Yes, trade was very brisk here about ten.	8
MAN Yes, I noticed.	9
(*Pause*)	
I sold my last one about then.	
Yes. About nine forty-five.	9a
BARMAN Sold your last then, did you?	10
MAN Yes, my last "Evening News" it was. Went about twenty to ten.	11
(*Pause*)	
BARMAN "Evening News", was it?	12
MAN Yes.	13
(*Pause*)	
Sometimes it's the "Star" is the last to go.	13a
BARMAN Ah.	14
MAN Or the . . . whatsisname.	15
BARMAN "Standard".	16

MAN Yes.   17
   (*Pause*)
   All I had left tonight was the
   "Evening News".   17a
   (*Pause*)
BARMAN Then that went, did it?   18
MAN Yes.   19
   (*Pause*)
   Like a shot.   19a
   (*Pause*)
BARMAN You didn't have any left, eh?   20
MAN No, not after I sold that one.   21
   (*Pause*)
BARMAN It was after that you must have
   come by here then, was it?   22
MAN Yes, I come by here after that, see,
   after I packed up.   23
BARMAN You didn't stop here though, did
   you?   24
MAN When?   25
BARMAN I mean, you didn't stop here and
   have a cup of tea then, did you?   26
MAN What, about ten?   27
BARMAN Yes.   28
MAN No, I went up to Victoria.   29
BARMAN No, I thought I didn't see you.   30
MAN I had to go to Victoria.   31
   (*Pause*)
BARMAN Yes, trade was very brisk here
   about then.   32
   (*Pause*)
MAN I went to see if I could get hold of
   George.   33
BARMAN Who?   34
MAN George.   35
   (*Pause*)
BARMAN George who?   36
MAN George . . . whatsisname.   37
BARMAN Oh.   38
   (*Pause*)

Did you get hold of him?   38a
MAN No. No, I couldn't get hold of him.
I couldn't locate him.   39
BARMAN He's not much about now, is he?   40
(*Pause*)
MAN When did you last see him then?   41
BARMAN Oh, I haven't seen him for years.   42
MAN No, nor me.   43
(*Pause*)
BARMAN Used to suffer very bad from
arthritis.   44
MAN Arthritis?   45
BARMAN Yes.   46
MAN He never suffered from arthritis.   47
BARMAN Suffered very bad.   48
(*Pause*)
MAN Not when I knew him.   49
(*Pause*)
BARMAN I think he must have left the
area.   50
(*Pause*)
MAN Yes, it was the "Evening News" was
the last to go tonight.   51
BARMAN Not always the last though, is it,
though?   52
MAN No. Oh no. I mean sometimes it's
the "News". Other times it's one of
the others. No way of telling before-
hand. Until you've got your last one
left, of course. Then you can tell
which one it's going to be.   53
BARMAN Yes.   54
(*Pause*)
MAN Oh yes.   55
(*Pause*)
I think he must have left the area.   55a

Last to Go, a revue sketch first performed in 1959, is a microcosm of Harold Pinter's dramatic universe. It presents in a condensed form the central paradox of his work: how is it that dialogue superficially so banal, repetitive and full of silences, and a story so slight and ambiguous, can interest and entertain us?

The fact that this text is so short allows us to ponder the question with the whole "play", as it were, present to our consciousness, and this is the reason I choose it for analysis. It has already been astutely commented on by Deirdre Burton in her book *Dialogue and Discourse: A Sociolinguistic Approach to Modern Drama Dialogue and Naturally Occurring Conversation* (1980). What I have to say here is indebted to her work and also, I hope, complementary to it. Deirdre Burton particularly admired the way *Last to Go* dramatically exploits certain features of real conversation, especially what is called "phatic" discourse; that is, speech whose primary function is to maintain conversational contact between people, rather than expressing or conveying any meaning. It was the pioneering anthropologist Malinowski who first identified this use of language and named it "phatic communion". Usually it is a one-sided operation, as when, for instance, a doctor murmurs, "Mmm, mmm," to indicate to a patient that he is attending to the latter's description of his symptoms. But *Last to Go* presents a conversation that is mutually and simultaneously phatic for *both* interlocutors, maintaining contact but not conveying much information between them. This accounts for the extraordinary amount of repetition in the dialogue. As Deirdre Burton observes, "the characters are continually questioning and confirming matters that they both already know, that they must surely know they both know, and that the audience certainly knows that they know."[*]

[*] Deirdre Burton, *Dialogue and Discourse: A Sociolinguistic Approach to*

The presence of the audience is, of course, crucial, making the dialogue an object of aesthetic rather than sociolinguistic interest; or, to put it less solemnly, funny and moving for us, but not for the speakers. We can formalize this point by putting the category of "phatic" in the perspective of Roman Jakobson's structuralist model of the speech act:[*]

CONTEXT

ADDRESSER   MESSAGE   ADDRESSEE

CONTACT

CODE

The ADDRESSER (speaker, writer) sends a MESSAGE (utterance, text) to the ADDRESSEE (interlocutor, reader) referring to a CONTEXT (which can be anything in the world, physical and mental, they both inhabit) using a CODE (e.g., the English language) and a means of CONTACT (which Jakobson defines generally as "a physical channel and psychological connection" – it might be a book or a telephone line or, as in conversation, the mutual presence-to-each-other of the speakers). The function of a particular speech act, or of an entire discourse, can be classified according to which of the component elements is emphasized or focused on. Thus, a "message" focused primarily on Context (like this essay, which is about Pinter's sketch) is Referential; a message focused on the Addresser, such as an expletive, relieving the speaker's feelings, is Emotive; a message focused on the Addressee (an order or instruction, for instance) is Conative; a message focused on its own code (such as a dictionary definition) is Metalingual; and a message that is focused on Contact (*e.g.*, the doctor's "Mmm, mmm,") is Phatic. But there is a final category, the Poetic, when the Message is focused on itself. "The set . . . toward the message as such, focus on the message for its own sake, is the POETIC function of language." Under "poetic", Jakobson includes any artistic use of language. It is important, though potentially confusing, to remember that poetic language doesn't only occur in poetry, or in novels and plays and other texts we call literary.

Modern Drama Dialogue and Naturally Occurring Conversation (1980), p. 13.
  [*] Roman Jakobson, "Linguistic and Poetics", in *Language in Literature*, edited by Krystyna Pomorska and Stephen Rudy (1987), p. 66ff.

Whenever we use language that calls attention to itself – make a pun, or fall into rhyme, for instance – we are making use of the poetic function of language. But that function doesn't *dominate* non-literary discourse. It is subordinated to some other purpose – to amuse or charm or persuade (much advertising uses the poetic function for this purpose). Correspondingly, utterances that in "real life" might be classified as referential, emotive, conative, etc., *become* poetic when they occur in an aesthetic context, in a play or sketch for instance. Language that is phatic for the Barman and the Newspaper-seller in *Last to Go* is poetic for us when we watch and listen to it being performed. How does this happen?

Before we pursue that question, let us look more closely at what Jakobson says about the category of the phatic:

> There are messages primarily serving to establish, to prolong, or to discontinue communication, to check whether the channel works ("Hello, do you hear me?"), to attract the attention of the interlocutor or to confirm his continued attention ("Are you listening?" or in Shakespearean diction, "Lend me your ears!" – and on the other end of the wire, "Um-hum!") This set for contact, or in Malinowski's terms PHATIC function, may be displayed by a profuse exchange of ritualized formulas, by entire dialogues with the mere purport of prolonging communication.[*]

This last observation seems very applicable to *Last to Go*. The sketch, we might venture to say, is on one level about two lonely people who rather than face their own solitariness, late at night, desperately keep a conversation going although they have nothing substantial to communicate. Neither of them wants to be the last to go (home).

It is important to recognize that Jakobson's categories are based on *dominance*. That is to say, speech acts are rarely focused exclusively on one function; it is a question of which function is dominant. The opening line of Pinter's sketch, for instance,

MAN You was a bit busier earlier

is ostensibly referential, though we infer from the triviality of its

---

[*] Jacobson, *op.cit.*, p.68.

content and the silence (indicated in the stage direction) preceding it, that its real function is phatic. The Barman's reply, "Ah" (line 2), is *manifestly* phatic, since it neither confirms nor disconfirms what the Man has said, but merely establishes that the Barman has heard him. The dialogue proceeds in this way for some lines – a pseudo-referential message from the Man being phatically acknowledged by the Barman, until the Barman ventures a referential (though redundant) observation,

BARMAN Yes, trade was very brisk here about ten

and the Man (redundantly) confirms it yet again:

MAN Yes, I noticed. (8–9)

This slight reversal of roles in the conversation brings the first phase or movement of the piece to an end. The Man now begins a new but parallel topic, concerning the time and nature of his last sale of the evening. This is a sublimely vacuous topic, spun out by the Man's repetition of the same information and the Barman's redundant checking:

MAN   I sold my last one about then. Yes. About nine
          forty-five.
BARMAN Sold your last then, did you?
MAN   Yes, my last "Evening News" it was. Went about
          twenty to ten.
          (*Pause*)
BARMAN "Evening News", was it?
MAN   Yes.
          (*Pause*)
          Sometimes it's the "Star" is the last
          to go. (9a–13a)

In performance, the pauses add greatly to the comic effect of the two men's effort to keep this contentless conversational ball rolling. Having covered all the possible variations of which newspaper is the last to go, they seem to have exhausted the topic, but after a silence the Man doggedly revives it by repeating what he has already said, and confirmed, earlier (11, 13):

          (*Pause*)
MAN   All I had left tonight was the
          "Evening News". (17a)

Then, after *another* pause, the Barman *again* checks this useless piece of information:

> (*Pause*)
> BARMAN Then that went, did it?
> MAN Yes.
> (*Pause*)
> Like a shot. (18–19a)

This phrase is so incongruous, both in application to the sale of the last newspaper at such a late hour, and in the context of the leaden-paced conversation, that it is sure to raise a gust of laughter from an audience in performance. (Harold Pinter, in the conversation referred to above, confirmed that this line invariably gets the biggest laugh of the entire sketch in the theatre.) Another reason for such an effect is that the opportunity to laugh provides relief from the tension of wondering whether the speakers will succeed in keeping the conversation going – a suspense heightened by the concentration of pauses at this part of the text. Silence, a characteristic feature of Pinter's drama, is extraordinarily potent on the stage, because of the audience's assumption that drama consists of speech or significant action.

An additional reason why "Like a shot" has a powerful effect is that, although a cliché, it is a figure of speech, a simile to be precise, and the first to be used by either speaker. One way of putting this is to say that the phrase "Like a shot" is *foregrounded* against a background of more literal, denotative language used by the speakers up to that point. For the Man, it constitutes a heroic effort (comically, pathetically heroic in the audience's perception) to dignify the banality of the last sale by a rhetorical flourish. In a livelier linguistic context it would hardly register as such. But that background of dull, repetitive, denotative language is itself foregrounded against the kind of language traditionally expected from drama – pointed, well-formed, eloquent, profound, witty – and thus makes *Last to Go* a modern or experimental piece of dramatic writing.

In other words, the poetic function of language is partly a matter of the way a given discourse is framed and perceived. A declaration of love in verse, for instance, might be primarily emotive for the addresser (a relief for his feelings) or primarily conative if sent to the addressee (persuading her to reciprocate) but if it is published in a literary magazine it is poetic, read "for its own sake". But you cannot turn *any* discourse into a work of verbal art simply by reading the message for its own sake. A railway timetable stubbornly remains a referential message, a dictionary remains a metalingual message, unless you select from and manipulate their component parts – in which case they would no longer perform their original functions.

What kind of selection and manipulation would be entailed? What is it that poetic messages, or messages capable of being received as such, have, that other messages do not have? Jakobson had a highly technical answer to this question: "The poetic function projects the principle of equivalence from the axis of selection to the axis of combination."[*] To expound this fully would take too long here,[†] but in effect it means that discourses which are either designed as works of verbal art, or capable of being read as such, are characterized by parallelism, symmetry, repetition, contrast, and other kinds of binary patterning. The most obvious example is the metrical and phonological patterning of regular verse, which is not required for the referential, emotive and conative functions of the message. In prose fiction and "prose drama", the system of equivalences is more difficult to spot, because prose and realistically rendered speech do not exhibit the overt formal patterning of verse, and because the variety of discourses and voices in these forms obscures what patterning there is. Nevertheless it can usually be discovered.

We receive *Last to Go* as a "poetic message", as a verbal work of art, on both the grounds referred to above: first because we encounter it in an aesthetic frame – as performed in a theatre or as read in a book of plays and sketches; and secondly because it stands up to being read as a message for its own sake, a quality which turns out on examination to have something to do with patterns of equivalence that can be perceived in it. Like all drama, this sketch is an imitation of various speech acts that can be classified according to the functions they would have in reality (referential, phatic, etc.), but that considered together, as a whole, constitute a poetic message, which we attend to "for its own sake" – that is, for the meanings it generates independently

[*] Jakobson, *op.cit.*, p.71.
[†] For further discussion, see my *The Modes of Modern Writing* (1977), *passim*.

of any "real" context. And both the plethora of meanings and the unification of them into a "whole" are related to the pattern of equivalences discoverable in the text. Like much modern realistic or naturalistic writing, *Last to Go* disguises its aesthetically necessary patterns of equivalence as contingency, as mere representation of typical behaviour. The surface justification for the amount of repetition in the dialogue is that people do actually repeat a good deal in dominantly phatic conversations. But one can also point to an effect in the dialogue something like echo and refrain in poetry: *about ten/about then; sold my last/ sold your last; Evening News it was/Evening News, was it?* There is a high degree of artifice here as well as an acute ear for the character of colloquial, uneducated speech. It would probably be possible to deceive someone into thinking that this dialogue was recorded from life, if one got two actors to tape-record it in a certain way – with much humming and hahing, coughs, grunts, overlapping of lines, elisions of words, nongrammatical pauses, background noise and suchlike features of "naturally occurring conversation". But, as written, the dialogue invites a much more stylized performance, bringing out its symmetries and echoes.

I have not yet mentioned the most obvious "equivalence" in the sketch – that between its beginning and ending, marked by the difference of its middle. Drama is a form of narrative, and narrative entails process and change. At first *Last to Go* presents a purely static situation. Two men are talking for the mere sake of talking. They endlessly recycle the same trivial information. Statements and questions that seem superficially to be referential in function are in fact purely phatic. But this stasis, and the pattern of verbal equivalences that underpin it, are disturbed in line 25:

BARMAN You didn't stop here, though, did you?

MAN   When? (24–5)

This is a deviation from the previous pattern of the text, whereby only the Barman asks the questions, and they are pseudo-questions, checking-formulae which contain their own answers (though they are answered anyway): "Ten, was it?" (4); "Sold your last then, did you?" (10); " 'Evening News', was it?" (12). The Man's "When?" in line 25 is a breach in the tacit rules of the game the pair are playing. It also implies either that the Man is extraordinarily stupid (since there is no doubt about what time is being referred to) or that his attention is wandering. The latter seems the likelier explanation. The Barman tries to pull the conversation back on to its safe course ("I mean, you didn't stop here and have a cup of tea then, did you?" (26)) but the Man moves on to another topic:

MAN   No, I went up to Victoria.
BARMAN No, I thought I didn't see you.
MAN   I had to go to Victoria. (29–31)

The "No" in line 29 is foregrounded against all the "yeses" scattered earlier through the dialogue, and the Barman is compelled to repeat this negative word in expressing agreement. He tries desperately to keep the conversation anchored to the previous topics ("Yes, trade was very brisk about then," 32) but the Man is mentally retracing his journey to Victoria, and the Barman has reluctantly to follow him.

MAN   I went to see if I could get hold of George.(33)

The dialogue now begins to take on a different character from the pattern previously established. With the introduction of the topic of George, statements and questions become genuinely referential. But the possibility of disagreement also raises its head, and with it, the possibility of confrontation, challenge and termination of the conversation. Either one of the men is wrong about George, or they are each thinking of a different George. In either case, the continuity of the conversation is jeopardized. In the event the desire to maintain phatic communion triumphs over the desire to establish the truth, but there is dramatic suspense about this outcome for some lines.

BARMAN George who?
MAN   George . . . whatsisname.
BARMAN Oh.
        (*Pause*) (36–8)

When the Man used the expression "whatisname" previously, the Barman was able to supply the missing name (15–16). Clearly unable to supply it in this case, he chooses to pretend that he knows who the Man is referring to.

BARMAN Did you get hold of him?
MAN   No. No, I couldn't get hold of him.
        I couldn't locate him.

BARMAN He's not much about now, is he? (38a–40)
This last line has the grammatical form of those earlier
questions from the Barman that are ostensibly referential, but in
fact phatic, merely recycling interrogatively the information that
has just been stated declaratively, like "Sold your last, then did
you?" (10) and " 'Evening News', was it?" (12). But this time
the Barman has hazarded additional information on his own
account, and thus laid himself open to referential challenge:

MAN   When did you last see him, then? (41)
The Barman equivocates and the Man, instead of pressing him,
identifies himself with the answer.

BARMAN Oh, I haven't seen him for years.
MAN   No, nor me. (42–3)
Emboldened by this admission, the Barman makes a very
specific referential assertion:

BARMAN Used to suffer very bad from arthritis.(44)
Why does he say this? Assuming that he doesn't really know
whom the Man is referring to, it could be because he actually
knew a George who suffered from arthritis, and is convinced
that the Man knows so little about *his* George that the two can
be happily fused into one for the phatic purpose of the
conversation; or it could be that he is reinforcing his claim to
know George by inventing this detail, as a writer will give a
fictitious character an air of reality by what Henry James called
"solidity of specification". At any rate, it proves a rash move in
terms of the conversational game they are playing, because it
leads to a direct challenge:

MAN   Arthritis?
BARMAN Yes.
MAN   He never suffered from arthritis.
BARMAN Suffered very bad.
         (*Pause*) (45–48)
This is obviously the dramatic climax of the sketch, the only
moment of conflict between the two *dramatis personae*. There is
a danger that if the topic is pursued much further it will be
revealed that one or both of the interlocutors is misinformed or
misunderstanding or lying, and the conversation will end
acrimoniously.

MAN   Not when I knew him. (49)
         (*Pause*)

This seems to continue the challenge, though it also offers a face-saving solution of their disagreement, *viz.*, that they must have known George at different times. If the Barman had replied aggressively, "Well, he did when *I* knew him", it would be necessary to establish when that was and to settle other factual matters to do with the identity of George, probably revealing the incompatibility of their respective accounts of him, and thus jeopardizing the continuance of the conversation. But in fact the Barman backs down:

BARMAN I think he must have left the area. (50)

This refers to an earlier topic, namely, the Man's failure to "locate" George. It is by way of being a confirmation of information already received, and thus brings the potentially divisive topic of George to an amicably indeterminate conclusion. The Man collaborates by reverting, after another pause, to the safe, manageable topic of the last newspaper to go:

MAN   Yes, it was the "Evening News" was the last
         to go tonight. (51)

To which the Barman eagerly responds with one of his typically redundant questions, reformulating information already received:

BARMAN Not always the last though, is it, though? (52)

To which the Man replies:

MAN   No. Oh no. I mean sometimes it's the "News".
         Other times it's one of the others. No way of
         telling beforehand. Until you've got your last one
         left, of course. Then you can tell which one it's
         going to be.

Superficially, the Man's reply seems another recycling of information already communicated in lines 11–16. But in fact there is a significant difference. Whereas in the earlier lines the Man had merely commented on which paper was the last to go, here he is talking about *predicting* which will be the last paper to go. This point is given emphasis by the fact that it is made in the longest single speech in the entire sketch. The phrase "last to go", which is the title of the whole piece, thus begins to acquire additional resonances, or equivalences.

The phrase "last to go", I suggested earlier, applies to the two men – neither wanting to be the last to go home, the last to be alone. But there seems to be another possible metaphorical meaning: death, and the fear of death. Out of a given set of people, you never know who is going to be the last to die, and therefore the next to die, until there is only one left: "then you can tell which one it's going to be." This might explain why the Man reverts, somewhat unexpectedly, in the very last line of the play, to the topic of George, adopting a line of the Barman's as if it is his own:

MAN   I think he must have left the area. (55a)

George's departure may have been from this life, not just from Victoria.

According to A. J. Greimas* all concepts are semantically defined by a binary relationship with their opposites (e.g. life versus death) or their negatives (e.g. life versus non-life), yielding the basic semiotic model, A:B::–A:–B (e.g., life is to Death as Non-Life is to Non-Death), and all narrative can be seen as the transformation of such four-term homologies into characters and actions. In *Last to Go* the life/death theme is represented as presence/absence. Life is presence, death is absence. Speech requires presence, and in phatic communion is used chiefly to maintain presence. The opposite of speech is silence, absence of speech, the "pause" that is such a characteristic feature of Pinter's drama. The negative of presence is represented by George, who is named in the dialogue but not physically present, thought to be in Victoria, but not "located" there; and the negative of absence is presence-about-to-be-terminated, such as the last newspaper to go, just before it goes. The semiotic structure of the sketch might therefore be summarized as: Speech is to Silence as George is to the last newspaper to go.

---

* A. J. Greimas, *Semantique structurale* (Paris 1966), *Du sens* (Paris, 1970) and *Maupassant. La Semiologie du texte: exercices pratiques* (Paris, 1976). I am indebted to Ann Jefferson's explication of Greimas' method in her review of the last-named book in *Poetics and Theory of Literature* II (1977) pp.579–88.

Playback:
Extracts from a Writer's Diary

A perfectly adequate and successful stage representation of a play requires a combination of circumstances so extraordinarily fortunate that I doubt whether it has ever occurred in the history of the world.

– George Bernard Shaw

A brief account of the genesis of *The Writing Game* was given on pages 215–17. For the benefit of readers not familiar with this play, the action takes place at the Wheatcroft Centre, a seventeenth-century farmhouse and barn in Dorset converted to accommodate short residential courses in creative writing. The dramatis personae are: Jeremy Deane, the secretary administrator of the establishment; Leo Rafkin, a fifty-something Jewish American novelist on sabbatical from his university job, and Maude Lockett, a successful forty-something English novelist, who are tutors on the course; Simon St Clair, a thirty-something London-based novelist and journalist who is the "visiting writer"; and Penny Sewell, a young married woman who is a student. The action may be summarized as follows:

Act One, Scene 1. Leo (a late substitute for a sick English writer) arrives and is shown the tutors' accommodation in the barn by Jeremy. Leo doesn't like what he hears about the course and decides to leave, but changes his mind when Maude arrives. When Jeremy reveals that Simon St Clair will visit for one night, Leo recalls that St Clair wrote a spiteful profile of him some years before. Maude's interest in Simon is hinted at. Her husband, Henry, an Oxford don, leaves a footling message, the first of several, on the answerphone, to which the others listen.

Scene 2. Maude and Leo come back to the barn after the first evening's socializing with the students. Leo makes a pass at Maude, which she rebuffs.

Scene 3. Next afternoon. Leo is rude to Penny about a chapter of her novel in progress. Maude attacks him for this.

Scene 4. Same evening. Maude reads to the students (whose presence is implied) from her novel in progress. She is interrupted by Jeremy asking if anybody has seen Penny Sewell, who is missing.

Scene 5. A few minutes later. Leo goes back to the barn alone and finds Penny asleep there. She wakes and asks him to tell her "how to write better". He describes how he wrote a story about an American who goes to Poland at a time of acute shortages, filling his suitcase with soap; he uses the soap to hire and abuse Polish prostitutes, then visits Auschwitz and realizes he is subconsciously seeking revenge for the Holocaust. Maude returns from searching the nearby river for Penny in a bad temper, not improved by finding her having a cosy chat with Leo.

Scene 6. Next evening. Leo reads his story, "Soap". Before he gets to the end half the audience walks out, offended by its sexual explicitness. Leo walks out too.

Scene 7. A few minutes later. Jeremy fails to mollify Leo. Maude and Leo argue about the treatment of sex in fiction. Disconcerted that Maude guesses the ending of his story, Leo starts revising it on his portable computer. Maude, aroused by the conversation and a few glasses of wine, leaves the door of the bathroom invitingly open when she goes to take a shower. Leo belatedly responds to this signal.

Act Two, Scene 1. The next afternoon. Simon St Clair has arrived and is leafing through Leo's story when Maude comes in to the barn, followed by Leo. Leo and Simon immediately begin to quarrel. Jeremy takes Simon to his accommodation in the main house.

Scene 2. Same evening. Simon St Clair gives his reading, a semi-autobiographical metafiction called *Instead of a Novel*.

Scene 3. A few minutes later. Back in the barn, Maude begins to flirt with Simon, who taunts Leo about his unfinished war novel. Leo throws a punch at Simon, whose nose bleeds. Penny comes in to give Leo a new piece of writing. While Maude is helping Simon to clean up in the bathroom, Jeremy tells Leo that she is notorious for "collecting young men." Maude retires to bed, and Simon asks Leo to exchange rooms. Leo refuses, but when Simon goes up to Maude's bedroom, Leo storms out of the barn.

Scene 4. Next morning. Leo prepares to leave before the end of the course, in spite of Maude's apologies. Penny comes in by appointment. Leo tells her that her new piece is a tremendous improvement and that she could be a "real writer" if she is prepared to work hard. She tells him that coming on the course has "cured her" of the wish to be a writer. Cast down, Leo is more responsive to Maude's conciliatory manner. He tricks her into thinking he is erasing his novel from his computer, as a way of announcing that he is going to abandon it. He teases Maude with the threat of writing a play about the events of the last few days.

I wrote the first draft of *The Writing Game*, then called *The Pressure Cooker*, in the summer of 1985 and submitted it (anonymously as the rules required) for the Mobil Oil play competition. It was not placed, but it was returned with a note saying that the judges had enjoyed reading it. My agent for drama and media work at Curtis Brown Ltd, Charles Elton, sent the play to a few London managements without success, then showed it to the director Patrick Garland, who liked it, and in turn passed it to John Faulkner, a senior administrator at the National Theatre, who also liked it and proposed a "rehearsed reading" at the Cottesloe, directed by Patrick. This took place on 16 June 1986. ("Bloomsday" – which I took to be a good omen.) I was fortunate to have a distinguished cast: Jack Shepherd as Leo, Eleanor Bron as Maude, Greg Hicks as Simon, Roger Lloyd Pack as Jeremy and Caroline Bliss as Penny. The performance went down well with the audience, especially the three "readings" (which constitute, in fact, the most original feature of the play), though the last two scenes sagged somewhat and clearly needed work. A week later, Leah Schmidt, who had taken over responsibility for the play from Charles Elton at Curtis Brown, called me to say that the National wanted to option it. I couldn't believe my luck.

I was right to distrust it. In a reshuffle at the National soon afterwards, John Faulkner left, and Peter Hall announced his intention of giving up the job of Artistic Director. While the search started for his successor, David Aukin was appointed to a new post of Executive Director. He liked *The Pressure Cooker*, but was unable to interest any of the resident directors, none of whom had come to the rehearsed reading, in doing it. He proposed a collaboration between the National and the Bristol Old Vic, where a friend, Leon Rubin, was Artistic Director. Rubin was enthusiastic about putting the play on in his Studio theatre with the possibility of a transfer to the National, but shortly afterwards he had a row with his Board and left Bristol. I suggested to David Aukin that we should approach the Birmingham Rep, where John Adams had just taken up the post of Artistic Director. The theatre wasn't ideal because the 900-seat main auditorium was too big and the 120-seat Studio too small for my play, but I was impatient to see it on any stage, and my connections with Birmingham made the Rep an obvious choice. After making encouraging noises, John decided against doing the play, which he said wouldn't fit into the youth-oriented programme he was planning for his studio. He also had artistic reservations about the script. "Is it really a radio play?" he asked rhetorically.

The National's option was running out. David Aukin was willing to renew it for another year, but Leah and I couldn't see much prospect of its being produced, so decided to try our luck elsewhere. Leah sent the play to the Royal Shakespeare Theatre, and I dropped a note to the Artistic Director, Terry Hands, whom I had tutored at Birmingham University in my first year as a lecturer, hoping he might take an interest in my play. He replied pleasantly, but neither Leah nor I ever heard another word from the RSC, and as far as I know the script is still mouldering in its archives. At about the same time I took up the offer of an old friend, Donald Fanger, Professor of Russian at Harvard, to pass the script to his friend Robert Brustein, distinguished director of the American Repertory Theater in Cambridge, Mass. Brustein wrote to say he liked the play and wanted to do a rehearsed reading with a view to a full production later. Meanwhile, however, a London producer, André Ptaszynski, partner in a firm called Pola Jones, had read the play and optioned it. Since his option covered American rights, the rehearsed reading in Cambridge went ahead without any commitment to a future production. This was staged in the foyer of the ART in January 1988, and both André and I attended it. It went down very well with the largely academic and anglophile audience, though the tension again perceptibly slackened in Act II, Scene 3, the "fight scene". Afterwards André and I went for a pizza and indulged in the favourite theatrical game of dream-casting. André suggested Dustin Hoffman for Leo.

First, however, he had to find a director. I was delighted when Mike Ockrent expressed strong interest, since I had much admired his production of Peter Nichols's *Passion Play* a few years earlier. He had some criticisms of my play, which were extremely acute, and prompted some revisions which much improved it. For example, he said he wished the characters could have more to do while they were talking – if Maude could be trying to make telephone calls in some scenes, for instance . . . This gave me the idea of introducing an answerphone, and another character – without the expense of hiring another actor. (It may have been the first time an answerphone figured in a stage play.) The "fight scene" was much improved by following Mike's suggestion that the conflict between the two men should arise out of their disagreement about the art of fiction as well as out of their sexual rivalry. And the last scene was strengthened by making Leo face the fact that the "big book" he has been working on for years will never work, which suggested the business with the computer.

We tried out the revised text at a private reading performed by actors from Mike Ockrent's production of *Follies*, very satisfactorily, and began to plan for a production of *The Pressure Cooker* (as it was still called) in the autumn. We began by trying to cast Leo, and never really got any further. André insisted on a star with box-office appeal, and Mike insisted that he had to be an American. We started boldly by offering the part to Dustin

Hoffman, and for some weeks he actually kept us dangling with the possibility of accepting it, because he wanted to act in the West End, but in the end he did Shylock in Peter Hall's production of *The Merchant* instead. We had no better luck with anybody else who met the criteria of both André and Mike. Not surprisingly, American stars weren't prepared to risk their reputations on a new play by a writer with no theatrical track record. André's option ran out at the end of 1988, and so did Mike Ockrent's availability.

At this point the Royal Court Theatre rang me up and asked if I would be interested in writing a play for them. I said I already had one and sent them *The Pressure Cooker*. Max Stafford-Clark, the Artistic Director, responded encouragingly and offered to option it. However, when we met to discuss his plans for producing it, he seemed to have changed his mind. He nodded agreement when his literary manager Kate Harwood said my play was too commercial for the Court and too literary for the West End. I took the point, but wondered why they had brought me to London to make it.

Early in 1989 André Ptaszynski mentioned my play to a young director called John Retallack who had just taken over the Oxford Stage Company, a subsidized touring company. Retallack obtained a copy of the play from Leah, and expressed keen interest in putting it on. We met for a convivial lunch in April, but in the weeks that followed he became very elusive and evasive and finally admitted that he had changed his mind, mainly because of negative responses to the play in his company, especially from feminists. (This was not a total surprise: I was told that an actress at the National had refused to read the part of Maude on these grounds.) Another director who expressed interest in the play that summer was Robin Midgley, who had taken over a touring company based in Cambridge. But as he wanted me to drop the three readings which I considered the play's most interesting feature, we didn't get beyond a first meeting.

In the autumn of 1989 I decided to have one more attempt at getting the play on to the stage, and, if that failed, to try adapting it for television. (Over the past twelve months I had been happily involved in the TV adaptation of *Nice Work* for the BBC.) I called John Adams at the Birmingham Rep, told him the history of the play since he had read it, and asked if he would like to see the revised script. He said yes. A couple of weeks later he phoned me on a rather bad line from London to say he had read the play on the train down and loved it. He didn't know what I'd done to it, but it now worked. The question was not whether the Rep would do it, but when; and he saw it as a main house play.

Naturally I was delighted, though having been disappointed so many times I kept the news to myself until the contract had been signed. I was rather dismayed when John talked about a production twelve or eighteen months hence. I pointed out that the television serialization of *Nice Work* was due for transmission that autumn, and it would be a pity not to exploit the publicity it would generate, especially in the West Midlands. John took the point, and proposed a production in May 1990. He mentioned that he didn't think *The Pressure Cooker* was a very good title, and I suggested *The Writing Game: a comedy*, which was adopted without further discussion.

What follows is a selection of passages from a diary I kept about the Birmingham Rep's production, with a postscript summarizing the play's subsequent fortunes.

Wednesday 21 March 1990 My play, *The Writing Game*, is due to be produced at the Birmingham Repertory Theatre, running for three weeks from Saturday 13 May. Rehearsals are due to start on Monday 9 April, or at the latest on Tuesday 17 April – that is, in two-and-a-half or three-and-a-half weeks' time. At the moment, not a single part of the five-character play has been cast, in spite of increasingly urgent efforts to do so over the last two or three months. I am told that this situation is by no means unusual in provincial theatre, but I find it rather nerve-racking. I have decided to keep an occasional diary as the play is cast and goes into rehearsal. Since time is limited, I will dictate the narrative into a tape recorder, have it transcribed, and polish it later on the word-processor.

This project, I must acknowledge, was suggested by Simon Gray's highly entertaining and instructive books about the trials and tribulations of mounting productions of his play, *The Common Pursuit*, in England and America, entitled *An Unnat-*

ural Pursuit and *How's That for Telling 'Em, Fat Lady?* respectively. Although I cannot hope to emulate the wonderfully comic paranoia of Gray's authorial persona, I shall try to be as candid as he seems to have been. If this narrative proves to have a more than private interest and value, it will be as the history of a play's gestation, development and performance, seen from the point of view of an author to whom the whole process is largely unfamiliar. Apart from a number of sketches which I contributed to two satirical revues produced at the Birmingham Rep in 1963 and 1966, *The Writing Game* is my first work for the stage to be professionally produced.

John Adams and I had no meetings until just before Christmas, when I went into the Rep and we talked about casting. He had already contacted me on the phone about commissioning a set from Roger Butlin, the designer who had done the sets for the Rep's recent productions of *Who's Afraid of Virginia Woolf* and *The Real Thing*, which I liked very much; so I was very happy to go along with that. John said on that occasion that he had only one substantial suggestion to make about revising the text: he didn't think that the opening scene in which Jeremy addresses the audience as if they are the newly arrived students ("Welcome to the Wheatcroft Centre! I hope you'll all have a wonderfully creative five days here . . .") would work in the huge space of the Rep's main auditorium. This was a scene I had inserted after the first reading of the play at the National, at the suggestion of my friend and Birmingham neighbour, David Edgar, who had read the play early in 1987, and given me the benefit of his dramaturgical wisdom. It had worked well at the American Repertory Theater reading, but John thought it was a device that belonged to the intimate scale of a studio production. I accepted this advice, and agreed to make the scene of Leo's arrival the opening scene of the play (which it had been in the first draft).

We met at my house in the week after Christmas to go through the text, agreeing any minor changes that either of us had thought about. It was a useful afternoon's work. I mitigated the explicitness of the language a little and made some other small adjustments. The latest version of the play is now dated January 1990 and that's the one we've been circulating. We've enquired about a great many well-known actors and actresses for Leo and Maude. We had a strong expression of interest from one quite starry actress, but to our great disappointment she withdrew, for unspecified reasons. Since then we haven't had any luck. In very few cases have the actors read the play and declined the part – usually they were "not available". But we have lost a lot of time waiting for them to make up their minds or trying to get answers from their agents.

Today there has been an interesting development on the other side of the Atlantic. In January, Bob Brustein of the American Repertory Theater in Cambridge, Mass., asked if he could see the revised text of *The Pressure Cooker*, and this afternoon Leah rang to say that she'd just had a call from Robert Orchard, the Contracts Manager at the ART, saying they want to produce the play in their 90–91 season, which begins in December. This is a pleasant surprise, inasmuch as it strengthens one's faith in the play. On the other hand the Birmingham Rep has some kind of option on the American rights, the exact nature of which is obscure to me. I told Leah I would speak informally to John Adams about it when I see him in London tomorrow.

Friday 23 March 1990 I went to London yesterday to meet John Adams at the offices of *Spotlight* (the famous and indispensable reference guide to actors and actresses) in Leicester Place, to interview some actors, including an actress I shall call Jane Doe, and Susan Penhaligon (both for Maude). A small but elegant office was set aside for our use, with bookcases filled with copies of *Spotlight* going back through the last few decades.

John told me that a script had gone off to Ed Asner in Los Angeles. Asner is, of course, a well-known American actor, and the star of a popular TV series, *Lou Grant*. His face appeared on the front cover of *Radio Times* on Tuesday, because he is starring in a new Jeffrey Archer serial on BBC1, *Not a Penny More, Not a Penny Less*, starting next week. He looked uncannily like Norman Mailer. I remembered that someone had once suggested him as a possible Leo, and his name was on one of the many lists I had drawn up in the last couple of months. It occurred to me that he might be in England for publicity to do with *Not a Penny More*, in which case we could show him the script. I phoned John and he agreed that we should pursue the idea. In fact Ed Asner is not in England, but his British agent says he is technically available, and seems to think it is worth our making an offer. Although he is rather older than the character I envisaged, John and I agreed that he could play it, perhaps with one or two minor modifications to the script. He meets the essential criteria of being American, Jewish (I think) and a star. However, it is of course an extremely long shot. We hope to know – we need to know – the answer by early next week.

I told John about the offer from ART. He said that he would have to consult people at the Rep because he had not been in such a situation before and didn't really know what all the implications were. He said he would like to postpone a decision until we had cast the play and had a better idea of whether this production had a realistic chance of moving to London.

We were looking through *Spotlight* when we got a message that Jane Doe was not coming. John said: "She can't like the script." Immediately I felt greatly downcast and discouraged. The whole business of casting this play has been a switchback of emotional highs and lows, excited expectation followed sooner or later by disillusionment and disappointment. John went off to find out the background to this message, and returned to say that Jane wasn't coming because her agent hadn't been able to find her to give her the details of the appointment. This made the news much less discouraging, though it confirms hints John has already received, that this actress has a somewhat troubled personal life and a difficult temperament. We expect to see her next week.

Susan Penhaligon arrived. We had some ice-breaking conversation about the BBC mini-series *The Heart of the Country*, written by Fay Weldon, which she was in a year or two ago. I had enjoyed it and her performance; she returned the compliment apropos *Nice Work*. She had not received the script of *The Writing Game*, nor had any chance to look at it, so we had to describe the story-line to her and the part of Maude. We had some discussion about whether she was too young for it – she admitted to being 40 but said she looks less than 40 on stage. It's a question that depends partly on who plays Leo. She gamely agreed to read on sight. John took her through her first scene and later she read Maude's monologue. I thought she did remarkably well, considering she had never read the script before. She's got the right sort of accent for the part and she has a kind of elegance and very English blonde good looks that go with it. It was agreed that we would get in touch with her again, with a view to another meeting when she had read the script. I said to John, after she had left, that I thought she was a very possible Maude. He agreed, though I thought his last words to her had been a little off-hand and that she had been slightly discouraged.

As there was nobody else to see, John and I drew up a short-list of men to be enquired about as reserves in the likely event of Ed Asner not accepting our offer. Earlier we had talked about possibilities for Penny and agreed that it might be a good idea to have a young actress with some kind of regional accent, perhaps Scottish, or Midlands (not Liverpool, as we don't want to stray into *Educating Rita* territory).

This morning, Friday, John rang, sounding rather weary and discouraged (partly, it turned out, because he had just read a hostile review of his production of Rattigan's *Flare Path* in the *Birmingham Post*) to say none of the men he had enquired about was available, for one reason or another. An American actor resident in England called Lou Hirsch is available. I don't know anything about him. He may be too young, I gather. And it's by no means certain that Ed Asner will receive the script before Monday apparently. So it goes.

Thursday, 29 March Yesterday was interesting and exhausting. John and I interviewed about a dozen actors and actresses at the Actors' Centre, which is situated over the Reject Shop in Tottenham Court Road, a location that out-of-work actors must regard as rather ominously symbolic as they make their way up the three flights of bleak stone stairs. The Centre consists of a quite cheerful and informal cafeteria with a menu that tends towards carrot cake and vegetarian lasagna, and a number of rehearsal rooms and interviewing rooms as drab and inhospitable as such places usually are.

Our first appointment was with Jane Doe. She is an extremely interesting and engaging person, but somewhat *distrait* in manner and emotionally volatile. She is not good-looking in the conventional sense, and she certainly hadn't dressed to impress: she wore a rather scruffy white sweater and straight black skirt and her hair was scrunched up in what looked like an elastic band. However I am sure she could make herself look attractive if she wanted to, and she has a most appealing voice, rather deep and husky. Maude is not, of course, *distrait* or emotionally volatile – quite the reverse. On the other hand she *is* a character with many different facets, and Jane has the ability to shift rapidly from one mood to another. She reminds me a bit of some women writers I know who have a slightly fey, unpredictable, dangerous quality about them. She could conceivably make Maude into a writer of that type.

We saw Susan Penhaligon again, and she read some further scenes for us. She obviously admires the play and does, I think, very much want the part. She said, "Maude is tremendously cool, isn't she?" and asked if Maude had a vulnerable side. I had to say that I didn't think she did, that she was a slightly duplicitous woman but quite in control of her life. However, the question lingers in my mind: perhaps Maude should have a weak point. Physically, and in manner and accent, Susan is much more like the character I envisaged than Jane. And Susan would perhaps be a more obvious object of Leo's sexual desire than Jane, though it depends on who is playing Leo. Jane is a feminist of a sophisticated, non-dogmatic kind. I found it encouraging that she was able to identify with Maude and didn't find the characterization in any way sexist. She did however have a feminist quibble with one line in the play, which rather interestingly and revealingly elicited a completely opposite response from Susan.

In the last scene of Act I, Leo and Maude are discussing the different ways in which men and women write about sex, and Leo says, "Most women in my experience don't believe their cunts are beautiful. That's why they write about sex with their eyes shut." The stage direction reads: *Maude is both shocked and aroused by this remark.* Jane Doe said she really didn't think she would be aroused by the word "cunt", which she described as a very male word, a violent word; and we talked about various possible alternatives. It was a line that John and I had discussed before, wondering whether the Birmingham audience would find it offensive. When we interviewed Susan Penhaligon for the second time I deliberately steered the conversation around to our doubts about this line, and she was very quick to defend it and say "No, you mustn't cut it, it's exactly right." She saw what I was trying to do with the line, that Maude is, in spite of herself as it were, aroused by the visceral force of the word and all it implies about Leo's sexuality.

So we really have rather a difficult choice between these two actresses. (There is no one else in the running at this late stage.) Susan would be the safe choice, Jane the interesting one. John and I agreed that it would depend on who plays Leo, which at that point of the day, as we broke for lunch, was still an alarmingly open question. Up till now John has always made light of my anxiety about the lateness of the casting process, assuring me that it is often like this; but it was clear to me from his frequent phone calls to and from his casting director Wiff Maton in the course of the morning, via the pay phone in the interviewing room, that he was getting genuinely rattled about the absence of any real prospect for Leo. We are, of course, still waiting for a reply from Ed Asner, but without real hope.

After lunch we saw two actresses for Penny, the second being Lucy Jenkins: a short, plumpish girl with a large, broad, open face and big eyes and dark curly hair. An engaging, friendly personality. She grasped the part immediately, and when she did it in a lilting South Wales accent it went very well indeed.

Whether or not we cast her, I'm convinced from the interviews that a dialect or regional accent would be a very good idea for this character. As well as making a contrast with the other voices, it seems to reinforce Penny's distance from the sophisticated, metropolitan, rather incestuous literary world, and underlines her innocence.

We then saw Patrick Pearson, my suggestion for Simon on the basis of his performance as Robyn Penrose's yuppie brother in *Nice Work*. He seemed to me physically perfect as he walked into the room. He is handsome, tall, slim, and says he is the same age as Simon is supposed to be. He went to Dulwich College, but not to University. He started reading for us, and was given a slightly hard time by John, who was, I think, testing him out. John was asking him to produce a more cut-glass, public-school accent, but I agreed with Patrick that ex-public-school boys in the seventies and eighties on the whole didn't flaunt their upper-class accents, particularly if they were working in the media. He did his lines very well, *Instead of a Novel* perhaps less well, but he had read the script only for the first time while sitting in the waiting-room that day. He turned out to have quite a lot of stage experience, including a part in the production of Peter Nichols's last play, which moved from Southampton to the West End for a while. John was quite impressed and we agreed that he was certainly a possibility. Then we interviewed some candidates for Leo, including Lou Hirsch, who was a pleasant surprise to both of us.

Lou is a Jewish American who has worked in England for quite a long time, without ever having had really big parts or being in the West End as far as I can tell, apart from playing George in *Of Mice and Men* at the Mermaid for a season. His chief claim to fame is that he was the voice of Baby Herman in the film *Who Killed Roger Rabbit?* But he is a very peppy actor with many of the qualities that we are looking for in Leo. First he has the priceless asset of speaking Leo's language as Leo would speak it. He has a nice deep voice and assured us that he can bellow if necessary, which it is in the Birmingham Rep. He loves the part, loves the play, and is dying to do it. He's a very engaging, amusing man, who would, I think, be great fun to work with. His interpretation of Leo would tend towards the comic and make the play light rather than heavy. He is smallish, I suppose about 5' 8". He's 41, but could make himself look a bit older with a bit of grey. He might be described as the Richard Dreyfuss type, small, feisty, humorous, sexy. The question is whether he could express the pain and the anger of Leo, particularly when Simon seems to be cutting him out in relation to Maude. He could certainly do the first act without any trouble at all. The second act is more of an open question, but both John and I agreed that he could do the part. He is not a well-known name, he won't particularly attract audiences, but it's very reassuring to know that at last we have an actor whom we could cast for Leo with reasonable confidence. The more I think about him the more enthusiastic I become, because I think, and I've always thought, that we would do better to cast an unknown American than a well-known Brit who didn't seem quite right and didn't sound quite authentic.

We asked Lou to stay behind and read with two potential Jeremies. The first of these was John Webb, who seemed to grasp the possibilities of the part instantly, and was very amusing in the first scene – Jeremy's biggest – when he receives Leo at the Wheatcroft Centre. When John Adams escorted him out of the room, Lou said to me, "He's good," a comment I thought worth passing on later.

We ended thinking it had been a good day, inasmuch as we could at a pinch cast all five parts from the people we saw. I suppose we're weighing up Jane Doe and Susan Penhaligon for Maude, waiting to hear from Ed Asner but prepared to fall back on Lou Hirsch for Leo unless some other surprising candidate pops up at the last minute, and weighing up Patrick Pearson and another actor for Simon. Decisions about the other two parts are not so urgent, but I would be happy with Lucy Jenkins and John Webb. Lou Hirsch, incidentally, told us that he has worked with Susan Penhaligon before in *Of Mice and Men* and is a friend of Patrick Pearson's, with the clear implication that he would be happy to act with them again.

[The play was eventually cast, twelve days before rehearsals were due to begin, as follows: Lou Hirsch as Leo, Susan Penhaligon as Maude, Patrick Pearson as Simon, Lucy Jenkins as Penny and John Webb as Jeremy.]

Tuesday 17th April Today we met for the first read-through, arranged for 2 p.m. to allow the actors time to travel up from London this morning. We assembled in the Boardroom at the top of the Repertory Theatre, with most of the heads of the various departments present. First the General Manager, Bill Hughes, welcomed the cast, introduced the various people present, and gave out practical information to do with pay, Green Room facilities, concessions, etc. Then all departed except for the cast, John, myself, designer Roger Butlin and the ASM, Philippa Smith.

John then gave a little chat designed to make the cast feel relaxed and at home, sketching out how he proposed to proceed, and indicating what the schedule of rehearsals was likely to be. The actors sat on each side of the Boardroom table. John sat at one end near them. I sat with Roger Butlin at the other end. This, though not pre-arranged, proved a rather useful seating plan, since John and I were able to exchange looks directly along the table and silently indicate whether we were happy or unhappy with something in the actors' delivery, though we did not actually begin to exploit this mode of communication until later on in the day. John began by saying that he wanted a simple read-through, and that if anyone had a performance prepared, they should keep it for tomorrow. The actors seemed to take him at his word, inasmuch as they rushed through the first act at breakneck speed, finishing in about 45 minutes, and without much subtlety of interpretation. I was looking at John's face, which became more and more thoughtful and quizzical as the reading progressed.

We broke for tea and the actors went down to the Green Room. John came over to me and said: "Sometimes with a read-through you think immediately, well, we've got the right cast and they've got hold of the play and all we need to do really is to refine and polish this reading; and with other read-throughs you think, *Hmmm*." And, he said, this is one where you think, *Hmmm*. In other words, there is quite a bit of work to be done. Both Roger and I agreed with this assessment. John said that he thought that instead of moving straight to the rehearsal room tomorrow, he would spend at least another day in the Boardroom just reading the text, because it was so much a play about words and language. When I went down to join the actors in the Green Room, Lou made a quip about "Well, what is it, a radical recasting?" which I fear I received with a rather sickly smile.

The read-through of Act II was rather more satisfactory. This was partly because Patrick Pearson did a good job on his part, and partly perhaps because Act II contains most of the recent rewriting and is therefore dramatically stronger than Act I. At the end of it Roger brought in a model of the set and explained the thinking behind it to the actors. He said the Birmingham Rep's stage was bigger than Covent Garden's, which caused Susan's jaw to drop. For this reason, Roger's set is mounted on a platform which is thrust out into the audience. The model is a very rough one, but the set looks attractive. John proposed that before the evening meal break (there was to be an evening rehearsal session to make up for the fact that there had been no morning session) we should all go down to the theatre and look at the stage, which we duly did. The actors stood on the set for the current production, Priestley's *When We Are Married*, and looked out into the auditorium. They didn't seem too intimidated by the vast space.

John began the evening session by telling the actors that he was going to spend at least another day reading the text. That evening he proposed that they should play a game developed by Max Stafford-Clark called "Actions." This consists of the following procedure: each actor has to decide what the line that he is about to speak is doing to the character to whom it's addressed, and to state this before speaking the line. Thus the first page of the play might be treated as follows:

> JEREMY *"Jeremy shepherds Leo"* Here we are. *"Jeremy educates Leo"* It's a converted barn, as you can see. *"Jeremy informs Leo"* There are two bedrooms, one up, one down. Bathroom and loo in there. *"Jeremy befriends Leo"* Maude hasn't arrived yet, so you can take your pick of the bedrooms.
> LEO *"Leo exploits Jeremy"* Which one do you recommend?
> JEREMY *"Jeremy entraps Leo"* Well, some people in the upstairs room do complain of the birds in the eaves.
> LEO *"Leo commands Jeremy"* I'll take the downstairs one. *"Leo challenges Jeremy"* It's a pretty old building, isn't it?
> JEREMY *"Jeremy educates Leo"* Seventeenth-century, like the farmhouse.

The "actions" I have specified here are examples, not necessarily those proposed by the actors, which I can't recall precisely. The point of the game is to make the actor think about the dramatic point of what he is saying and to discover in the lines things which might otherwise remain latent and unexpressed. Sometimes it can discover meanings not intended by the author. The action *"Jeremy entraps Leo"* in the extract above, for instance, anticipates a moment later in the play when Maude thanks Leo for choosing the downstairs bedroom, because it's damp and has beetles in it; Leo had no chivalrous motive, and is disconcerted to discover these facts about his room, but it was John Adams' suggestion, not mine, that Jeremy deliberately lured Leo into making this choice. Often there is a good deal of discussion and debate as to the appropriate action-word. The rules of the game specify that it must be a transitive verb taking a direct object, which makes the game quite difficult, and sometimes the players have to invent a kind of nonce-word to express their meaning.*

On the whole the actors responded enthusiastically to this challenge. Lou was perhaps the most sceptical. He was afraid it might limit the actors' development of their roles; John hastened to say that it was not meant to yield a definitive interpretation, but was merely an exercise to bring out the possible meanings of the words of the text. It certainly had the effect of producing a more nuanced and subtle reading from all of the actors. As a result I felt rather more cheerful at the end of the reading than I had done earlier in the day.

Wednesday 18 April Rehearsals this morning began at 10.30. We went through the play, pausing occasionally to play the Actions game on certain portions of the text. The actors seemed much better today, particularly Susan. The Actions game has certainly been useful for her. She is thinking a good deal about Maude's character and again questioned whether Maude could really be so cool and calculating about her sexual life, and whether there mustn't be some kind of hurt underneath it all. This made me think of somewhat revising or amplifying Maude's dialogue in the final scene of the play. We have made a number of small adjustments to the text already. For instance Lucy, who plays Penny, does not correspond to the text's description of Penny as a waif-type with long straight blonde hair, so that has to be changed. Lou suggested one or two changes to more American idiom in his lines; for instance, "punch you in the nose" rather than "punch you on the nose." Patrick's reading of the story gets better and better, and is likely to be quite a hit, I think, in

* The method, and the rationale behind it, are described in more detail by Max Stafford-Clark himself, in his book *Letters to George: the account of a rehearsal* (1989).

the eventual production. John and I seem to have developed a good understanding, and communicated a great deal to each other by nods and winks. I am impressed by his ability to make the actors dig into their minds and find a motive for even the shortest and ostensibly least expressive lines, like "Oh."

Susan's question about Maude's marital history made me think that this was perhaps a rather weak point in the text. Also, perhaps as a result of doing Henry's voice myself in the read-throughs, I have begun to feel that it's rather improbable that a fatuous and pompous man like him would have a totally open marriage with Maude. Accordingly this evening I re-wrote some lines in the final scene of the play, so that Maude tells Leo a bit more about her marital history: "Married to the first man I slept with, who happened to be my tutor. So preoccupied with child-bearing and child-rearing that it was years before I realized I wasn't the last of his special tutees. I didn't have a lover until I was thirty-five," and so on. And the earlier exchange in which Leo said, "And you have your adoring young men" and Maude said, "It's a perfectly amicable arrangement, so much more civilized than divorce and much less expensive" becomes:

LEO   And you have your adoring young men.
MAUDE Why shouldn't I?

Thursday 19 April Today was the first rehearsal with moves. We are using the basement of a church hall in Newtown a mile or two from the Rep. It's actually a "Church Centre", designed to serve a council housing estate of tower-block flats and little terraced houses built, I should think, in the late Sixties or early Seventies. The estate is surrounded by a biggish area of scruffy grass ("park" would be too grand a term) and visible just over the brow of a low green hill is an enormous redbrick factory, now derelict and empty, its windows smashed, looking like the rusting hulk of a beached liner. It is a quintessential Birmingham scene: planners' housing, industrial decline, urban pastoral.

Our basement room is rather bare and bleak and chilly but big enough for a correct layout of the stage, which seems enormous. It's fortunate that my play has a barn or converted barn as its setting, rather than an ordinary room, since the Rep's stage is barn-like in dimensions. John's method at this point is to let the actors work out their own moves and not to intervene very much, and not to bother at all about delivery. It's exciting when an actor discovers a move that seems right. For instance, Lucy (who seems more and more likely to be extremely good) made us all laugh by one particular move. Leo, seated at his computer, tells Penny that her story is saturated in the pathetic fallacy. Her line is, "What's that?" Lucy gave it great point by suddenly seating herself in front of Leo at the other side of his desk and leaning on it, saying challengingly, "What's that?" Her expression as Leo read sarcastically from her "Lights and Shadows" piece was also very amusing.

Lou had what seems quite a good idea for the scene after his reading. The stage direction in the text had him knocking back a glass of whisky at the sink unit as the lights go up. He suggested that he should be sulking inside his room, that Jeremy is trying to coax him out, and that Maude's remark, about it not perhaps being a good idea to resume the reading, draws him out of his lair.

I showed Susan my suggested rewrites of the last scene with reference to Maude's marital background, and she was highly delighted with them. She has decided to play Maude as a woman who enjoys her sexual power and feels no guilt or uncertainty about it, her vulnerable spot being about her writing – the fact that she is a completely intuitive writer who doesn't know where her ability really comes from. This seems a good way of doing it. I grow more and more reassured about Susan, and correspondingly perhaps a little less confident about Lou. He hasn't yet settled into a consistent style of performance, and there is a danger that he will seem too much of a rough diamond, not convincing as a university-based writer. He is having some difficulty with Leo's reading, which is perhaps symptomatic.

Friday 20 April Today we did the walk-through of Act II. John was delayed by some meeting at the theatre, so the actors started without him. They moved about the stage with their scripts in their hands, occasionally blundering into the furniture or each other as they worked out their moves. One of the problems of the vast space of the Rep's stage, even when reduced by clever design, is that an actor can find himself stranded yards away from another character whom he should be eyeballing in the next line. For instance, in the fight scene, when Lou says "That's it," and, according to the stage directions, makes a lunge at Simon and shouts "Fight, you son of a bitch," it's impossible for Lou to lunge: he has to walk about twelve paces. I am also a little worried about Lou Hirsch's gait. He is taking short steps, slightly pigeon-toed, with his arms hanging loosely down. This adds to the comedy of his character, but at times I feel the need for a more assertive kind of body language.

Talking of body language and the importance of posture in the King of the Road pub, at lunchtime, John said that there had been an experiment which showed that students listening to a lecture sitting upright with their arms extended, and their hands open as if to receive something, absorbed 30% more information than students who listened to the same lecture without any instructions as to posture. I wondered if we couldn't ask our audience to adopt the attitude of arms extended and hands cupped. Patrick said he thought the audience should be told, "You will enjoy this play more if you sit with your legs apart."

Monday 23 April This week I have agreed to stay away from rehearsals, as the actors will be mainly concerned with trying to learn their lines. I called the Rep this morning to arrange for a taxi to collect the rewrites that I'd done over the weekend, and Wiff told me that Timothy West has agreed to do the voice of Henry. That's good news.

Friday 4 May I spoke to John at about 9.30 a.m. this morning on the phone before we both left for the rehearsal, about the notes I had kept back from the previous day's discussion with the cast. The most important was my anxiety that we should handle the topic of the Holocaust sensitively. I pointed out that we were skating on thin ice in touching on this tragic subject in the context of a comedy. I said that it was necessary for Lou to create a kind of area of seriousness around this theme when Leo is talking to Penny about his story, and that this requires Lou to draw on his own Jewishness at this point. We want to avoid any impression of treating the subject lightly or glibly. There is also perhaps a slight danger of this in Maude's line "Oh you don't need to be a clairvoyant to work it out: Poland – Jews – soap." The second general point I had to make was that it seemed to me one reason why Patrick's reading was so effective was that he had learned his story, so was able to maintain eye contact with the audience while telling it. I said I doubted whether Lou or Susan could hold the audience in the enormous space of the Rep if they were actually reading their stories from the page, as they are planning to do (and as would be the case in "real life"). John accepted both these points.

The morning's rehearsals went very well. John began by reblocking the opening scene so that Lou now delivers his early lines from inside the bedroom while he is unpacking his bag, popping out to confront Jeremy over the question of prose and poetry. This made the opening scene much more natural and made Leo seem less passively depressed at the very beginning. Then we did Leo's scene with Penny, Act I Scene 4, which has become known as The Lesson Scene. After running it once, John made the point about the sensitivity of the Holocaust theme, subtly pretending that it was a spontaneous idea of his and not something he and I had talked about beforehand. Lou immediately responded to this, and gave a very good rendering of his long speech to Penny about his story when he did it again. He gave a wonderfully expressive little shrug as he said, "I'm Jewish, you see." John got quite excited by this and began to encourage Lou to draw on his Jewishness, not only in this speech but in the play as a whole.

We obviously don't want to overdo it, and Lou is very anxious not to be the stereotype stage Jew, but the whole discussion seemed to have an electrifying effect on his performance.

We next reblocked Act I, Scene 2, or the Romeo and Juliet Scene as it is now known. Susan had been unhappy with this scene and asked if we could do some more work on it. The key seemed to be to make Leo more confident of pulling Maude, right up to the point where she actually goes into her bedroom and shuts the door. Now, instead of clinging on to the stairs and wheedling her, as he had been doing, Lou addresses Susan (who is standing on the stairs and landing) sprawled in his swivel chair, communicating a cocky confidence that he's going to get his way. Both the actors were much happier with this version of the scene.

Altogether it was a very good morning's work. I made a number of new cuts in the text. It is interesting that when there is a problem about acting a particular passage, it usually turns out that the dialogue is unnecessary or somehow wrong.

In the afternoon we did a run of the complete play. Wiff and the production manager John Pitt were present. They seemed to be quietly amused. Of course, both were familiar with the script. It's very difficult rehearsing a comedy because all the lines are familiar to everybody concerned, and it's hard therefore to judge the effectiveness of particular jokes and situations. I thought the run-through went pretty well, though there were a number of line fluffs.

Thursday 10 May I've been so busy over the last few days that I haven't had time to record any notes until now. On Monday, the British May Day holiday, I flew to Frankfurt to appear with Malcolm Bradbury in a kind of festival of contemporary British writing organized by the British Council. We have done this double act so often that we are in danger of becoming the Peter Cook and Dudley Moore of modern English letters. It was a long and tiring day and evening – an almost continuous sequence of interviews, meetings and socializing. We were interviewed together for German radio by a German lady who suddenly stopped in some confusion and confessed that she had been questioning me under the impression that I was Malcolm. Not so much the Pete and Dud, perhaps, as the Rosencrantz and Guildenstern of English letters. The next morning, after a leisurely breakfast and a short stroll around Frankfurt with Malcolm, I flew back to Birmingham, arriving at 1 p.m. I drove home, changed and went out immediately to the rehearsal rooms for the run-through.

This went quite well and Lou got through all his major speeches except one without a fluff. He and Sue still however tend to make small, but to me troubling, verbal errors. For instance Lou renders Leo's description of Maude's writing,

"Comedy of manners, plus love interest, plus a little gynaecology" as: "Comedy of manners, plus a little love interest, plus a
little gynaecology." The extra "little" spoils the rhythm of the
sentence and takes some of the humour from the final phrase.
When Leo says to Maude, "I thought I might share your
room," Sue has been replying, "Oh I don't think that would be
such a good idea," although there is no "such" in the text.
When you analyse it, you realize that "not such a good idea" is
a phrase usually applied to something that has been done in the
past and is now regretted: it is therefore not appropriate here.
One of the incidental interests of the rehearsal process is
discovering the precise meaning of ordinary words and phrases,
and also the way in which meaning is affected by context.
Towards the end of the "fight scene" Leo asks Penny, in the
script, "What did you think of the reading?" Lou has been
saying, "What did you think of Simon's reading?" This
bothered me, but it seemed so trivial an alteration that I didn't
bother to correct him, until it occurred to me that it was entirely
out of character for Leo to refer to Simon by his Christian name
– he never does so anywhere else in the play. Accordingly, the
line has been changed to: "What did you think of Mr St Clair's
reading?"

On Wednesday I arrived at 10.30 a.m. at the rehearsal rooms to
find Lou being given instruction in the use of a portable
computer. This is slightly bigger and more sophisticated than
the one we were first given, but it is still extremely small, light
and compact. I therefore had to change Maude's line, "Don't
you get tired of lugging that apparatus around with you
everywhere?" to "Don't you get tired of carrying that contrap-
tion around with you everywhere?" However it is a very suitable
machine for unpacking and packing and unpacking again, on
stage. We spent a good deal of the morning on this business
with the computer at the beginning and end of the play. The
actors become more comfortable if they have things to do on
stage while they are talking. Lou seems to be in better spirits
these days, and his performance is acquiring more shading and
variety. John is continuing to pursue the Jewish theme to this
end. Lou himself is second-generation American, with Jewish
grandparents on both sides who came from Poland and

Romania. He occasionally puts on a heavily Jewish act, or cracks Jewish jokes, to indicate how far he could go in this direction. I call this version of the play, "Scribbler on the Roof." He rattles off a rhyme:

> Roses are reddish,
> Violets are bluish,
> If it wasn't for Christmas,
> We'd all be Jewish.

We went down to the King of the Road for lunch, as usual. John indicated the audiences that the cast should expect for the first three nights. He said there would be three or four hundred people on Saturday, the first preview night, which he said would look like quite a lot, though it doesn't sound many to me. On Monday the audience will be a large one, because it is the night when all the staff of the Rep come with their families. The Press night on Tuesday however would be about half full, he predicted, which seems rather unpropitious. I do hope that the spurt of publicity we have had this week will raise the attendances, since it makes so much difference to a comedy to have a large, responsive house.

Friday 11 May Reading Simon Gray's *How's That For Telling 'Em, Fat Lady?* a few months ago I discovered that it is traditional for the author of a new play to give some small gift to each member of the cast on opening night. When I was in Holland recently I picked up from my Dutch publisher a dummy book used for display purposes. It looks exactly like a bound novel but the pages in it are entirely blank. This reminded me of Simon's text, *Instead of a Novel*, in the play, and I thought it would make an amusing first-night gift for him, especially if I could have the title, *Instead of a Novel* by Simon St Clair, printed on the spine. I then thought of doing something similar for the other members of the cast, since each character has either written a book or hopes to do so. So I phoned Jimmy Thompson, the University Librarian, on Wednesday and asked if he could possibly arrange for his bindery, at very short notice, to cover the spine of four copies of *Nice Work*, so as to obscure the original lettering, and to print on top the names and titles of my fictitious texts: *Wise Virgins* by Leo Rafkin, *Dissuasion* by Maude Lockett, *Moroccan Musings* by Jeremy Deane and *Lights and Shadows* by Penny Sewell, plus *Instead of a Novel* by Simon St Clair on the dummy. When I came back from Wednesday's rehearsal there was a message on the answerphone to say that the books were already ready for collection. I collected and paid for them yesterday (Thursday) morning.

I went to the Rep at 2.30 p.m. for a press call, essentially a photographic session on the set, which I saw for the first time. I could have looked at it before, but I wanted to wait till it was complete, to get the full effect. It is very attractive, and as the afternoon wore on it became more and more obvious that it was a successful acting space. The actors seemed quite comfortable with it. Negotiating the spiral staircase needs some care, but it is a very interesting feature in itself. The set looks extremely attractive in various lightings, and when silhouetted against a backlighting it is rather reminiscent of constructivist stage sets in Russia in the 1920s. The barn effect is established by some big suspended beams and it doesn't seem too vast.

I had only one serious reservation about the set, which began to worry me more as the technical rehearsal proceeded. Roger has designed a sliding frosted-glass door for the bathroom. This is visually interesting, but seems to me out of place: if you were converting a barn for use by transient visitors of both sexes, you would have a bathroom door that gave more privacy. When it is illuminated from within, the audience can see quite clearly the outline of a figure inside the glass door. The lavatory is off to the right and out of view, but the shower is directly behind the glass door; and although there is a shower curtain, it's impossible for Susie to get into the shower at the end of Act I without either taking off her dressing gown and underclothes and revealing that she is naked, or appearing to take a shower with these clothes on.

My stage direction assumed that the door is opaque and that Maude leaves it open a crack through which steam and the noise of the shower emerge, alerting Leo to the fact that Maude has left the bathroom door unlocked. This encourages him to go inside. As directed by John, Susie goes into the bathroom, closes the door, undresses fairly visibly behind the door, steps naked into the shower, pulls the shower curtain behind her, then reaches an arm from behind the shower curtain to open the door a little. Leo then becomes aware of this, gets up, takes off his jacket, throws open the bathroom door, steps inside and shuts it behind him, and takes off his shirt very visibly behind the door. Meanwhile the noise of the shower increases to a crescendo. This is visually and theatrically fairly stunning, but powerfully erotic rather than funny, like a scene out of a Tennessee Williams play. And the joke of Henry's telephone ringing immediately after Leo stepped inside the bathroom seemed to fall flat, partly because one was still looking at Leo through the glass.

This morning (Friday) we resumed technicals at 10 a.m. and began with the shower scene again. This time it seemed more polished, and certainly visually effective, but I had basically the same reservations about it. The effect could perhaps be mitigated by making the door more opaque without being totally so, and making Maude leave the door open ambiguously instead of deliberately opening it. I gather that Susie is also unhappy about this latter gesture, because it is too crude a sexual invitation. I spoke to John about it. He takes all the points but says he wants to see the effect in a full run-through before he makes up his mind. His view is that if Leo does not go into the bathroom with a clear invitation from Maude, then in terms of sexual politics it looks as if he is exercising a kind of male power and virtually raping her. But I think we must get some ambiguity into this scene. Perhaps it could be done by making Leo enter the bathroom more hesitantly, half-expecting to be ordered out.

Act II went very well. Lou has thought of another way of bringing the bust of Aubrey Wheatcroft into the play. As he stalks out of the room at the end of Scene 3, leaving Maude and Simon giggling erotically upstairs, he turns to the bust and says, "Up yours too!", which makes quite a funny exit line. The cast have also added a little bit of business to do with *Nice Work*. When Maude unpacks her bag in Act I scene 1, she takes a copy of the novel out of her bag and when Jeremy leans inquisitively over her shoulder to look at it, Maude says "I'm reviewing it." Jeremy grimaces dismissively.

The dress rehearsal went very smoothly, with only a couple of fluffs. Afterwards, John and I compared notes in the Green Room over one of its proletarian high teas. Our only point of disagreement – but it's a fairly serious one – concerns the shower scene at the end of Act I. John wants to go with the scene as he directed it. I still feel, as Susie and Lou both feel, that the effect is too heavily erotic for the play. To use John's own shorthand, it is too much Marlon and not enough Woody. While we were talking, Sue came in to have a snack and joined in the argument, on my side. John began to get a little uptight and upset, but he promised that he would try it in the way we were suggesting this evening, though it will not be possible to do it with proper lighting and sound effects because there will be no technicians present.

We reassembled in the theatre at 7 p.m., sitting in the front stalls, while John and I went through our notes, and occasionally the actors went up on the stage to practice some new moves or very small changes in the dialogue. John deliberately left the shower scene to the end. We then tried out the alternative method of doing it, viz.: while Maude is partially undressing upstairs, Leo is typing at his desk and takes his jacket off as if to get down to work, so that there is a kind of counterpoint between Maude's undressing and his undressing, simultaneously, but for quite different reasons. Maude comes quietly down the stairs, goes into the bathroom, shuts the door and then opens it slightly. The door will be made less transparent, so that a certain amount of light comes through it, but it will be impossible clearly to distinguish any shape behind it. Then as Leo types at his computer, steam begins to come through the open door. Leo clocks this, is puzzled, gets up from the desk and comes round in an arc, slightly downstage, peering at the door as if to ascertain the source of the steam, then stops thoughtfully. The penny drops, he gives a little comic shrug or grimace and goes into the bathroom, shutting the door behind him. The telephone rings. Curtain. The cast and I are happy with this, which gives the end of the act a much lighter, more comic note. John is, I think, half-convinced.

Sunday 13 May Yesterday, after wrapping up my first-night presents for the cast, I went into the theatre in the afternoon for the second and final dress rehearsal. Susie was hovering backstage and gave me and John "token presents", as she called them – little soap ducks and a card. John seemed rather flustered and embarrassed, saying that he never did this himself, and also warning that he never wished his actors good luck on a first night. My card was a reproduction of the Van Gogh painting of books, and bore a nice message thanking me "For all your help and support. There has been such a good feeling working on this." As it happened, this "good feeling" was to face its severest test later in the afternoon.

The dress rehearsal began at 2.30 p.m. It had been agreed that we would try out the revised ending to Act I, the one preferred by myself and Susie and Lou, which we had blocked out the previous evening. Act I proceeded reasonably well, with only a few fluffs. The actors were, on John's advice, not trying to do anything like a performance, but more of a technical run-through. As a result of our discussions about the door of the bathroom the previous day, the stage staff had that morning fitted an extra layer of plastic film to make the door less see-through. As the play act proceeded, however, this extra layer of film began to slowly unpeel, and as we approached the crucial conclusion to Act I it was half hanging off the door inside the bathroom. John accordingly went down to the front of the stalls and asked the actors to stop for a minute or two while he and an assistant stage manager stuck the film back again. This, of course, didn't help the actors' concentration for the remainder of the scene, and Lou forgot to take off his jacket at the time that had been agreed – i.e. when getting down to work on his computer. There was no crescendo of water noises, merely a naturalistic rendering of the shower very slightly magnified.

It was undoubtedly a rather flat and feeble conclusion to the act, though it was difficult to decide how much this effect was due to the interruption of the performance. John and Roger and I discussed it animatedly throughout the interval. It was an interesting example of how important a set is, and how its design can both release unexpected sources of energy and expression and also counteract the author's original intention. By making the door semi-transparent, Roger had certainly made it into an interesting feature, but it had become from my point of view too powerful. It had drawn John, as a director with a feeling for the possibilities of light and sound, into creating an effect which I found – and the actors found – striking but inappropriately heavy. I explained again the effect that I had intended: the door is opaque and conceals an area into which the audience cannot see and about which it can only speculate. When Leo throws open the door the space should be full of steam and light and quite impenetrable. When he shuts the door the audience uses its imagination to work out what is going on in the shower between him and Maude. The stage is empty. The telephone rings. Given the previous function of the telephone in the act, this should bring the first act to a conclusion with a laugh. (Mike Ockrent had certainly thought it would when he read this version of the script for the first time.) In the course of the discussion John said to me, "You can direct it yourself" – a suggestion he immediately and wisely withdrew. It was, however, an indication that he himself was in a rather nervous and excitable state. Roger was apologetic – needlessly so, because it wasn't really his fault, but the result of a very tight schedule which left so little time for consultation, and of my own inexperience, which had prevented me from specifying exactly what kind of bathroom door I wanted.

The second act began without our having resolved the issue. I went back to my seat and sat there rather unhappily, unable to concentrate on Act II because I was worrying about the end of Act I all the time. John was prowling around the auditorium, and towards the end of the act came and sat down next to me. He whispered in my ear that he had consulted various people in the theatre (about a dozen members of the tehnical and administrative staff were present) and that all of them thought that "his" ending to Act I was the more effective; that he himself was sure that the ending we had just seen would be a flop (a judgement with which I had to concur); that to carry out my intention we would have to rebuild the door of the bathroom; that this could not possibly be done in time for the first night, though it could conceivably be done on Monday. He therefore proposed that for the performance that evening we should proceed with "his" ending to Act I and see how it went down with the audience. We would have Sunday to think about it, and Monday to discuss it. I felt I had no alternative but to agree. He said all we had to do now was to encourage the actors and get them in good spirits for the opening night, which was now of course less than three hours away.

We went down onto the stage to talk to the cast. John explained what we were going to do about the shower scene. Lou and Susan were unhappy; and although I said that I thought the ending had been a failure that afternoon, I could not pretend to have any great enthusiasm for John's crescendo ending. John, seeing that the actors agreed with me, began to get very upset and almost in mid-sentence changed his mind and said, as if washing his hands of the business: all right, we would do it as Susan, Lou and myself wanted. We were, of course, very unwilling to proceed in flat contradiction of the director's wishes. Susie asked if there couldn't be some sort of compromise. She pointed out that she did not particularly want to have to take all her clothes off in the bathroom and that her contract had not required her to do so, but that she was more concerned with the question of being true to the spirit of the play. The atmosphere was now quite highly charged, with John issuing a stream of new instructions to Karen, the Deputy Stage Manager, and then cancelling them immediately, as the argument proceeded.

At this point, feeling very unhappy about the situation, I made a suggestion which had occurred to me in the course of my ruminations during Act II, but which I hadn't had an opportunity to bring up before, namely, that the telephone ring, which certainly had not had its intended comic effect in the dress rehearsal, should be brought forward so that it rings just as Leo is about to fully open the bathroom door and step inside, causing him to stop, check, look back at the telephone, give a kind of comical shrug or grimace as if to say "Tough luck, Henry," and then step into the bathroom. John immediately latched onto this. At first he wanted to integrate it into "his" ending, but I pointed out that we would have to lose the crescendo of sound, otherwise we wouldn't hear the telephone. So we went back to "my" ending, with the telephone ring brought forward. Susie and Lou practised the scene just once, without any undressing. Lou produced a quite neat little comic reaction to the telephone ring. John said he thought it was a great improvement on the dress rehearsal, and he was happy with it, if we were. With the sense of a serious crisis narrowly avoided, and breathing sighs of relief, we sat down in the front stalls for a few notes on other aspects of the dress rehearsal. One encouraging bit of news which Lou had passed to me was that we were going to get an audience of over 500. Since they will all be paying customers (the Rep does not believe in papering the house) this was a good augury both of public interest in the play and of a responsive audience for the first performance. An invited audience, John says, will often sit on their hands.

By the time we had finished giving our notes, which were few in number and not very significant, it was about 5.45 p.m. I had to go home to eat a meal and change, having left my presents for the cast at the stage-door office for distribution after the dress rehearsal. I thought they might enjoy a surprise at that point in the evening.

I returned to the theatre, with my wife Mary and my daughter Julia, at about 7.15 p.m. for the 7.30 p.m. curtain-up. Was I nervous? I suppose I was a little tense, but not uncomfortably so. I was basically convinced that the play would be reasonably successful, and certainly not a failure. Now that the matter of the shower scene had been settled, I was satisfied that we had done everything we could within the time available to make it a success. And I was encouraged by the prediction of a large audience, since comedy depends so much upon the infectiousness of laughter. In the foyer we met John Adams, who was certainly much more nervous than I. He said jokingly that the cast backstage were all desperately wishing they'd never gone into the acting profession, but at that moment he looked as if he wished he'd never gone into the directing profession. We went into the auditorium, which by the time the lights went down looked about two-thirds full. It was filled from side to side up to about row O.

The music of "Greensleeves" began to play – a good choice by John, because it got the audience into a pleasantly receptive mood. Then the voice of Jeremy was heard offstage saying, "Here we are!" and John Webb and Lou made their entrance. Almost at once they began to get laughs or chuckles from the audience. They were both acting extremely well. As the scene proceeded I became a little worried that the number and intensity of the laughs did not increase quite as quickly as I had hoped, and Susie's entrance was a little strained. A sign of her nerves was that she was late producing the copy of *Nice Work* from her bag, so that Jeremy had to linger rather a long time pushing an ashtray about on the coffee table to give himself time and space to react to the book. However, the scene began to roll along very smoothly after that, and the business of Henry's first phone call went extremely well and provoked a lot of laughter. As the scene ended, with a blackout apart from two spotlights on Leo and Maude, there was a great burst of applause from the audience. In my experience it is extremely rare for the Rep audience to applaud between scenes, and I knew at that moment that we were home and dry. (In fact the audience applauded after every scene throughout the evening, except for one or two where there was a slow fade of the lighting, or business on stage, which made the ending of the scene somewhat ambiguous.)

The rest of the act went extremely well, the audience being responsive and attentive. Lou was acting infinitely better than he had ever done before, presumably as a result of this audience response. The audience was relishing his Americanness in this very English context, and they obviously found his character likeable as well as slightly absurd. Maude's reading went well, and she got quite a few chuckles and a real laugh on the "walking the dog" joke. Leo's story also provoked a lot of laughter, especially his miming of the students walking out. There never seemed any danger of any real members of the audience walking out at this point, as some people had feared. As usual, the laughs often came at unexpected places or with unexpected intensity. One of the biggest of the first half was produced by Leo's comment on prostitution: "The girl does it because she wants the money, and the guy does it because he wants to get laid. A lot of marriages are based on the same principle." As John Adams said to me in the interval, this line produced a kind of "Mexican Wave" laugh, which started on one side of the auditorium and took, as he hyperbolically put it, about three minutes to reach the other side. He said he'd never witnessed anything quite like it in a theatre before.[*]

---

[*] This delayed-action effect was repeated every night. Someone (was it David Aukin?) later said to me that it was the result of the men in the

The revised conclusion to Act I worked perfectly well, though Lou again forgot to take his jacket off while still working at his computer, and the telephone ring seemed a little feeble as a sound effect. Lou introduced an additional and effective little bit of business: on realizing that Maude has left the door open for him to enter the bathroom, he looks heavenward and gives a little triumphant shake of the fists with both arms. Although it wasn't quite perfect, the scene did work in the way that I had intended, namely, the audience began to giggle as soon as they realized that Maude had left the bathroom door open deliberately and that the penny was taking a rather long time to drop inside Leo's head. At the interval John was generous enough to say, "You were right and I was wrong."

The second act also went very well, though it did not quite confirm the feeling John and I had always had that it was very much stronger than Act I. One reason may have been that Patrick, although extremely good, is perhaps milking his lines just a little too much. He could afford to "throw away" parts of his solo reading. I shall try tactfully to make this point to him. He made the end of the reading very serious, almost tragic, and his concluding statement, "The rest of the novel consists of 250 completely blank pages," was received in stunned silence. In the rehearsed readings, if I remember rightly, it was taken as parodic, and got a laugh. But Patrick was certainly not aiming at a laugh. I'm not sure whether this is a good thing or a bad thing for the next scene, but it was certainly effective in itself.

The most pleasing thing about Act II from my point of view was that the business with the computer at the very end, when Leo appears to be destroying his novel, worked superbly. The main surprise or disappointment was that the actual last line of the play seemed to fall flat. Leo says he is thinking of trying a completely new form and turns to Maude, who is reading her students' manuscripts, and says "I've got this idea for a play." As the penny drops, Maude slowly turns to face him in consternation. This did not produce the laughs of recognition that I had expected. I discussed it later with various people and we couldn't decide whether it was because the audience hadn't

audience waiting to see if their wives laughed before they felt free to laugh themselves.

taken the point that Leo was about to write a play about the events at the Wheatcroft, or whether they were taken by surprise by the fact that there was no continuation of the conversation.

In spite of this slightly anticlimatic ending, the applause was warm and sustained. There were several curtain calls for the cast, who quite justifiably looked delighted. When we went back stage, they were all burbling with pleasure at the responsiveness of the audience. Lou said that he had been absolutely amazed how many laughs he was getting from the very beginning of the first scene, and that this gave him a tremendous boost of confidence, which certainly showed in his performance on the night. Susie, I think, was to some extent the victim of first-night nerves, and I would expect her performance to improve in the coming days, though it was perfectly adequate tonight. The other three actors were excellent. Lucy made quite an impression on the audience – Penny, of course, is the character they tend to identify with. I thanked them all, warmly and sincerely. Susie had a couple of bottles of champagne chilled and I was toasted in the rather bleak, institutional corridors of the Rep's backstage area. The cast were very elated by the success of the evening, and also obviously pleased by their presents. John Webb gave me a hug. Lou was bubbling over with enthusiasm. He was impressed by the quickness and sophistication of the audience. "They even got the Beckett joke," he said incredulously.

Susie and her husband Duncan went off for a quiet meal together, as did Patrick and his girl-friend, Lisa. Mary and Julia went home, and I went along with John and and some others to the Prince of Wales, the Rep's local, for a final drink. Roger Butlin was delighted with the way the show had gone and told me, not for the first time, what a thrill it was to design the set for a new play. He takes enormous pains with the detail of the set, and is always tinkering with it and adding new refinements (like a box of candles in case of power-failure just inside Leo's bedroom) which will never be noticed by 99% of the audience. John's summing up of the evening was that it had been a great success, and I should feel very pleased. But he had a feeling from people he had spoken to that Act II was not quite as strong as we had hoped it would be. We shall try and tighten it up when we give notes to the cast on Monday afternoon. John and his partner Amelda Brown gave me a lift home, and we said goodnight well pleased with ourselves, and the night.

The more I think about it, the more convinced I am that it was a very considerable achievement by all concerned to make a play like this work so well in the huge space of the Rep's main auditorium, and that if it works there it could certainly sit happily on any London stage.

Tuesday 15 May I went into the theatre at 2.30 p.m. on Monday for a meeting with John and the cast. We both gave them some notes and they practised one or two bits of modified business and blocking. Susie seemed a little bit edgy. When John said that he thought the last scene was lapsing into a slightly self-indulgent, cosy, now-we're-coming-to-the-end sort of feeling, she reacted quite sharply, saying that she had thought the scene had gone very well, and that she would have to think about whether she could respond to this note. I said I thought the last scene had gone well, and John didn't press the point. He and I then went off to have a private conference with Patrick about his reading, while the rest of the cast started a line-rehearsal of Act I. This seems to be standard practice on the second day, or following a weekend: the cast sit together, rapidly reciting their lines without trying to act them, or even to give them expressive intonation – just making sure that they've got them right. From a distance it sounds like the old Latin Low Mass being said by priest and acolytes in an empty church.

John invited me upstairs to his office, where he gently reproached me for contradicting him in front of the actors about the tempo of the last scene. I accepted that it had been rather tactless, though he also agreed that he should have found time to meet me and discuss our common notes before we met the cast. It's all part of the absurd pressure of his daily routine. He said some very kind things about the play: that whether or not it transferred to London, it was a play which would go on being performed in the future by provincial companies, because it was interesting and informative and entertaining. Of the London managements who had turned it down in the past, he said, adopting Leo's argot: "They're arseholes." I said I thought they would be kicking themselves when they saw this production, which I considered could sit on any London stage, and he agreed. On this hubristic note, we parted amicably.

I went off to record an interview for Channel Four, then home to eat and change my shirt and then off to the Rep again for the second preview. This is traditionally the night when employees of the theatre, their friends and families and certain local bigwigs associated with the theatre attend. The house was full, which is a pretty awesome sight, 900 people in this steeply-raked fan-shaped auditorium. I was sitting quite far back in row N, on the aisle. The first act started rather more slowly and quietly than on the first night. The audience applauded between scenes, however, and the response steadily warmed. Leo's reading went wonderfully well, as did the following, final scene of Act I. The ending of Act I was done in a much more polished way than on the first night and worked extremely well. Feedback in the interval was very complimentary and encouraging.

The second act was perhaps marginally better than on the first night, but I still felt a slight sense of disappointment after the success of Act I. There were plenty of laughs, but there were also flat spots. Patrick got more light and shade into his reading, though there is still a slightly stunned feeling in the audience at the end of it. It seemed to me that Susie was finding it rather a strain to project to this enormous audience and that Lou was getting a little hoarse. I was convinced that he was starting a cold and would lose his voice before the press night. The closing scene, however, went extremely well. There was an extraordinary reaction, a kind of shiver of expectation, in the audience, as Maude says to Leo, about the computer, "Show me how it works."* That little sequence worked even better than on the

---

* This happened every night, and we were well into the run before I worked out what was happening: the audience thought Maude was going to erase Leo's novel accidentally. They were remembering a line in Act II, Scene 1, when Maude says to Simon, "You have to be careful with those things. One hears the most frightful stories of whole books being swallowed in a single gulp because someone pressed the wrong key." In fact, that speech was in early versions of the play long before I thought of the business with the computer in the final scene, and I had never made

first night. And as a result of some work we had done in the afternoon, the last line of the play worked much better too. Leo now says to Maude, "I've just had this idea for a play," which seemed to make the penny drop for the whole audience.

John and I went backstage. Lou was in good spirits and delighted by the way his reading had gone. John gave him a few notes as he was washing the grey out of his beard. He made no mention of having a cold or sore throat, so I presume that it was my imagination that his voice was getting hoarse. Everybody I have spoken to has been warm in his praise, and this has obviously been the key to the play's success. It's ironic in view of our anxieties about his performance in rehearsal, but it vindicates our decision to cast him. As I sat listening to the dialogue tonight, I realized that it was because Leo is played by an authentic American that he has the audience's permission, as it were, to use language which they would find offensive coming from a British character or perhaps even a British actor playing an American character. When, for instance, he says sarcastically to Maude, of his character Zimmerman, "Yeah, he meets a radical feminist who convinces him he should cut off his balls," there is an enormous roar of appreciative laughter from the audience.

John and I went to the bar at the front of the house where there was a drinks party for members of the company and the Directors. A couple of young ladies who work in the administration of the Symphony Hall, now approaching completion in the Convention Centre next door, accosted me, and said how much they had enjoyed the show. One of them said she had a friend who had been taught by me and believed that she was the model for one of the characters in *Small World*. She mentioned a name which meant nothing to me. I asked which character she thought she was based on, and my interlocutor said a red-haired nymphomaniac (presumably Fulvia Morgana). I said I should be so lucky, to teach a red-haired nymphomaniac. I asked them if they had any criticisms of the production, and the only one they could come up with was that when Susie came in from

the connection myself. One of the most effective moments in the whole play was therefore a complete fluke.

having been searching for Penny by the river, with her trouser-leg covered in mud, it was obvious from the soles of her shoes that they were brand new and had never been worn outside the theatre since they were bought. I passed this on the stage-management staff.

Wednesday 16 May Last night was press night. I went to meet Leah Schmidt and Charles Elton who had come down from London to see the play, and were staying overnight at the Copthorne Hotel. It was a showery, squally evening, and we got quite wet walking back from the Copthorne to the theatre. I had been told there were about 700 people in the house – much better than John had predicted last week. I myself was sitting at G39, rather nearer than I'd sat in previous performances.

From the first scene it was obvious that this was going to be a much more subdued audience than those of the first two nights. Lines that got a laugh on previous occasions got merely a few chuckles, and lines that had got chuckles were received in silence, though it was always an attentive and amused silence. The lady sitting next to me was continually quaking with silent merriment. The audience did not clap after the first scene as they had done on the two previous occasions, and this set the pattern for the rest of the evening. Real laughter began to come with Leo's story and the following scene, which went extremely well. However, after the very vocal response of the audience at the first two performances, this was a slightly disappointing Act I, particularly as it was the press night. In the interval Leah said that this was very often the case at a press night – that it somehow inhibited the audience's response. I don't quite understand why, since the critics can constitute only a tiny proportion of the audience. Perhaps the rest feel that they are being assessed too. Act II went, I thought, very well, and for the first time I didn't feel it was falling below the level of Act I. This may have been because Act I itself had been rather more subdued, but, for whatever reason, this did seem to me, all in all, the most balanced performance so far, even if it hadn't reached the peaks of certain moments in the two previews. The audience applauded very warmly at the end.

Wednesday 23 May Sunday breakfast was somewhat spoiled by negative reviews in both the papers we have delivered: a very dismissive one in the *Sunday Times*, by John Peter ("wobbly motivations, arthritic dialogue and plodding stagecraft") and a longer, less destructive piece by Irving Wardle in the *Independent on Sunday*, which was impressed by the dialogue, but found the narrative structure old-fashioned and unconvincing. Both critics compared the play unfavourably to my novels (Wardle said that "it was as though the designer of the Mark II Concorde had come up with the invention of the wheel") which I suppose might have been expected. I couldn't help thinking that they were somewhat ungenerous, in view of the success of the play with audiences all this week. And it seemed to me that they had put paid to any hopes of moving the production to London.

Later I picked up a copy of the *Observer*, and lo and behold, there was a very pleasant review by Michael Coveney, predicting that "with some fine tuning and smart re-casting it will become a West End hit." So the critics are equally divided. For: the *Telegraph*, the *Guardian*, the *Birmingham Post*, the *Observer*, and the *Sunday Mercury* (Birmingham). Against: *The Times*, the *Independent*, *The Sunday Times*, the *Independent on Sunday*, and the *Birmingham Mail*.

Friday 1 June The play ends its run tomorrow. I haven't been to see it so far this week, partly because I had reached a kind of saturation point by the end of last week. On Saturday Mary and I invited the cast round for drinks and a light lunch. The weather was beautiful, and we were able to sit in the garden. Susie brought her husband, Duncan, and Patrick brought his girl-friend, Lisa. John Webb walked to Edgbaston from the City Centre along the canal path. He told an amusing story about the electric strip sign on the front of the Rep, which carries information and advertising in a continuous loop. According to John, the other day it was saying: "EMPTY MESSAGE EMPTY MESSAGE EMPTY MESSAGE . . ." Presumably somebody had forgotten to program the device, but it looked like a comment on my play, which was advertised on a large poster just underneath.

Saturday 2 June Yesterday evening I went to see the penultimate performance of the play, after an interval of a week and a half. The actors were noticeably more relaxed and confident, particularly in their moves and bits of business. Susie had added all kinds of little variations of gesture and intonation to her performance. Lou's has perhaps become too relaxed. He didn't generate enough amusement at the beginning of his reading, with the consequence that the sexual explicitness towards the end of it became tricky to handle. A woman left her seat at the end of that scene, and I think she may have been walking out in protest. Susie's line at the beginning of the next scene, that if such things happen, the British middle classes would prefer not to hear about them, got a huge laugh and a round of applause. I think they were applauding the sentiment.

Tuesday 5 June I took my mother-in-law to the theatre on Saturday evening, at her own request. I was doubtful whether a pious Catholic widow of eighty-eight would enjoy it greatly, but as she is pretty deaf I decided it wouldn't scandalize her too much. Mary's youngest sister Margaret was also visiting us to see the play. I had wondered whether to just leave them at the theatre, since I had seen the show so often, but as it was the last performance I decided to stay, and I am very glad that I did. It was a wonderful audience, that responded to almost everything in the text in the way that I had intended (apart from my mother-in-law, who fell asleep in Act II), and the actors threw themselves into their performances with great gusto. It was certainly one of the most successful performances of the run, and a very nice way to end it. I was particularly pleased by the way the long third scene of Act II went. The cast played the literary debate leading up to the fight with real passion and conviction, and the audience seemed to respond to every nuance. This scene has always been tricky, and it's tempting to try and solve the problem by drastically curtailing the literary debate. But this performance showed that it *can* work as written.

After the cast had taken their well-deserved curtain-calls, and the house lights came on, a man who had been sitting behind us got to his feet and declared loudly to his companion, in the characteristic no-nonsense tones of a Birmingham businessman, "Well, I really enjoyed that. It was in English, and you could understand it." I'm not quite sure what plays he was, by implication, comparing with mine, but the spontaneous and sincere expression of enjoyment was very gratifying. It is a commonplace that the appeal of the theatre for actors is in the contact with a live audience; but this contact is equally fascinating to writers. In no other medium can the writer observe and measure the reception of his work so closely and intimately. Publishing a novel is, by comparison, like putting a message in a bottle and casting it into the sea. Occasionally the bottle is washed back on to the shore with a review or a reader's letter inside, but these responses represent a tiny fraction of your actual audience. One of the satisfactions of artistic creation, if it is successful, is that it is a benevolent exercise of power: power, because you are controlling other people's behaviour, benevolent because you are giving them pleasure. Sitting in an audience in the theatre, you can experience the exercise of that power, when the play works – and, by the same token, experience mortification and frustration when it doesn't. The theatre, it seems to me, is essentially about wooing, manipulating, controlling and delighting audiences. So is all art; but the fact that a play is never (unlike the words of a novel after publication, or the images of a film after release) fixed, but always open to modification at the next performance, invites endless experiment in trying to make it work perfectly. Writers, directors, designers and actors are therefore involved in a continual, obsessive, ultimately impossible pursuit of the perfect performance, in which every word and gesture and silence will work together to keep the audience rapt in aesthetic bliss for the duration of the show. The goal is unattainable, but the quest inexhaustibly fascinating.

Mary collected her mother and sister from the theatre so that I could say my farewells to the cast. There was no last-night party, because all the actors wanted to get back to London. Susie went off quickly with her young son and his nanny, who had brought him up to see the show. Susie told me the other day that by the time she had paid for the nanny, her Birmingham digs, and her travel expenses, she was out of pocket on the production, but that she didn't regret doing it. A rather humbling disclosure, which also helps to explain why it was so difficult to cast the play.

I had a quick drink with Lou, Patrick and John in the Rep bar. Lou declared that whatever happened to the play in the future, he was sure no company could do it better than they had. I agreed, of course. Lou has enjoyed his part more and more in the course of the run. He was particularly delighted that he had been applauded tonight in the middle of his reading for the way he mimed the students' walking out – he said he'd been waiting three weeks for that.

Patrick had two friends with him who had been his contemporaries at drama school, and remarked that they had never seen him do anything as flamboyant and sexually ambivalent as Simon before. Patrick himself is quite enraptured with the part, and said that he would happily play it for another year, whether in London or the Outer Hebrides. On that we all shook hands and said goodbye. There was a feeling of satisfaction and good fellowship at what we had achieved, but a sense of sadness and anticlimax too. I wish we could have had a proper party to mark the end of the run, because, whatever happens to the play in the future, it will always belong to this cast in a special way.

26 June Today I received, via Curtis Brown, my royalty statement for *The Writing Game*, which came with a computerized breakdown of the figures for the complete run. There were twenty-one performances, of which three were matinées. The total attendance by paying customers was 60% of capacity (plus 4% complimentaries). I found this figure slightly disappointing, but the three matinées had been very badly attended and pulled the overall average down. (Rep matinées are patronized mainly by old-age pensioners taking advantage of reduced seat prices – not the ideal audience for my play; the cast had reported performing on these afternoons in an eerie and baffled silence.) Even so, it was apparently the most successful play the Rep had put on for at least a year, barring the Christmas show. Lou also told me – I don't know on what authority – that it had broken records for a new play in this theatre. Just over 12,000 people saw it. The Rep took about £70,000 excluding VAT, of which my share was about £7000 (half of which I had received already in the form of an advance). This is about half of what I would earn from the sale of 12,000 copies of a novel in hardback. The play may earn me more in the future. But in any case I feel well rewarded for all the hours of work I have put into it. It is no exaggeration to say that participating in the production of *The Writing Game* has been the most intensely interesting experience of my literary career to date.

POSTSCRIPT

Later in the summer of 1990, Nathan Joseph, who has a small production company called Freeshooter, optioned *The Writing Game* for a London production. He had seen the Birmingham Rep's production at the second preview, and enjoyed it, but took the view that it needed recasting with bigger stars to be viable in the West End. We then commenced another epic search for actors. As before, the main difficulty was casting Leo. A well-known actress agreed to play Maude if a suitable Leo could be found, but we were unable to attract either an American actor with British box-office appeal, or a British actor who would be plausible in the part. Eventually, in June 1991, after countless telephone consultations, faxes and meetings, Nathan sadly admitted defeat, and his option lapsed.

Meanwhile, the American Repertory Theatre in Cambridge, Mass., had mounted its production in March of that year, directed by Michael Bloom. The part of Leo was played by David Margulies and Maude by Christine Esterbrook, both actors with considerable experience, including Broadway. I flew to Boston for the last week of rehearsals, the previews and first night, and went through a condensed version of the same excitement, anxiety, backstage drama, rehearsal arguments, highs and lows of elation and disappointment that I had experienced in Birmingham the previous year. The style of the production was very different from the Rep's – broader, more farcical, and, to British taste, slightly over-the-top. (Christine Esterbrook brought the house down by making Maude get completely drunk in the last scene of Act One, culminating in a superb falling descent of the spiral staircase before inviting Leo into the shower.) Nathan Joseph came to see the production and hated it. But the audiences loved it, and the theatre was full or nearly full for most of the short run. I had never experienced such laughter and applause as the play got on its first night, a Saturday. People shook my hand afterwards and murmured "triumph" into my ears. On Monday morning, however, the *Boston Globe* reviewer described the play as unfunny. Other reviews were favourable, but the *Globe* was the one that mattered as regards the play's future prospects in America, and it was small consolation to be told that it invariably trashed ART productions.

In March 1992, the Manchester Library Theatre put on the play for a three-week run, directed by Chris Honer. It was a thoughtful, intelligent production, and a very creditable one given the theatre's limited resources. I attended some rehearsals and performances, but not with quite the same involvement and enthusiasm as before. I still hankered after a first-class production in London or New York. The latter seemed the likelier possibility when a New York producer, Jack Temchin, wrote to me at about this time asking if he could option the play with a view to producing it, initially off-Broadway. He had seen Michael Bloom's production at the ART, and proposed to ask him to direct in New York. Of course, it would need to be recast . . .

So the long quest resumed. More letters, more faxes, more phone calls (one made from a hotel in Sussex cost me over a hundred pounds). I met Jack in the course of a book-promotion tour in America and got on well with him. But the company (Theaterscope) he and his partner ran was a small one, and Jack found it an uphill struggle to interest major stars, without whom he couldn't raise the money to mount a production. The casting problem was almost a mirror-image of the one in England: Maude now presented the trickier problem, since the actress ought to be English, but would need a green card to work in America. Eventually a Big Star of the British stage and screen, who had moved to America and was looking to make her New York stage debut, agreed in principle to play the part. (She had been my first suggestion for the Birmingham production, but we had not been able to get in touch with her at that time.) A major Jewish American actor of the right age expressed interest in playing Leo. A reading was arranged in New York in November 1992, in front of an invited audience of about fifty people. If the chemistry worked and they both wanted to do it, we were made. In the event she was wonderful, but it seemed as if he had already decided that he didn't want to do the part, and this proved to be the case. Some months later the British Big Star agreed to do the play, without preconditions, in an American regional theatre with a track record of moving shows to New York. But on the day it was announced in the press, she withdrew in order to act in a new play by a well-known British playwright transferring from London to Broadway. (This production in fact never happened.) If I hadn't already experienced so many disappointments over *The Writing Game* I suppose I would have been by now devastated by this turn of events, but it just seemed par for the course.

Jack's option, which had already been renewed once, expired in the summer of 1993. He asked to renew for another twelve months. I said he could have till the end of the year – then, if he had made no significant progress, I wanted to have a go at adapting the play for television. Over the past few years Waldemar Januszczak, now Head of Arts at Channel Four, who had seen *The Writing Game* in Birmingham, had written to me periodically expressing interest in doing the play in his "Without Walls" slot. (Usually dedicated to arts documentaries, it does feature the occasional drama.) When Jack Temchin regretfully bowed out at the end of December, the way was open. I had a meeting with Waldemar and Michael Custance, an independent producer, in January 1994. We agreed on the format of the screenplay: it would be a multi-camera studio play with just a little exterior location scene-setting; it would not attempt to "open out" the original stage play, but remain as faithful to it as possible within a ninety-minute duration. With the money available it would have been difficult to do anything else, but we all agreed that this was the appropriate form for *The Writing Game*. In March we met with the veteran director, Stuart Burge, who agreed to direct. Channel 4 greenlighted the production shortly afterwards. I wrote the first draft screenplay in April, and the second draft in May. Because of Stuart's and my availability, rehearsals had to start in late May or the whole project would have to be postponed for months. It seemed an

incredibly tight schedule, but Michael and Stuart were convinced that we had a better chance of getting top actors at short
notice. They were absolutely right. Within a few weeks they
assembled a wonderful cast. George Segal as Leo, Susan
Wooldridge as Maude, Michael Maloney as Simon were the
principals; Penny was played by a very promising young actress
called Zara Turner, and Jeremy, by a pleasing symmetry, was
played by Ralph Nozzek, who had been in my very first work for
the professional stage, the revue *Between These Four Walls* at the
Birmingham Rep in 1963. Securing George Segal, the perfect
Leo and a Hollywood star, almost effortlessly in a matter of
days, seemed like a dream after the tortuous negotiations and
disappointments of the past five years, and I hardly dared to
believe it until I met him in the rehearsal rooms in a Chiswick
working men's club.

As usual, the main task of adaptation for me was condensation: I had to cut some 30–40 minutes out of the playtext. The
surgery required seemed drastic, but some of the cuts, and
other changes, I would want to keep in any future stage
production of the play. In particular, I believe the problem of
the final scene, which to many people has always seemed to lose
momentum, has finally been cracked. It turned out to be a
simple matter of bringing forward Penny's interview with Leo,
so that his reconciliation with Maude moves to its resolution
without interruption.

The cast rehearsed for three weeks and then the production
moved down to Southampton for a day's location shooting, and
three days' recording in the Meridien studios. This proved to be
an exhausting, nail-biting, heroic struggle against the clock. On
the last day they started at nine o'clock in the morning and they
wrapped at two o'clock the next morning. The enthusiasm and
commitment of all concerned in the production was remarkable, throughout.

By the end of August the film had been edited and delivered
to Channel 4. I watched a tape of the finished production, and
was very pleased by what I saw, but had to wait some time to
see how it would be generally received. For programming
reasons transmission was delayed until Sunday 18 February
1996. The previews (comments in the TV listings) were
prominent and positive. Against strong competition on the

other three channels, *The Writing Game* attracted an estimated
1.2 million viewers (roughly equivalent to a full house at the
Birmingham Rep six nights a week for four and a half years).
The reviews, however, were sparse, and mixed – the longest
being a Simon St Clair-style hatchet-job in the *Guardian*.

Meanwhile, a young French actor and director, Armand Eloi,
has translated the play with his novelist wife, Beatrice Hammer,
and is making strenuous efforts to mount a production in Paris.
He has been told that it is too commercial for the subsidized
theatre and too literary for the commercial theatre. To stand a
chance, it must have stars. "*Plus ça change,*" as we say in
England . . .

February 1996

Index

Note: numerals in **bold** indicate substantial quotation and/or discussion of an artist's work.